Jesus Risen

Jesus Risen

An Historical, Fundamental and Systematic Examination of Christ's Resurrection

WITHDRAWN

Gerald O'Collins, S.J.

Paulist Press
New York/Mahwah

Library of Congress Cataloging-in-Publication Data

O'Collins, Gerald.
    Jesus risen.

    Bibliography: p.
    Includes index.
    1. Jesus Christ—Resurrection. I. Title.
BT481.033 1986   232'.5   86-18660
ISBN 0-8091-0393-1 (cloth)

Published by Paulist Press
997 Macarthur Boulevard
Mahwah, New Jersey 07430

Printed and bound in the
United States of America

Contents

Abbreviations

CD   K. Barth, *Church Dogmatics* (Edinburgh, 1936–69).

DS   *Enchiridion Symbolorum, definitionum et declarationum de rebus fidei et morum*, ed. H. Denzinger, rev. A. Schönmetzer (25th ed.: Freiburg, 1973).

ETh   *Encyclopedia of Theology. A Concise Sacramentum Mundi*, ed. K. Rahner (London, 1975).

OBC   H. Küng, *On Being a Christian* (London and New York, 1977).

par(r).   and parallel(s) in other Gospel(s).

PG   *Patrologia Graeca*, ed. J.P. Migne, 162 vols. (Paris, 1857–66).

PL   *Patrologia Latina*, ed. J.P. Migne, 217 vols. (Paris, 1844–55).

SM   *Sacramentum Mundi* (London and New York, 1968–70).

ThI   K. Rahner, *Theological Investigations* (London, 1961–84).

Introduction

La seule excuse de vivre,
c'est attendre la Résurrection.
—Léon Bloy

The resurrection from the dead of the crucified Jesus deserves serious attention from any thoughtful person, whether believer or non-believer. It claims a quite extraordinary intervention from God in human history. Millions of Christians have accepted the truth of this claim, which—among other profound consequences—carries a promise of deep and everlasting happiness in a transformed life beyond death. It is clearly a good thing to investigate Jesus' resurrection. In fact, the great importance of the issues involved could even suggest a certain obligation to inquire and reflect about this central article of Christian faith.

But where should we "station" ourselves in approaching the question of Jesus' resurrection? The academic captivity of much Western thinking on this topic has privileged out of all proportion the scholarly setting. In the professor's study, the university lecture hall or the seminary classroom, the relevant New Testament texts and the events behind them have been analyzed and reconstructed in a variety of ways over the last two hundred years. More recently academics have also taken to radio and television in order to explain to a wider public what we may conclude about the resurrection from the New Testament.

Undoubtedly it was and is essential to interpret properly the biblical texts and establish what lay behind the Easter proclamation of the early Church. At the same time, however, respect for the scholarly desire to settle the historical origins of the Easter message should not allow us to slip over a highly pertinent fact. Millions of people have turned to and interrogated Jesus' resurrection in very different contexts.

Alone at home a sudden painful awareness of one's own mortality

1

can make Christian belief about Jesus' fate after death vitally significant. One may also look at the resurrection out of the agony of some shattered personal relationship.

In general, situations of normal and abnormal suffering can offer a most profound way to appreciate, and even experience the resurrection. The two criminals crucified alongside Jesus symbolize for all time this possibility. Theirs was a case not of "bad things happening to good people," but of "bad things happening to bad people." The Gospels do not claim that those two men were unjustly sentenced to death. But in their suffering they hung on crosses next to Jesus. What then does his resurrection mean from the angle of those who, in normal or abnormal ways, find themselves crucified with him?

When viewed from the dining-room in an old people's home or from a ward for the terminally ill, the resurrection looks different from the challenge it presents at a desk in an air-conditioned library. An academic's interests will not coincide with the way in which the members of an Asian refugee camp or the survivors of a devastated Lebanese village might draw hope from Jesus' resurrection. If asked to dispose of the remains of an aborted fetus, what is a distressed Christian nurse to think about resurrection for the born and the unborn? Experiences of actual and threatening evil provide a privileged approach to Jesus' new life beyond death.

The presence of fifty thousand nuclear warheads around our world yields a view of the resurrection which no earlier generation has ever had. These weapons now make it possible to exterminate human life on this earth. What does Jesus' victory over death mean when examined at the entrance of an Eastern or Western missile base? What can the risen Lord promise this generation, which possesses the power to end the human story everywhere and forever? Our advanced opportunities for annihilating the human species give a new slant to any evaluation of Jesus' resurrection as a message of hope for men, women and their world.

From the very beginning of Christianity worship has proved a third "station" from which believers continue to absorb and understand the resurrection. They may do so in some beautifully celebrated Easter Vigil service or in Saint Peter's Square at midday on Easter Sunday. More often it will be in the context of everyday worship that they hear the resurrection preached and experience its impact on their hearts. Either way it is through prayer together that these Christians encounter the person and power of the risen Jesus in their midst (Matt 18:20).

In short, not only historical study but also human hope and Christian worship open up ways for considering Jesus' resurrection. To read and reflect on the Easter stories with the aid of the latest biblical commentary can be valuable and should always be much more than an empty intellectual exercise. Yet other kinds of commentary on the Easter message come from the experiences of those who suffer materially and spiritually or from those who find only meaningless horror in the advanced preparations for the nuclear extinction of the human race. Thirdly, we ignore at our peril the commentary on and access to the Easter story provided by community worship—as at least two of the Gospel writers seemed to have realized clearly (Luke 24:30–31, 35; John 20:19–23).

Apropos of that third approach to the resurrection, it is worth recalling the famous question which Margareta put to Faust:

> Please tell me what religion means to you.
> Although I think you very good and kind,
> I doubt if worship weighs much in your mind.[1]

Unless and until worship counts for us, neither Jesus' resurrection nor, for that matter, religion itself can say much to us. In Faust's case this was all the more poignant as he had been saved from suicide when he heard the hymns and bells inviting Christians to worship on Easter Sunday.[2]

We can express as follows the difference between the three approaches to the resurrection. Scholars can use their critical reason to penetrate the Easter mystery. Those who suffer and worship can let themselves be penetrated by that mystery. All three groups take up valid attitudes toward Jesus' rising from the dead.

In short, we should respect and try to open up various opportunities for experiencing and interpreting Jesus' resurrection, not destroy them in the name of just one, absolutized approach to this crucial matter. Different settings offer mutually enriching possibilities for understanding, expressing and verifying what the resurrection might mean. In this book I plan to keep open various contexts for appreciating and interpreting the Easter story. We can learn something about that story not only by working in the scholar's study but also by suffering in a hospital or singing in a church. In fact, those who attempt a purely academic approach and refuse to remember prayer and suffering are sure to go wrong. Their intellectual efforts to grasp resurrection can stand in the way of the resurrection working in them and on them.

Likewise we need to recognize the severe impoverishment involved in reducing our entire inquiry to one such question as: "Well, did it happen?" There is a large range of distinct or at least distinguishable issues to be tackled about Jesus' resurrection. What was the event which re-

liable traditions from early Christianity claim to have happened? What
did it reveal about God? How does the truth of Easter imply and illuminate other truths of revelation? Why can we accept faith in Jesus as
risen from the dead? How does this resurrection deliver people from the
evils which they experience and suffer? What does the resurrection of
Jesus say about human hope and divine love? How is the good news of
this resurrection communicated?

Obviously these questions overlap and intertwine. Yet it is impossible to raise, let alone answer, all questions at once. Hence I will take
up these issues one by one, distinguishing but not finally separating
them from each other.

As such this book looks at the resurrection of Jesus, but it does not
wish thereby to downplay and belittle his crucifixion. Christian liturgy
has always held together these events as the two sides of the one paschal
mystery. This death and resurrection are not just two events which simply followed each other. Without his resurrection, Jesus' crucifixion
would have had no final meaning. Without that death, his resurrection
might seem cheap and unmerited. At the same time, however, to lump
together the crucifixion and resurrection as if they were two aspects of
only one event does not do justice to either. They are certainly distinguishable, although not separable, events. From the New Testament
times on, Christians have used both *spatial* and *temporal* language to express this distinction. The crucifixion and resurrection meant that Jesus
first "descended" into the realm of death and then "ascended" into
heaven to "sit at the right hand of the Father." He died and was buried
before being raised "on the third day." In this book I give my attention
to the resurrection but wish to recall consistently that distinguishable
but inseparable event which preceded it, the crucifixion of Jesus.

Certainly by now it should be clear that this work is written from
the standpoint of one who accepts Jesus' personal and bodily resurrection from the dead. It could be called an exercise of "Easter faith seeking
understanding (*fides paschalis quaerens intellectum*)." But I hope that this
version of resurrection faith will still manage to be intelligible not only
to those who endorse it but also to those who either do not share this
faith or are unsure whether they share it.

If this book is an exercise of "Easter faith seeking understanding,"
I dare not claim to possess this faith with anything like perfection. How
many of us let our personal and public lives become simply filled and
guided by the Easter mystery? Which of us systematically and gener-
ously acts out our faith in Jesus risen from the dead?

The cross is the characteristic sign and symbol of Christianity.
Even so, Paul will not say, "If Christ has not been crucified, your faith

is futile." Instead he insists, "If Christ has not been raised, your faith is futile" (1 Cor 15:17). It was the resurrection of the crucified Jesus which created and sustains the essential Christian identity. Yet which of us can allege, "I really identify myself and measure my whole life by this truth"? Paul takes the resurrection as *the* basis for living and dying. As a baptized and believing Christian do I truly walk in newness of life under the Lordship of the risen Christ (Rom 6:3–4; 14:9)? My "Easter faith seeking understanding" will always remain defective and limited. However, I can console myself with the thought that one does not have to be perfect in order to be useful. A very imperfect living of and identification with the Easter faith might still hope to yield something worth hearing.

Finally, a word about sources. In constructing its account of Jesus' resurrection and what it entails, this book will draw from the scriptures and also from the rich variety of ways the resurrection has been expressed in Christian life, liturgy and teaching. A summary history of how Jesus' victory over death has entered the experience, tradition and theological reflection of believers sets the stage. After that historical introduction I can take up the thematic issues.

I should like to express my profound gratitude to many colleagues, students and other friends in Rome and elsewhere. By their experiences, observations and questions they have clarified my vision of Jesus' resurrection from the dead. In particular I want to thank Josef Graf, George Hunsinger, Dan Kendall, Maria Franca Lamaro, Philip Rosato, Mimi Sbisà, Elizabeth Mary Strub, Willibrord Welten, Jared Wicks, Christopher Willcock and those who took summer courses with me at the University of Notre Dame and the University of San Francisco. I want to thank very much Hilva Martorana and Leslie Wearne for typing the book with their usual expertise. With deep gratitude and affection I dedicate this work to Don Frank and Donna Orietta Pogson Doria Pamphilj and their children (Jonathan and Gesine).

Gerald O'Collins, S.J.
The Gregorian University, Rome
25 May 1986

1

The Resurrection in the Story of Christianity

The New Testament understands and interprets Jesus' resurrection in a variety of ways. Christian formulations from the thirties and forties which were picked up by Paul and Luke, in particular, highlighted the fact that this resurrection had taken place. Known individuals and groups testified to the event: "The Lord has risen indeed, and has appeared to Simon [Peter]" (Luke 24:34). In 1 Corinthians 15:5 Paul quoted a similar piece of kerygma ("He appeared to Cephas [= Peter], then to the twelve"), and referred also to the witness of a large body of early Christians: "Then he appeared to more than five hundred brethren at one time, most of whom are still alive, though some have fallen asleep" (1 Cor 15:6).

Besides testifying that Jesus had been personally raised from the dead, the authors of the New Testament let us see or at least glimpse six further distinguishable consequences of this event. It revealed the crucified Jesus in his true identity as God's Son (Gal 1:12, 16). It saved and justified sinners (Rom 4:25; Acts 5:31). It called human beings to a new life of faith (1 Cor 15:1–2, 11), hope (1 Cor 15:12ff) and love (John 17:26). The message of Easter was to be communicated to the world (Acts 2:14–36).

In these opening chapters I plan to sample the history of Christianity to see how believers understood and interpreted the resurrection of the crucified Jesus. I want to concentrate on the Patristic era, the Middle Ages, and the twentieth century. What approaches to the Easter mystery emerge in these various periods?

The memorable statement with which Tertullian (c. 160–c. 225) began his *De resurrectione carnis* (*On the Resurrection of the Flesh*) characterized an approach to the resurrection which would last for many centuries: "*Fiducia Christianorum resurrectio mortuorum, illam credentes hoc sumus* (The resurrection of the dead constitutes the confidence of Christians. By believing it we are what we claim to be)."

Even before Tertullian, early Christian writers like the author of the Epistle of Barnabas (c. 85) and Clement of Rome (fl. c. 90) show us that the event of Jesus' own resurrection, while accepted and confessed in the standard creeds, was not a distinct theme to be considered in its own right. Our hope for resurrection from the dead quickly assumed prominence. In the Patristic period the Easter kerygma about Christ's resurrection found in 1 Corinthians 15:3ff did not play an important role. What was taken up and really shaped Christian thinking came a little later in that chapter:

> Christ has been raised from the dead, the first fruits of those who have fallen asleep. For as by a man came death, by a man has come also the resurrection of the dead. For as in Adam all die, so also in Christ shall all be made alive. But each in his own order: Christ the first fruits, then at his coming those who belong to Christ (1 Cor 15:20–23).

Even in that classic of Christian apologetics, the *Contra Celsum* by Origen (c. 185–c. 254), 1 Corinthians 15:3–8 turned up only three times, while verses from the rest of that chapter were quoted or appealed to twenty times. Although the factuality of Jesus' own resurrection as such slipped somewhat into the background, what was said about it by the Fathers of the Church? What did they propose about the origins of the Easter story?

(1) *Verifying Jesus' Resurrection.* The New Testament indicates how the message of Jesus' resurrection not only won acceptance but provoked different kinds of negative reactions. Jewish leaders in Jerusalem claimed that Jesus' disciples had stolen his corpse (Matt 28:11–15). According to Acts 17:32, in Athens Paul's proclamation of Easter provoked a good deal of scorn and skepticism. Within the Church itself some deviant tendencies and misunderstandings about the resurrection had to be confronted (1 Cor 15:12ff; 2 Tim 2:17–18). In the post-apostolic Church we also find writers facing and dealing both with (Jewish and

pagan) denials of the resurrection and with Christian misinterpretations of it.

Justin Martyr (c. 100–c. 165) in his *Dialogue with Trypho* (nr. 108) responds to the charge of body-snatching which Matthew had earlier reported. In *De Spectaculis* (nr. 30) Tertullian mentions another rebuttal of the resurrection: the local gardener, fearing that many visitors would come and damage his vegetables, removed Jesus' corpse from the tomb. On finding the tomb to be empty, the disciples wrongly concluded that resurrection had taken place. Apparently the gardener was supposed to have said nothing to disturb their "good faith."

Within or on the margin of Christianity various Gnostic and Hellenistic misunderstandings of the resurrection came to the fore in the second century. Gnostics promoted a one-sided theology of the resurrection which cut it off from the whole history of Jesus, suppressed its bodily nature and turned it simply into the heavenly exaltation of Christ. Over against Gnosticism Christians emphasized the true incarnation of the divine Logos and, on the basis of the Word really "becoming flesh," maintained the resurrection of the flesh.[1]

As part of their version of Christ's exaltation, some Gnostics wanted to appropriate Peter for themselves and portrayed him as a recipient of special revelations.[2] The orthodox reacted by no longer associating Peter's ministry with his having been an eye-witness of the risen Lord (1 Cor 15:5; Luke 24:34; Acts 2:32). Instead Clement of Rome (nr. 5), Tertullian[3] and others based Peter's role on his martyrdom. In at least two places the New Testament reports kerygma (that also functioned as creed for those who accepted this proclamation), in which early Christians confessed the appearance to Simon Peter (1 Cor 15:5; Luke 24:34). The reaction to Gnosticism meant that this appearance did not enter the ancient liturgical summaries of faith (DS 1–76), which— as in the case of the Apostles' Creed ("suffered under Pontius Pilate")— included the Roman procurator as a kind of witness to the crucifixion rather than including any Christian witness to the truth of Jesus' risen life.

In his *Contra Celsum*, Origen aimed among other things to meet the objections brought against Jesus' resurrection by Celsus, a second-century pagan philosopher whose *True Discourse* (c. 178) is the oldest literary attack on Christianity of which we have some details. (a) Celsus suggested that the story of Jesus' resurrection was on the same level as "the legends" about Pythagoras, Orpheus, Heracles, Theseus and others returning from the dead—legends used to convince and exploit "simple hearers" (*Contra Celsum*, II, 55). (b) The alleged witnesses to the risen Christ were either hysterical and hallucinated or else ambitious liars.

While he was alive he did not help himself, but after death he rose again and showed the marks of his punishment and how his hands had been pierced. But who saw this? A hysterical female, as you say, and perhaps some other one [? Peter] of those who were deluded by the same sorcery, who either dreamt in a certain state of mind and through wishful thinking had a hallucination due to some mistaken notion (an experience which has happened to thousands), or, which is more likely, wanted to impress the others by telling this fantastic tale, and so by this cock-and-bull story to provide a chance for other beggars (*ibid.*; see also *ibid.*, II, 70).[4]

(c) Celsus further argued that if Jesus really wanted to establish the divine truth of his resurrection from the dead, "he ought to have appeared to the very men who treated him despitefully and to the man who condemned him and to everyone everywhere" (*ibid.*, II, 63). In his *Against the Christians* Porphyry (c. 232–c. 303) was to make the same point: Jesus should have appeared not only to his insignificant disciples, but also to his Jewish opponents, to Pilate and Herod, and even better to the members of the Roman Senate. (d) As Porphyry would do later, Celsus cast doubt on the trustworthiness of the evangelists by noting the conflicts between their accounts. For example, Mark and Matthew have one angel announcing the resurrection to the women, whereas Luke has two (*ibid.*, V, 52). (e) Like Porphyry after him, Celsus held that our true reality is the spirit imprisoned at present in the body. This view of human existence could not entertain the possibility of resurrection either for Jesus or for anyone else.

Origen did well in his replies to these difficulties. (a) He pointed out the differences between the case of Jesus who was crucified publicly and the fantastic tales about men alleged to have descended to Hades and returned from there to life on earth (*ibid.*, II, 56). (b) Celsus suggested that Mary Magdalene was "hysterical." But "there is no evidence of this in the scriptural account [John 20:14–17] which was the source upon which he drew for his criticism" (*ibid.*, II, 60). Moreover, Origen noted that, according to Matthew 28:9–10, the risen Jesus appeared to Mary Magdalene and another woman (*ibid.*, II, 70). Origen admitted that the hallucination hypothesis "would not be unreasonable if the visions had occurred by night." But daytime hallucinations do not occur among sane persons like Jesus' disciples, who "were in no way mentally unbalanced and were not suffering from delirium or melancholy" (*ibid.*, II, 60). Against the accusation (favored by Celsus) that the disciples invented the "fantastic tale" of the resurrection, Origen observed that they faced the danger of death by preaching this message. A "clear and certain proof" (which ruled out the hypothesis of deliberate deception) he found in "the argument from the behavior of the disciples, who devoted themselves to a teaching which involved risking their lives" (*ibid.*, II, 56). Their sufferings and unshakable hope revealed the strength and sincerity of their conviction about Jesus' resurrection:

> [Jesus] both rose again and convinced his disciples about his resurrection, and convinced them to such an extent that they show to all men by their sufferings that they are looking for eternal life and for the resurrection which has been exemplified before them in word and deed, and that they deride all the troubles of life (*ibid.*, II, 77).

(c) Origen had much to say in answer to the objection that the risen Jesus failed to appear to his enemies and to the general public. Origen took Celsus' point seriously and reported it again, this time in terms of the contrast between the publicity of Jesus' ministry and the secretiveness of the Easter appearances. Origen quoted Celsus as follows:

> At the time when he [Jesus] was disbelieved while in the body, he preached without restraint to all; but when he would establish a strong faith after rising from the dead, he appeared secretly to just one woman [*sic*] and to those of his own confraternity (*ibid.*, II, 70).

Origen began by drawing a parallel between the Old Testament Theophanies and the Christophanies of the risen Christ. He did not linger over the point to explore the differences. But for those like Celsus who were sympathetic to the Old Testament and even accepted the divine appearances recorded by the Jewish scriptures, the *prima facie* parallel offered some justification for the limited appearances of the risen Christ:

> Just as it is recorded that God appeared to Abraham or to one of the saints, and that this appearing was not happening all the time but only at intervals, and just as he did not appear to all, so also I think that the Son of God appeared in much the same way to the apostles as God appeared to the saints in the Old Testament (*ibid.*, II, 66).

Origen named the revelation of Jesus' divinity as the reason why "all those who formerly saw him could not look upon him." When Jesus "had put off the principalities and powers" and risen from the dead, "he no longer had anything about him that could be seen by the multitude" (*ibid.*, II, 64). Origen distinguished sharply between the possibility for neutral and hostile persons of seeing the humanity (of the earthly Jesus) and the divinity (of the risen Christ): "His human characteristics were visible to all, while the divine characteristics *could* not be seen by all" (*ibid.*, II, 70; italics mine). Elsewhere Origen mitigated this claim that it was *impossible* for the ill-disposed to see the divine glory of the risen Christ. Thinking of an Old Testament example and perhaps also of the effect produced by the angel of the Lord upon the guards posted at Jesus' tomb (Matt 28:4), Origen argued that it could have been dangerous for the opponents if the risen Christ had appeared to them:

> It would not have been right for him to have appeared to the man who condemned him and to those who treated him despitefully. For Jesus had consideration both for the one who condemned him and for those who treated him despitefully, lest they should be smitten with blindness as the men of Sodom were smitten when they conspired in lust for the beauty of the angels lodged at Lot's house. . . . Jesus, then, wanted to show forth his divine power to each of those able to see it, and according to the measure of his individual capacity. In fact, perhaps he avoided appearing simply because he was considering the mean abilities of people who had not the capacity to see him (*ibid.*, II, 67).

Ultimately Origen held that two factors had been involved in limiting the Easter appearances. On the one hand, in his risen existence Christ's divinity was objectively "more brilliant." Hence "not even with the apostles themselves and the disciples was he always present or always apparent, because they were unable to receive his divinity without some periods of relief." On the other hand, some enhanced and graced powers of perception were needed by those subjects who experienced these passing encounters with the risen Jesus. He "appeared after his resurrection not to all men but only to those whom he perceived to have obtained eyes which had the capacity to see the resurrection [= to see him in his risen state]" (*ibid.*, II, 65).

(d) In dealing with the differences between the Gospels on such matters as the number and the actions of the angels at Jesus' tomb, Origen showed a desire to harmonize the accounts into a coherent, historical narrative. At the same time, nevertheless, he spoke of these variant details as also "manifesting some allegorical meaning which concerns the truths which are made clear to people who have been prepared to see the resurrection of the Logos" (*ibid.*, V, 56). We could translate this response into modern terms. The Evangelists all accepted the resurrection and wrote for people who (largely or even wholly) also already believed in the risen Christ. The divergences of detail in the Easter reports came not only from the sources but even more from the Evangelists' intention to express for their different audiences various insights about the rich meaning and truth of the resurrection. It should be added that Origen refused to be drawn on minor variations of detail, which he believed to be "relevant" to gospel "commentaries" rather than "to the present undertaking" (*ibid.*). In his rebuttal of Celsus he concentrated, as we have seen above, on such major points as the New Testament witness to Christ's post-resurrection appearances.

(e) It would be a mistake, however, to present the debate between Origen and Celsus as if it were primarily a matter of interpreting the Easter texts of the New Testament. The challenge was to justify the very notion of resurrection which Celsus' dualistic anthropology ruled out in advance. Origen saw the need to make sense of resurrection in itself, but largely left this as unfinished business.

> Celsus did not understand the doctrine of the resurrection, which is deep and hard to explain, and needs a wise man of advanced skill more than any other doctrine in order to show it is worthy of God and that the doctrine is a noble conception (*ibid.*, VII, 32).

Where Origen faltered was in his answer to the objection that Christian teaching represented no advance over the Jewish, or at least the Pharisaic, idea of resurrection. Celsus disparaged

> . . . as stale stuff the doctrine of the resurrection of the dead and of God's judgment giving reward to the righteous but fire to the unrighteous. He thinks he can overthrow Christianity by saying that in these matters Christians teach nothing new (*ibid.*, II, 5).

Origen's reply was beside the point. He should have agreed that by the time of Jesus many Jews believed that there would be a general resurrection for judgment of both the righteous and the unrighteous. The Christians, however, taught something new when they proclaimed (i) that the final resurrection of *one* individual (Jesus) had taken place before the universal resurrection of the dead, and (ii) that this individual would play a decisive role in the divine judgment at the universal resurrection to come.

In his apologetic for Jesus' resurrection from the dead Origen dealt directly with the event itself and the Easter appearances. But he also added an argument which came into its own with a number of Patristic writers:

> Those who believe in the resurrection of Jesus . . . show considerable fruit from their faith in that their moral life is healthy and that they have been converted from the flood of iniquity (*ibid.*, V, 57).

This was not to argue directly about the event of the resurrection itself but to point to the public effects of Easter faith in the lives of contemporary believers. Athanasius (c. 296–373) made out a similar case. Christ's living impact on his followers provided evidence for the reality of his resurrection from the dead several centuries earlier:

> Anyone who likes may see the proof of glory in the virgins of Christ, and in the young men who practice chastity as part of their religion, and in the assurance of immortality in so great and glad a company of martyrs (*The Incarnation of the Word of God*, 48).

In the *City of God* Augustine (354–430) pointed to another form of public evidence for Jesus' resurrection—its proven capacity to win wide and deep acceptance, even though in itself it seemed incredible and even though the witnesses to the risen Christ were only "rude and lowly" persons:

> It is incredible that Christ should have risen in his flesh and, with his flesh, have ascended into heaven; it is incredible that the world should have believed a thing so incredible; it is incredible that men so rude and lowly, so few and unaccomplished, should have convinced the world, including men of learning, of something so incredible and have convinced men so conclusively (22, 5).

In these terms, the publicly verifiable faith of Christians, as well as the quality of their moral practice (Origen, Athanasius), lent plausibility to the claim that the crucified Jesus had truly risen from the dead. In various forms this argument from observable effects (in the life and history of the Church) to their original cause (Jesus' resurrection) has continued to maintain its appeal.

(2) *The Basis for Hope.* As we have already seen, in the Patristic era the event of Christ's resurrection was generally not treated as a distinct theme but very often taken as grounding Christian hope for resurrection.[4a]

At the end of the first century Clement of Rome comforted his readers with the assurance of their coming resurrection:

> Think, my dear friends, how the Lord offers us proof after proof that there is going to be a resurrection, of which he has made Jesus Christ the first-fruits by raising him from the dead (1 Clement, 24).[5]

To strengthen hope in future resurrection, Clement noted some "processes of resurrection" going on all the time in nature: the succession of day and night and the crops which come into being from the seed that "decays" in the earth. Clement clinched his case by recalling the Arabian Phoenix:

> Look at that strange portent that occurs in the East (in the neighborhood of Arabia, to be precise). There is a bird known as a Phoenix, which is the only specimen of its kind and has a life of five hundred years.
> When the hour of its dissolution and death approaches, it makes a nest for itself out of frankincense and myrrh and other fragrant spices, and in the fullness of time it enters into this and expires. Its decaying flesh breeds a small grub, which is nourished by the moisture of the dead bird and presently grows wings. This, on reaching full growth, takes up the nest containing the bones of its predecessor and carries them all the way from the land of Arabia into Egypt, to the city called Heliopolis. There, in the full light of day and before the eyes of all beholders, it flies to the altar of the Sun, deposits them there, and speeds back to its homeland; and when the priests consult their time records, they find that its arrival has marked the completion of the five-hundredth year (nr. 25).

Given the fact that the Phoenix was "the only specimen of its kind," one might have expected that fabulous bird to have first brought to mind Christ and his resurrection. Instead for Clement the Phoenix symbolized immediately the resurrection we should hope for:

> When the Creator of all things has even made use of a bird to disclose the magnitude of his promises to us, need we find it such a great wonder that he has a resurrection in store for those who have served him in holiness and in the confidence of a sound faith? (nr. 26).[6]

Here "resurrection" expressed at once (a) the great hope of *Christians* which was (b) closely connected with two things: a fear of coming judgment and a serious ethical commitment ("a resurrection in store for those who have served him in holiness").

(a) The future resurrection from the dead became a favored theme in the writings of apologists[7] and in the acts of the martyrs. Christians could face a cruel execution because they enjoyed a certain hope of rising from the dead. When the persecutions ceased, monastic movements drew their inspiration in part from the notion of a living martyrdom endured through the promise of a resurrection to come. In all of this much more interest was shown in our resurrection than in that of Christ. Here early Christian art followed suit. From the outset the Phoenix became a symbol for the resurrection of the dead, and was not reserved to Christ himself. Christian artists used Daniel among the lions (Dan 6:16–24), the resurrection of Lazarus (John 11:1–44), and even Jonah, to express their hope to be raised from the dead. After Matthew had explicitly associated Jonah's "three days and three nights in the belly of the whale" with Jesus' "three days and three nights in the heart of the earth" (12:40), the last case is startling. Nevertheless, hope in resurrection bulked so large that in Christian art and literature the Jonah-image was applied not only to Jesus himself but sometimes much more to our coming resurrection from the dead.[8] In his *Adversus omnes haereses* Irenaeus (c. 130–c. 200) made that application (IV, 19, 1; 52, 1; V, 5, 2). In the *De resurrectione* Tertullian argued that Jonah's remaining intact, despite his stint inside the whale, guarantees that our human body will be raised intact (32, 3).

(b) Along with the hope for the coming resurrection went the warning of a final judgment. The Epistle of Barnabas (written between 70 and 100 A.D.) contrasted the fate of the man who practices "the precepts of the Lord" and for whom "there will be glory in the kingdom of God" with that of "one who prefers the other Way" and who "will perish together with his works. To this end are the ordinances of resurrection and retribution" (nr. 21). Among other Fathers of the Church, Cyril of Jerusalem (c. 315–386) gave a central place to the resurrection of the dead; he named our hope for resurrection as "the root of every good work" (*Catecheses*, 18, 1. 20).

(c) I noted above how Clement of Rome bolstered hope in resurrection from the dead by introducing such "arguments" as the legend of the Phoenix. In general, early Church writers were more concerned to establish a case for our resurrection than that of Christ himself. Often they invoked the created world to support the plausibility of their hope. As Clement had done, Tertullian appealed to the divine power shown in the change of seasons and in the return of daylight after the darkness of the night (*De resurrectione*, 12). These and other natural phenomena such as the grain which decays and rises in greater fertility led Tertullian to enunciate a principle: "All things are preserved by being destroyed" (*Apology*, 48, 7). In the case of the resurrection of our flesh, however, there will be change rather than a real destruction involving the substitution of another bodily existence. To establish this point ("That which is changed is not destroyed"), he used an argument which the second-century apologist Athenagoras (*De resurrectione*, 17) had drawn from the changes which the human body already experiences during the present life: "For a proof that a thing can be changed and none the less be itself, the man as a whole does during this life in substance remain himself, yet changes in various ways" (*De resurrectione*, 55).[9]

Besides the order of created nature, other sources provided arguments in support of the Christian position. In his *First Apology* (1, 21, 1) and *Dialogue with Trypho* (69, 2) Justin Martyr drew on pagan myths about the after-life to add credibility to Christian hopes for resurrection.

In the face of heretics who denied the coming resurrection of our flesh Tertullian recalled the truth—not of Christ's resurrection, but of the incarnation. If the dead are not going to be raised, then the Logos has not become incarnate (*De resurrectione*, 9). His incarnation gave a dignity to human flesh which guarantees that it will be raised to consummate the work of redemption. To adapt Tertullian's lapidary expression (*"caro salutis est cardo"*), by the very fact of becoming flesh the Logos became the pivot for the complete salvation which will be our resurrection (*ibid.*, 8).

In supporting their hope for resurrection, Tertullian and others dealt with difficulties of a "physiological" nature. What will happen to those who have been eaten by cannibals and wild beasts (*ibid.*, 4, 32)?[9a] In our risen state will eating, drinking and sexual activities continue? Apropos of our digestive tract and genital organs, Tertullian faced the objection from critics of the resurrection. These essential parts of the body should also function in our life after death. But if they do not, why have a risen body at all?

> . . . they argue also about the function of its [the flesh's] members, either alleging that they ought to continue for ever in their activities and effects, as being appurtenances of that identical bodily constitution; or else, because it is agreed that the functions of the members will cease, they cancel the bodily constitution as well, seeing its continuance is, they say, not credible without the members, as neither are the members credible without their functions.

Tertullian explained that even though the genital and other organs cease to function, they should and will be maintained so as to have "a man in full being" (*ibid.*, 60). Even at the time this response would not have been very convincing. But it illustrated a key and persistent challenge for those who profess hope in resurrection. What account can they give of the continuity (and transformation) between bodily existence here and hereafter?

Besides fending off objections against Christian hopes for the future life, certain writers in the early Church also protested against reductionist and deviant versions of what lies in store for us. Thus Tertullian argued against a "merely" symbolic interpretation of the resurrection (*De resurrectione*, 1, 21–22), and rejected notions of reincarnation (*Apology*, 48, 13). But the main debate was normally with those who took a strongly dualistic view and argued for the immortality of the soul rather than the resurrection of the whole human person. Tertullian reported them as follows:

> Some, maintaining that the resurrection begins from the release of the soul, interpret "come forth from the tomb" as "escape from the world" (on the ground that the world is a habitation of dead men, that is, of men who know not God) or even "escape from the body" (on the ground that the body, in the guise of a tomb, encloses and imprisons the soul in the death which is this world's life) (*De resurrectione*, 19).

Finally, it should be noted that in the early centuries some Christians endorsed various rather material views of our future state. Revelation 20:1–5 encouraged the Chiliastic (or Millenarian) theory that the risen Christ would return to reign on earth for a thousand years before all things were finally consummated. Justin endorsed a millenarian view (*Dialogue*, 80f). Irenaeus toyed with the idea of an idyllic millennium (*Adversus omnes haereses*, V, 35, 1). Tertullian was not totally clear in his opposition to millenarianism. Origen, however, castigated those who expected to rise and dwell in a heavenly Jerusalem where they would eat, drink and enjoy sexual love (*De principiis*, 2, 11, 2).

This section has sketched some expressions of Christian hope built on Christ's resurrection. His resurrection was also experienced and articulated in the celebration of the liturgy. Let me turn to that now.

(3) *Liturgy and Christ's Resurrection.*   The early Church celebrated the resurrection of Christ (a) in every Eucharist, (b) in every Sunday liturgy and (c) especially in the Easter liturgy. The Christian communities remembered the past story of his dying and rising and expressed their own hope for a resurrection to come. But they experienced these liturgies above all as Christ's passage through death to a new life now being actualized and realized in their midst and for their advantage.

(a) John 6 had already linked the Eucharist to our resurrection (6:53–54, 57–58) and through that to Christ's resurrection (6:62). The Eucharistic prayer of Hippolytus followed suit.[10] The "Markan" liturgy of Alexandria built on 1 Corinthians 11:26 to do the same: "As often as you eat this bread and drink this chalice, you should announce my death and confess my resurrection."[11] In reassuring his Ephesian and Roman readers about his imminent martyrdom, Ignatius of Antioch interpreted it in terms of the Eucharist and his hope to share in Christ's resurrection (Rom 4, 6; Eph 20). The anti-Gnostic struggle in the second century saw Irenaeus associate the Eucharist with the resurrection of the flesh (*Haer.* IV, 18, 5; V, 2, 2–3).

(b) On Sunday, "the day of the Lord" (Rev 1:10), the Eucharist not only recalled his past triumph over death but also anticipated the experience of the future resurrection, world judgment and new creation. The Epistle of Barnabas noted that "we rejoice in celebrating the eighth day; because that was when Jesus rose from the dead, and showed himself again, and ascended into heaven." It called Sunday "the commencement of a new world" (15, 8–9).

At the end of the fourth century Etheria observed the services in Jerusalem and its neighborhood. She reported the liturgy on early Sunday morning, a vigil service which paralleled the Easter vigil and made present the death and resurrection of Christ (*Peregrinatio*, 24–25, 27).

(c) It was above all the Easter vigil liturgy which offered Christians the richest redemptive experience of Christ's "Pasch" or "Passover" and through baptism and Eucharist shared with them most deeply the saving significance of his resurrection from the dead.

Jesus died and rose at the time of the Passover, the Jewish spring festival celebrated by slaying and eating a lamb in memory of the people's exodus from Egypt and the deliverance from slavery to freedom (Exod 12; Deut 16). Mark (14:12, 14, 16) and the other Synoptic Gospels placed the institution of the Eucharist within the context of a Passover meal. Saint Paul associated baptism with the deliverance from Egypt: "Our fathers were all under the cloud, and all passed through the sea, and all were baptized into Moses in the cloud and in the sea" (1 Cor 10:1–2). In a later letter he reminded the Roman Christians that their baptism brought a participation in Christ's dying and rising:

> Do you not know that all of us who have been baptized into Christ Jesus were baptized into his death? We were buried therefore with him by baptism into death, so that as Christ was raised from the dead by the glory of the Father, we too might walk in newness of life (Rom 6:3–4).

In short, from the beginning of Christianity the resurrection of the crucified Jesus had been linked with what came before (the exodus led by Moses, and the Jewish Passover rite), and with what followed afterward (the Christian Eucharist and baptism). The Easter vigil celebration of the resurrection drew together the biblical story of salvation with the present sacramental experience of it.

For several centuries two explanations were offered of the "paschal" mystery of the crucified and risen Christ or "second Passover." Some derived this new "Pasch" from the Lord's passion (*ex passione*). They could appeal to Paul: "Christ, our paschal lamb, has been sacrificed" (1 Cor 5:7). Others explained the "Pasch" as a *"diabasis"* or *"transitus."* In the light of John 13:1 ("Now before the feast of the Passover, when Jesus knew his hour had come to depart out of this world to the Father . . ."), Augustine took together the two traditions and saw the Lord's "Pasch" as his "passage through the passion (*transitus per passionem*)" to resurrection (*Catech. rud.* 23, 41, 3; *Epist.* 55, 1, 2; *Enarr. in ps.* 120, 6).

The Easter celebration was the privileged occasion for participating in the Lord's Passover, particularly for those who were baptized and received Communion for the first time. Sacramentally they repeated and experienced Christ's passage through death to new life. Their baptism during the night of the resurrection was a *mimesis* or real imitation of his dying and rising, as Saint Cyril of Jerusalem, Theodore of Mopsuestia (c. 350–428) and others explained. There could be no "more suitable day for baptism than the Pasch," according to Basil of Caesarea (c. 330–379) in his thirteenth homily on baptism: "This day is the memorial of the resurrection, and baptism is a power of resurrection. Hence it is on the day of [Christ's] resurrection that we shall receive the grace of [our] resurrection" (PG, 31, 424D–425A).

In his homily *On the Pasch* (composed between 166 and 180) Melito of Sardis left a brilliant testimony to the risen Christ's redemptive power experienced here and now.

> It is he who has made us pass from slavery to freedom, from darkness to light, from death to life, from tyranny to the eternal kingdom, making of us a new priesthood and a people chosen forever (*ibid.*, 68).

Melito presented the risen Christ as proclaiming himself victor over the forces of evil and holding out salvation to all.

> "I am the Christ," he says. "It is I who destroyed death, who triumphed over the enemy, who trampled Hades underfoot, who bound the strong one and snatched man away to the heights of heaven; I am the Christ.
>
> "Come then, all you nations defiled by sin, receive the forgiveness of sin. For it is I who am your forgiveness, the pasch of your salvation, the lamb slain for you; it is I who am your ransom, your

life, your resurrection, your light, your salvation, your king. I am bringing you to the heights of heaven, I will show you the Father who is from all eternity, I will raise you up with my right hand" (*ibid.*, 102–103).

In one of his *Theological Orations* Gregory of Nazianzus (329–389) described as follows the Easter experience of being brought alive with the risen Christ:

Yesterday I was crucified with Christ; today I am glorified with him. Yesterday I died with him; today I am made alive with him. Yesterday I was buried with him; today I am raised with him (PG, 397B).

In the first centuries of Christianity the liturgical experience of redemption through Jesus' resurrection remained vitally alive. One permanent witness to that experience is the *Exultet* or Paschal Proclamation. Earlier forms of this prayer of praise reach back to the end of the fourth century. In the late twentieth century, when sung in the Easter vigil service, the *Exultet* continues to celebrate joyfully the Christian community's gratitude for being saved through the resurrection of the crucified Jesus.

THE MIDDLE AGES

In dealing with the Middle Ages I plan to concentrate on Thomas Aquinas (c. 1225–1274) whose treatment of Christ's resurrection was both innovative and traditional.

The Christological controversies of the fourth and fifth centuries led up to the classical formulations of the Council of Chalcedon (A.D. 451) about Christ's one person and two natures. Often his resurrection was discussed only in connection with the incarnation, and sometimes not at all. Chalcedon itself had nothing to say about the crucifixion and resurrection. In the centuries which followed the Council an all-absorbing theology of the incarnation generally monopolized attention. Thus twelfth-century theologians debated endlessly and sometimes bitterly one aspect of the mystery of the incarnation, the question of the *homo assumptus* or Word of God assuming a human nature. In Christ's actions what belonged to his humanity and what belonged to his divinity? Bernard of Clairvaux (1090–1153) stood apart from these debates with his freedom from abstract speculation and concern for a real spirituality inspired by the risen and glorified Christ.[12] Aquinas also differed from

many theological predecessors and successors in that even though his
Christology centered on the incarnation, nevertheless, he was ready to
treat Christ's resurrection at considerable length. Right down to our
own day many have failed to do that. Jesús Solano's standard textbook
on Christology, *Sacrae theologiae summa* 3 (Madrid, 1956), was so much
under the shadow of a Chalcedonian preoccupation with the incarnation
that this 326-page work included less than one page on the resurrection.
Bernard Lonergan's lecture notes for his course on Christology at the
Gregorian University betrayed the same "obsession" with the incarnation. They ran to 546 pages but included no more than a few incidental
remarks (425–427) about the resurrection. [13]

   What elements emerge from a study of Aquinas' treatment of Jesus'
resurrection? First, let me take up questions 53 to 56 of his Christology,
Part 3 of the *Summa theologiae*. Then we can turn to Part 4 of his *Summa
contra gentiles* to see what aspects of the resurrection he decided to include in that classic work of medieval apologetics.

(1) *Question 53*.   In the *Summa theologiae* Aquinas opens his discussion
of the resurrection by assuming the fact and seeking to expound its
meaning. The first article of question 53 asks whether "it was necessary
for Christ to rise again." Easter faith is to be explained and interpreted,
not challenged. Aquinas starts from where he actually is—a believer in
the risen Christ. As we will see in the next chapter, this procedure does
not satisfy Wolfhart Pannenberg. He proposes a starting-point outside
the circle of Easter-faith, with the intention of justifying this faith more
successfully. For him the process expressed by the dictum *fides paschalis
quaerens intellectum* should be reversed: "I examine the historical evidence
from the New Testament in order that I might find Easter faith." However, others like Karl Barth, Rudolf Bultmann and Karl Rahner (who
will also be discussed) agree with Aquinas that the theologian properly
begins from belief in the resurrection and not from the methodological
fiction of some neutral starting-point.

   Aquinas responds to his opening question by offering five reasons:
Christ rose again (a) to commend the divine justice, (b) to instruct our
faith, (c) to raise our hope, (d) to set in order the lives of the faithful, and
(e) to complete the work of our salvation. Aquinas explains the last reason for Christ's resurrection as follows: "Just as by dying he endured
evil in order to free us from it, so too by rising he was glorified that he
might move us toward what is good." Romans 4:25 is then cited to support this exposition of the two sides of the salvific process: "He was
handed over for our sins and rose again for our justification."

This procedure of elaborating reasons to show why the fact of the resurrection was "necessary" invites the following general comment. Undoubtedly it is desirable for theologians to explain how some article of Christian faith is intelligible in itself and consistent with other truths. However, an appeal to some principles as a means of clarifying some fact can only too readily deteriorate into an argument from principles to facts. If not here, only too often elsewhere, Aquinas and other medieval theologians are disposed to maintain that so-and-so is the case about such matters as Jesus' human consciousness because they hold this state of affairs to be fitting or downright necessary. Although the introduction of scientific historical methods has forced theologians to be more conscientious about establishing facts, the argument from principles (whether real or alleged principles) to facts still persists in subtler forms. One or two latter-day examples will turn up when we come to the question of Jesus' empty tomb.

An examination of Aquinas' five reasons reveals the following points. Reasons (b) and (c) suggest our *subjective* appropriation of Christ's resurrection through the decision to believe and hope. Reasons (d) and (e) concern the role of that resurrection in so-called *objective* redemption. Reason (a) connects the crucifixion and resurrection as the two events which make up the one paschal mystery. Whereas Christ's crucifixion constitutes his humbling himself to death out of love and obedience, the resurrection is the exaltation which the divine justice brings to those who humble themselves for God's sake. The theme of vindication which is adumbrated here will be fully expounded in Barth's interpretation of the resurrection as "the verdict of the Father." For Barth, Christ's passion and death express the Father's "No," his resurrection the Father's "Yes" (CD 4/1, 283ff, especially 297ff). Like Barth, Aquinas acknowledges the unity of cross and resurrection and locates this unity ultimately not in the area of meaning (as Bultmann does) but in *the action of God* who exalts the humble.

From the outset Aquinas seems aware that he dissents from those like Anselm of Canterbury (1033/34–1109) whose attention is monopolized by the obedient life and death of Jesus. Anselm's *Cur Deus homo*, a work which deeply affected medieval scholastics, Calvin, Melanchthon and many other theologians right down to the mid-twentieth century, manages to discuss the redemption while completely ignoring Christ's resurrection. The third objection in article 1 of Aquinas' question 53 introduces a position which has then haunted Western theology—and for that matter Christian living—for a very long time. If "Christ's passion sufficed for our salvation," it was not necessary for him to rise from the dead. So long as full credit for our redemption is ascribed to his death, his resurrection will become at best a highly useful (if not strictly necessary) proof of Christian claims. Aquinas replies: "Christ's passion effected our salvation, properly speaking, by removing evils, but the resurrection did so as the beginning and model of all good things." This answer anticipates a fuller treatment which Aquinas will offer on "the causality of Christ's resurrection" in question 56. Within an Aristotelian scheme the suffering of Christ is classified (under the general heading of final causality) as a meritorious cause; his resurrection is interpreted as both efficient and exemplary cause of our justification and resurrection.

Here Aquinas presents himself as faithful to that central conviction of the early Church's liturgy: both the crucifixion and the resurrection are sacramentally actualized in baptism and the Eucharist. Believers experience salvation coming to them through the crucified and risen Christ. Aquinas expresses theologically what Christians celebrate liturgically: Christ effected our redemption through both his dying *and his rising*.

Article 2 of question 53 ("Was it fitting for Christ to rise again on the third day?") sounds innocuously medieval, and Aquinas' answer seems to content itself with an undisturbed Chalcedonian belief. Resurrection on the third day formed a highly appropriate testimony to the God-man. To confirm our faith in his divinity, we required a prompt return from the dead, not a resurrection postponed until the end of the world. At the same time, some interval between death and resurrection was needed to show that he was truly man and had truly died. A death followed by immediate resurrection could have suggested that his death had not been genuine.

In the course of his discussion Aquinas raises two objections which still retain their vitality. First, surely Christ's resurrection should not have been deferred but should have taken place on the same day (objection 2)? This line of argument would reduce the "gap" between crucifixion and resurrection and eventually identify them as two aspects of the one event. An opposite objection (nr. 1) would propose instead that Christ's resurrection should have been postponed until the end of the world.

> Members ought to be in conformity with their head. But we who are his members do not rise from death on the third day, since our rising is put off until the end of the world. Therefore, it seems that Christ, who is our head, should not have risen on the third day, but that his resurrection ought to have been postponed until the end of the world.

In the 1960s G.W.H. Lampe mounted a similar argument from the solidarity based on "the truth of the incarnation." By becoming man, the Son of God entered fully into our human condition both during lifetime and after death. Hence his body decayed in the grave, as do the bodies of other men and women. His "resurrection cannot be of a different order" from our resurrection.[14]

Elsewhere I have taken up Lampe's case.[15] Here it is interesting to note the style of Aquinas' reply to the problem raised against a third-day resurrection by Christ's solidarity with us:

> The head and members conform in nature, but not in power. For the power of the head excels that of the members. Hence, to show forth the excellence of Christ's power, it was fitting that he should rise on the third day, while the resurrection of others is put off until the end of the world.

Aquinas' biological notion that the head of a body possesses more power than the other limbs may be antiquated, but it points to an essential distinction which Paul indicates between Christ's resurrection and that of others. Even in 1 Corinthians 15 the apostle's readiness to assimilate our resurrection to Christ's has its limits. Only Christ "became a life-giving spirit" (1 Cor 15:45). No one else was or will be "raised for our justification" (Rom 4:25). This difference, which Lampe glosses over, is respected in their various ways by different modern writers. Thus Rudolf Bultmann, as we will see in the next chapter, speaks of Christ "rising into the kerygma" and interprets the Easter-faith of the primitive Church as expressing the saving value of the crucifixion. But Bultmann does not talk of *our* rising into the kerygma nor understand Easter-faith as affirming precisely the same kind of meaningfulness in our personal death.

Article 3 of question 53 ("Was Christ the first to rise from the dead?") looks like a harmless attempt to relate Christ's own resurrection to the various raisings of dead persons reported in the Old Testament and in the Gospels. One distinction introduced by Aquinas deserves retrieval. Whereas Christ enjoyed a "true and perfect resurrection" which excluded even the possibility of ever dying again, the other dead persons "returned to life in such a way that they were to die again." Such "imperfect" resurrection, which meant the resumption of biological life under the normal conditions of space and time, might be better called resuscitation or reanimation. At all events, Aquinas clearly distinguished between Christ's resurrection, on the one hand, and the raising of Lazarus and other such cases, on the other. This distinction had not always been made by the Church Fathers. Curiously it was there, however, in the argument Porphyry brought against the Christian expectation of a final resurrection for all men and women. Would that alleged resurrection resemble the resurrection of Lazarus or that of Christ?

> If it conforms to that of Christ how can the resurrection of the one who was born without any intervention of seed accord with that of the sons of his seed? And if it conforms to the resurrection of Lazarus this does not seem appropriate, because the resurrection of Lazarus was accomplished with a body not yet corrupted, with the same body in which he was recognized as Lazarus, whereas our bodies will be raised after having been scattered for many centuries (*Fragment*, 92).[16]

Porphyry denied, of course, the raising of Lazarus, the resurrection of Christ and the general resurrection to come. Nevertheless, like Aquinas he appreciated that some distinctions were to be made between the three cases and, specifically, that the claimed raising of Lazarus did not coincide with claims about Christ's resurrection.

(2) *Question 55.*   The last article of question 53 ("Was Christ the cause of his own resurrection?") and the whole of question 54 (on "the quality of the risen Christ") remain the least promising sections of Aquinas' discussion. Much of what he says here about the reunification of Christ's body and soul proves at best unexciting, at worst quaintly medieval. Hence I move straight on to the treatment of "the manifestation of the resurrection" in question 55.

In the first article ("Should not Christ's resurrection have been manifested to all men?"), like Origen Aquinas accepts that there were post-Easter appearances only to "certain special" persons and that these encounters differed from any later Christian experiences of the risen Lord. Some twentieth-century authors deny or doubt this difference. Apropos of the meeting with the risen Christ to which Paul refers in 1 Corinthians 15:8, John Macquarrie observes: "It is not unreasonable to suppose that it is . . . on a par with the encounters which subsequent believers may have had with the risen Christ."[17] We are dealing here with something enormously important and cannot afford to let Macquarrie (and others) off lightly. What is at stake is human access to God through the risen Christ. Do the official witnesses to the resurrection play an indispensable role, or can believers—at least in principle—know the risen Lord independently? In this regard, could faith prove ultimately free from the necessity of being mediated socially through the testimony of certain privileged apostolic witnesses? Should we acknowledge a democracy of experience vis-à-vis the risen Christ, so that as regards the possibility of such an experience all post-apostolic generations would be on an equal footing with the original apostolic witnesses?

Like Barth centuries later (CD III/2, 448f, 454f; IV/3, 281ff), Aquinas points to the way revelation worked: "Christ's resurrection was not manifested to everyone, but to some, by whose testimony it could be brought to the knowledge of others." Equivalently Aquinas is distinguishing two groups of believers: (a) the official witnesses to the risen Lord, who received the "foundational" revelation and whose activity brought the Church into being, and (b) those later Christians whose encounter with God in Christ remains dependent upon those apostolic witnesses. A second line of argument emerges when Aquinas discusses the (first) objection, that "since Christ's passion was manifested to all . . . the glory of the resurrection ought to have been manifested to all." In effect, Aquinas holds that the divergent status of Christ's death and resurrection explains the different publicity of the two events. As Christ suffered with a body subject to the normal laws of human existence, his passion and death were in principle open to ordinary observation. But we cannot presuppose the same publicity for that event in which he rose in glory to assume a heavenly mode of existence with his Father. Rather than constituting "a return to the familiar conditions of life," the resurrection was a passage "to an immortal and God-like kind of life" (article 2).

Aquinas' position here requires strengthening through more scriptural backing. John's classic distinction between those who have seen and believed and those who "have not seen and yet believe" (John 20:29) pointed to the unique role of the apostolic witnesses who met the risen Christ, testified to that experience and founded the Church. These witnesses saw for themselves and believed. In proclaiming the good news of the resurrection and gathering together those who had not seen the risen Lord and yet were ready to believe, those original witnesses did not rely on the experience and testimony of others. Paul also drew attention to the difference between the fundamental post-resurrection encounters and all later experiences of the risen Lord: "Last of all" Christ "appeared also to me" (1 Cor 15:8). This episode constituted Paul's apostolic calling and the basis for his mission (1 Cor 9:1; Gal 1:11ff). Other Christians shared with him the gift of the Holy Spirit and life "in Christ." But they did not experience that fundamental meeting with the risen Lord which made Paul a witness "by whose testimony" the resurrection "could be brought to the knowledge of others."[18]

Article 2 ("Was it fitting for the disciples to have seen the resur-

rection itself?") raises the point that no New Testament witness claims
to have been present at the resurrection itself. How then can we speak
of "witnesses to the resurrection"? Aquinas remarks reasonably that the
apostles could testify to the resurrection because they saw him alive
whom they had known to be dead. The apparently trivial issue adumbrated here recurs in a debate initiated by Willi Marxsen in the 1960s.

The other article which deserves our attention in question 55 is
number 5 ("Should Christ have demonstrated the truth of the resurrection by proofs [*argumentis*]?"). Here we reach a question which continues
to divide many theologians and other Christians into two opposed fac-
tions: the role of evidence for Christ's resurrection. Aquinas states the
key issue in objection 1: "Faith is required regarding Christ's resurrection. Hence proofs are out of place here." In more developed and sophisticated forms this contention has haunted later theology. As we
shall see in the next chapter, it is often a matter of safeguarding the freedom, certainty and gifted quality of faith.

Aquinas agrees that "proofs" in the sense of "scientific" proofs
drawn from human reason remain useless for demonstrating things of
faith. But "proofs" in the sense of visible signs may be at work to manifest the truth, as was the case with Christ's appearances manifesting the
truth of his resurrection. By these "very evident signs he showed that
he was truly risen from the dead." "The merit of faith," Aquinas explains, "arises from this, that at God's bidding man believes what he
does not see." John's Gospel portrays Thomas seeing the bodily reality
of the risen Christ and going beyond that visible evidence to believe in
his divinity: "My Lord and my God" (John 20:28). The fact that certain
visible signs provide the means by which someone comes to faith does
not "totally rob faith of its substance." Yet "a more perfect faith" would
not "require such aids to belief."

Let me draw attention to two noteworthy features of Aquinas' position. He refuses to suspect and depreciate visible signs, even if he allows that a readiness to believe without such signs characterizes "a more
perfect faith." In other words the believer accepts and takes advantage
of such signs as are given, but does not unconditionally demand them.
Second, in Aquinas' view, accepting the truth of the resurrection is
equivalent to believing in God. Although article 5 is explicitly concerned with "proof" for Christ's resurrection, this turns out to be a matter of believing in God through visible signs. Chapters Four, Five and
Six of this book will expound the resurrection of the crucified Jesus as
the event par excellence through which the tripersonal God is revealed
and invites human faith. For Christians believing in God is essentially

believing in a God who has raised Jesus and will also raise us from the dead (Gal 1:1; 1 Cor 6:14; 15:15; etc.).

(3) *Question 56.* Finally, we reach question 56, where Aquinas applies Aristotelian notions of efficient and exemplary causality to Christ's resurrection. As well as forming the exemplar to which we must conform, the resurrection—or rather the risen Christ—constitutes the instrumental cause both for our present justification ("the resurrection of the soul") and for the future completion of justification in our bodily resurrection. "Christ's resurrection" functions as "the efficient and exemplary cause of our resurrection," inasmuch as "Christ's humanity, according to which he rose again, is as it were the instrument of his divinity and works by its power" (art. 1, reply to obj. 3).

A summary of Aquinas' contributions in Part 3 of the *Summa theologiae* should include the following items. In the face of a long-standing preoccupation with the incarnation, he maintains the essential place of the resurrection within an adequate Christology. His point of departure is his belief in the resurrection, not some allegedly neutral position. He insists that our redemption came through both the crucifixion *and the resurrection.* While he takes Christ's dying and rising as two events in a single process, he refuses to identify them. Likewise he points to that essential difference between our resurrection and Christ's resurrection which makes resurrection after three days intelligible in the latter case. Further, Aquinas distinguishes Christ's "perfect" resurrection from any "imperfect" resurrection (= the reanimation of a corpse). He maintains a fundamental difference between the apostolic encounters with the risen Christ and those of later believers. Finally, he recognizes "visible signs" attesting the resurrection, even if he refuses to allow that ordinary human proofs apply here.

A comprehensive treatment of Aquinas' thought on the resurrection would not only draw on other works like his commentaries on scripture and on the *Sentences* of Peter Lombard but also discuss questions 57–59 of his *Summa theologiae* (on Christ's ascension, his "sitting at the right hand of the Father" and his power as judge). Here I want to restrict myself to Aquinas' reflections on the resurrection in his *Summa contra gentiles,* book 4.

(4) *Summa contra gentiles.* In the Middle Ages Jesus' resurrection naturally featured in works aimed at converting Jews to Christianity. It likewise entered apologetics directed toward Islam, although in this case

Christian scholars were generally more concerned to show that the Bible was superior to the Koran and that Jesus Christ's divinity put him above Mohammed. Aquinas aimed at a broad audience in his *Summa contra gentiles:* Muslims, Jews, Cathars and non-believers affected by the philosophy of Averroes. He appealed to reason (rather than revelation) to demonstrate Christian truth.

Curiously in this classic work of apologetics for non-believers Aquinas does not take up Jesus' own resurrection as a distinct theme to be examined in its own right. Here he fails to follow the lead of Origen's *Contra Celsum* and joins forces rather with Clement, Justin, Tertullian and the other early Christian writers who aimed to recommend hope in our resurrection from the dead.

Aquinas begins by stating clearly the nature of our coming resurrection which is not to be falsely spiritualized and reduced simply to the life of grace:

> There are . . . some who are perverse in their understanding of this
> and they do not believe in the future resurrection of bodies, but at-
> tempt to ascribe what we read about the resurrection in the Scriptures
> to a spiritual resurrection in which some arise from the death of sin
> by grace (IV, 79, 5).

Aquinas bolsters the case for a bodily resurrection by noting "the natural desire of man to tend to happiness," the fact that there can be no "ultimate happiness" without resurrection (IV, 79, 11), and the sense in which resurrection is the natural destiny for the whole human being.

> Resurrection is natural if one considers its purpose, for it is natural
> that the soul be united to the body. But the principle of resurrection
> is not natural. It is caused by the divine power alone (IV, 81, 14).

Aquinas' argument for the reasonableness and naturalness of our future resurrection both recalls early Christian apologetics and anticipates some contemporary approaches. In the second century Athenagoras had argued in his *De resurrectione* that since we cannot achieve the full purpose of our life in this world, this must happen in a future life. Since we are made up of a body and soul, it is natural to expect that our body and soul will both participate in the life to come (nrs. 18–25). In our own century Wolfhart Pannenberg presses the cause of resurrection as a bodily-cum-spiritual fulfillment which can be reasonably expected for the whole human person.[19]

Aquinas pushes beyond Tertullian and other early Christian apologists for our resurrection in his argument that we will rise "numerically the same" (IV, 81, 10; see IV, 80 and 81 *passim*). Yet often we find him tackling identical issues. He devotes a chapter to showing that "among the risen there will be no use of food or sexual love" (IV, 83). He concludes that in the resurrected state

> . . . all the business of the active life—it seems ordered to the use of food, to sexual activity, to the other necessities of the corruptible life—will come to a halt. Therefore, only the occupation of the contemplative life will persist in the resurrection (IV, 83, 24).

We saw above how Tertullian excludes eating, drinking and sexual activity in the life to come. At the same time, Tertullian maintains that although the digestive and genital organs will cease to function, they will remain parts of the risen body so as to have "a man in full being." In the name of "integrity" Aquinas also holds that when risen from the dead, men and women will retain these organs: "They will . . . have all the members of this sort, even though there be no use for them, to reestablish the integrity of the natural body" (IV, 88, 2).

As regards the pleasures of heaven, Aquinas aims to rebut "the error of the Jews and of the Saracens, who hold that in the resurrection men will have use for food and sexual pleasure as they do now" (IV, 83, 14). But he is also aware that from the time of the early Church, Christian millenarians have held similar views. Here his apologetic about the resurrection is as much concerned to correct insiders as it is to convince outsiders (*ibid.*).

On one hilarious (minor) objection Aquinas upstages the Church Fathers. We saw earlier that Tertullian and Athenagoras dealt with the difficulty raised against the chance of resurrection for those persons unfortunate enough to have been devoured by wild beasts and cannibals. Aquinas investigates the question of bodily resurrection for the cannibals themselves and not just for their victims. How can "a man's identical body" be "restored to life" when "the same flesh is found in many men" (IV, 80, 4 and 5)? This problem seems particularly acute for those cannibals whose diet is restricted to "human flesh" and even more for those whose "parents, too, have eaten only human flesh." Aquinas believes that "if something was materially present in many men," it "will rise in him in whom it was the first time" (= the cannibals' victim). That would seem to exclude any chance of bodily resurrection for any individuals and families misguided enough to eat only human flesh. However, "what is wanting" in such cases "can be supplied by the power of God" (IV, 81, 13).

Like Origen's *Contra Celsum*, the *Summa contra gentiles* remains an
interesting work of Christian apologetics. But unlike the *Contra Celsum*
it has practically nothing to say directly about the resurrection of Jesus
himself. Its contribution lies elsewhere.[20]

TO THE TWENTIETH CENTURY

To write the full history of what Christians have made of Jesus'
resurrection, or failed to make of it, would require volumes. It calls for
a proper examination of the whole story of the veneration of the Holy
Sepulchre in Jerusalem. What, for instance, could we glean from the
records of pilgrimages to the Holy Land and, for that matter, from their
brutal counterpart, the Crusades which ran from the eleventh to the
fourteenth century? Then we would need to look hard and searchingly
at the relevant liturgical texts of Christianity, both Eastern and Western. Many musicians, sculptors, painters, and illuminators of manu-
scripts have enjoyed the advantages of their genius in expressing the
nature and consequences of belief in Jesus risen from the dead. Easter
hymns, books of prayer and popular devotions can reveal how ordinary
Christians understood and articulated their resurrection faith. A comprehensive study would also look at Easter sermons, funeral sermons
and the symbols chosen by believers to adorn the graves of their de-
ceased relatives.

In Europe, North America, Australia and elsewhere, cemeteries
bear witness to a change which began with the Renaissance, was sub-
merged by the Reformation and Counter-Reformation and then seriously set in with the eighteenth century: a certain erosion of Easter faith
in the Western world. Young men with lowered torches, broken col-
umns and other such expressions of a human life now terminated began
to replace symbols of hope in the resurrection. Deism and the Enlightenment reduced belief to three basic ideas: God, freedom and immortality (which did not necessarily include bodily resurrection as such).
Immanuel Kant (1724–1804) saw morality as the essence of reasonable
religion. Hence Christianity should remain unaffected by the contin-
gent truth or otherwise of Jesus' resurrection from the dead. Faith in
human progress and various styles of hope for a this-worldly perfection
eventually replaced for many Western people any expectation of a full
salvation to come through sharing in Christ's victory over death. By the
mid-nineteenth century philosophers, social reformers and others not
uncommonly rejected not only bodily resurrection but also the personal
immortality of the human soul.

By that time the resurrection of Jesus himself had been the target of fresh rejection for a century or more. In 1774–78 came the posthumous publication of selections from the writings of Hermann Reimarus (1694–1768). He represented Jesus as a preacher of messianic illusions who died in failure. The disciples then stole the corpse, fabricated the story of the resurrection and set up the Christian Church. Earlier in the eighteenth century David Hume (1711–1776), as part of his case against miracles, made his position clear on Christ's resurrection. He went beyond Celsus and Porphyry to maintain that no number of witnesses (whether friendly or hostile) would ever be sufficient to establish it.

Orthodox believers rose to the defense. In part 2 of *A View of the Evidences of Christianity* William Paley (1743–1805) argued that it was impossible to account for the Easter faith of the first disciples without supposing that Jesus really rose from the dead. Giovanni Perrone (1794–1876) in part 1 of *On the True Religion Against Unbelievers* put the case for Christ's resurrection (taken together with his miracles and prophecies) verifying the revelation he brought. Many Roman Catholic and other apologists maintained that the miracles of Jesus and especially "the greatest of the miracles," his resurrection, demonstrated the truth of his claims to divinity.

The first part of this chapter showed how the early Church directed its interests more to the final hope supported by Jesus' resurrection and to the present (redemptive) experience of the risen Lord in the community's sacramental life. These interests have not by any means disappeared in the nineteenth and twentieth centuries. One thinks, respectively, of Jürgen Moltmann's *Theology of Hope* (New York & London, 1967) and of the theme of the paschal mystery in the liturgical renewal largely led by Belgian and German Benedictines which prepared the way for the Second Vatican Council's Constitution on the Sacred Liturgy (1963). At the same time, however, with Deism, the Enlightenment and their aftermath, three other themes came very much to the fore: the *factual* (historical) status of Jesus' resurrection, its *revelatory* value, and the nature of *faith* in the crucified and risen Jesus. Of course, these themes had not by any means been overlooked in the early Church. Nevertheless, they caught the attention of many theologians in modern times. The next chapters will examine some major writers who have taken up these themes.

2

The Resurrection in
Modern Theology

To complete my sampling of the ways Christians have understood and
interpreted the resurrection of Jesus Christ, I want to spend this and the
next chapter examining eight twentieth-century theologians. The first
pair pick themselves naturally: Karl Barth (1886–1968) and Rudolf Bultmann (1884–1976).

Barth helped to pioneer a renewed interest in Christ's resurrection—particularly through his *Epistle to the Romans*. In its second edition
of 1922 that book marks the real beginning of twentieth-century Protestant theology.[1] To prevent this investigation of Barth's view of
Christ's resurrection from becoming confused and confusing, it seems
advisable to make use of a distinction between the middle and the late
Barth. His Anselm study (*Fides Quaerens Intellectum*) of 1931 forms the
turning point.[2] It would be inaccurate to maintain that Barth's later theology represents a total break with his work in the 1920s, but it is in-
contestable that certain important shifts take place.

Despite his rejection of liberal theology, Barth's *Romans* displays a
certain Christian "existentialism" affected by the anthropology of Kierkegaard and Dostoevsky. This is the period when he revels in paradox
and dialectical thinking and has not yet become uncompromisingly
Christocentric. His Anselm book shows how he has rethought the theological task in terms of "faith seeking understanding." The new phase
is definitively inaugurated with the publication of the first volume of the
Church Dogmatics in 1932. The influence of Kierkegaard's and Dostoevsky's existentialist philosophy gives way to a concentration on the Word

34

of God. Dogmatic thinking based on the analogy of faith displaces dialectical thinking. There is a shift toward the unqualified dominance of Christology.

In approaching Barth's views on Christ's resurrection, it will help to put five questions and to note any changes between his middle and later periods. Does he attribute a central importance to the resurrection? Is he ready to describe it as an historical event? How does he link the crucifixion and the resurrection? What is his view of Jesus' empty tomb? What relationship does he maintain between the resurrection and the *parousia* or Jesus' second coming?

(1) *The Centrality of the Resurrection.* It can seem that Christ's resurrection forms the central theme for the Barth of the 1920s. During this period *The Resurrection of the Dead* appears, in which Paul's teaching on the resurrection in 1 Corinthians 15 is taken as "the clue" not only to the meaning of the whole letter but also to the apostle's other writings.

> Here Paul discloses generally his focus, his background, and his assumptions with a definiteness he but seldom uses elsewhere, and with a particularity which he has not done in his other epistles as known to us. The epistles to the Romans, the Philippians and the Colossians cannot even be understood, unless we keep in mind the sharp accentuation which their contents receive in the light of Corinthians 15.

Barth's evaluation of this chapter carries further implications. 1 Corinthians 15 is judged "vitally important" for "understanding the testimony of the New Testament generally."[3] To all appearances no stronger acknowledgment of the centrality of Easter could be expected.

And yet a second look at *The Resurrection of the Dead* shows how Barth's real intention requires that we modify our assessment. Ultimately he aims at elucidating the truth of revelation. The resurrection of the dead "as such is only to be grasped in the category of revelation and none other." It expresses the "miracle" which God performs in revealing himself to man (145f). Barth makes a similar assertion in his *Romans:* "The resurrection is the revelation; the disclosing of Jesus as the Christ, the appearing of God and the apprehending of God in Jesus" (30). The resurrection is not merely credited with a central function in revelation; it is absorbed into revelation. As we will see, Bultmann's view of the resurrection resembles that of the middle Barth.[4]

The later Barth, while continuing to affirm the centrality of Christ's resurrection, declines to interpret it simply as an expression of revelation. The revelatory function remains essential, but the resurrection is no longer merged into revelation. From the early to the later volumes of the *Church Dogmatics* we meet a reiterated insistence on the factual reality of the resurrection and the appearances of the risen Christ. These appearances form the "Archimedean point" upon which all biblical witness rests (CD I/2, 117). The "central," indispensable place which the event of the resurrection holds in the New Testament finds expression in the following terms:

> While we could imagine a New Testament containing only the history of Easter and its message, we could not possibly imagine a New Testament without it. For the history and the message of Easter contains everything else, while without it everything else would be left in the air as a mere abstraction. . . . It is the key to the whole. . . . Either we believe with the New Testament in the risen Jesus Christ, or we do not believe in him at all (CD III/2, 443).

Barth is no longer satisfied to speak simply of the "message" of the resurrection. Such an expression could allow us to reduce the resurrection simply to its revelatory value and its function in the Church's proclamation. The actual occurrence of the resurrection as "history" must be safeguarded.

(2) *The Resurrection as Historical Event.* The middle Barth appears reluctant to speak of the resurrection as an historical event, separate from and subsequent to the crucifixion. He classifies it as a "non-historical happening."

> The raising of Jesus from the dead is not an event in history elongated so as still to remain an event in the midst of other events. The resurrection is the non-historical relating of the whole historical life of Jesus to its origin in God (*Romans*, 203, 195).

At most, Barth admits that the resurrection may be called "historical" in the sense that certain persons at a particular time and place came to know it and proclaim it. He writes: "The resurrection is . . . an occurrence in history, which took place outside the gates of Jerusalem in the year A.D. 30, inasmuch as it there 'came to pass,' was discovered and recognized" (*Romans*, 30). Yet even this admission receives a significant qualification which robs it of its proper force. At this stage Barth shows himself indifferent to the "when" and "where" of the testimony to the resurrection. As regards the "human eyes" of the first witnesses,

. . . time and place are a matter of perfect indifference. Of what these eyes see it can be equally well said that it was, is, and will be, never and nowhere, as that it was, is, and will be always and everywhere possible (*Resurrection*, 143).

The assertion that the resurrection was "discovered and recognized" by a particular group of men at a definite time loses its importance. We are asked to discard any assertion that the original resurrection witnesses enjoyed an experience which was unique and irrepeatable. No difference in principle between any earlier or later "discovery" of the resurrection can be allowed.

When he reaches his *Church Dogmatics* period, Barth jettisons the tendency to underplay the element of historical reality. The resurrection constitutes a particular event in the temporal course of Jesus' history, an innerworldly, spatiotemporal occurrence in its own right, "a separate event, different from his death, following it in time."[5] As a new deed of God the resurrection creates a new history:

Jesus has a further history beginning on the third day after his death. . . . It is a second history—or rather, the fragments of a second history—of Jesus. It is the Easter history, the history of the forty days between his resurrection and ascension (CD III/2, 441).

Barth's changed attitude means that he becomes ready to defend the proper place of historical inquiry into the resurrection. An "impartial and painstaking investigation" of New Testament texts in "their character as historical documents" can create a "neutral and objective" knowledge as the presupposition to the "genuine and fruitful knowledge" of love and faith. Barth clearly has Bultmann in mind and challenges an imposition of Heideggerian existentialism on the New Testament, a denial of the miraculous and the hermeneutical method which approaches the text with questions already raised by the situation of human existence. He asks for

. . . a consideration of what the texts say (and do not say) in their attestation of this event, without measuring them by an imported picture of the world and history, without reading them through these alien spectacles, without prejudice as to what is possible or impossible . . . without imposing questions which they themselves do not ask, but entering into their own questions and remaining open to their own replies (CD IV/2, 149f).

What Barth ultimately wants is the decision of faith, not the acceptance of a well-attested historical event. Faith itself remains unattainable by historical research. Although the resurrection occurs in history, the acknowledgment of it arises through the intervention of the Holy Spirit.

Nevertheless, Barth's increased sense of historical realism allows him to press the claims of a "neutral and objective" knowledge preparatory to the "genuine" knowledge of faith. Can the resurrection then be "proved" by historical investigation? Does he agree with Wolfhart Pannenberg that prior to our commitment of faith we could in principle know the resurrection? Barth declines to move to this position. Various conditions must be fulfilled before we can speak of some alleged event as proven according to the canons of modern historical scholarship. We would need to know (a) the outline of the event in its "How," both (b) independently of the standpoint of the onlooker and (c) within its general and specific context, as well as (d) in its analogies to other events. Barth takes a firm stand on our incapacity to satisfy condition (b) by offering "external objective assurance" based on "outside impartial witnesses." When they call for "a decision of faith" in the face of the Easter message and "not for the acceptance of a well-attested historical report," the New Testament witnesses decline to meet this requirement. Not even the list provided by 1 Corinthians 15 forms an attempt at such a proof. We could falsify Paul's intention even by trying to deduce a proof from this passage (CD IV/1, 335). 1 Corinthians 15:5–8 may not be regarded as "a citation of witnesses for the purposes of historical proof" (CD III/2, 452).

Barth's argument invites two comments. First, he limits the possibilities of objective, historical proof by admitting evidence only from outsiders, "impartial witnesses" who report something which remains "external" to them and independent of their "standpoint." Does objectivity always require such neutrality on the part of the witnesses? Surely it is possible to be a highly involved "insider" and yet testify in a way which would yield reasonable assurance that the event in question has truly taken place? Second, Barth repeats in the *Church Dogmatics* what he has already maintained in *The Resurrection of the Dead*—that Paul does not intend the list of witnesses in 1 Corinthians 15 as a proof for Christ's resurrection. "The point of the passage" is not "historical demonstration" (*Resurrection*, 132). In a review of that book Bultmann disputes this interpretation of the apostle's intention.[6] Bultmann agrees with Pannenberg that Paul does wish to offer what amounts to a proof for the resurrection, even if—unlike Pannenberg—Bultmann deplores this procedure.[7]

Barth's definitive position on the "historical" character of the resurrection seems too good to be true. It looks like claiming genuine historical reality for the resurrection and yet denying historians the right to pronounce on the matter. On the one hand, the (believing) acknowledgment of the resurrection arises through the intervention of the Holy Spirit and remains unattainable by historical research. On the other hand, the resurrection enjoys a true historical reality, so that it would be "a fundamental misunderstanding" to interpret it as though it had "not happened in time and space in the same way as the death of Jesus Christ." Since normal methods of inquiry fail to establish the resurrection, it may be classified as "saga" or "legend" (not as "myth"). (Barth understands as sagas or legends events which—unlike myths—did in fact occur. Their details, however, were of such a nature that they evade verification by the historical method.)

Barth admits then that when we move from Good Friday to Easter, we enter "a historical sphere of a different kind," but only in the sense that we pass beyond the historically verifiable (CD IV/1, 336f, 334). We remain in "the sphere of history and time *no less* than in the case of the words and acts and even the death of Jesus" (italics mine). Barth scorns as "superstition" the view that "only the historically verifiable could take place in time" (CD III/2, 442, 446). Such a position has puzzled Pannenberg and many others. What happens in the spatio-temporal sphere of history must surely be open to historical inquiry. To the extent that Jesus' resurrection is placed on an historical par with the episodes of his life and death, it must like them become a proper object of the historian's attention.

Barth's changed attitude toward the concrete objectivity of the resurrection carries with it a new conviction that the apostolic witnesses play a unique, unrepeatable function. For later Christians Christ "is no longer present and revealed" as "he once was in the forty days" (CD IV/1, 319f). In the course of writing the *Church Dogmatics* Barth increasingly stresses the objective and corporeal nature of the apostles' encounter with their risen Lord. At first he speaks of "the Easter story, Christ truly, corporeally risen, and as such appearing to his disciples, talking with them, acting in their midst" (CD I/2, 114). Later he elaborates this by explaining literally the Johannine and Lucan portrayal of the risen Christ eating with the twelve and inviting them to touch his body (CD III/2, 448). The resurrection

> . . . involves a definite seeing with the eyes and hearing with the ears and handling with the hands, as the Easter-stories say so unmistakably and emphatically, and is again underlined in 1 John 1. It involves real eating and drinking, speaking and answering, reasoning . . . and doubting and then, believing (CD IV/2, 143).

Barth's eagerness to make this point leads him to use language which risks reducing the resurrection to the resuscitation of a corpse. Jesus Christ, he declares, is "risen—bodily, visibly, audibly, perceptibly in the same concrete sense in which he died" (CD IV/1, 351).

Barth is rightly concerned to safeguard the real objectivity of those encounters, which took place between the disciples and the risen Christ in the days following the crucifixion and which "established, awakened and created faith" (CD III/2, 445). But Barth ventures into a minefield of problems by associating that objectivity with Christ's body being perceived by the disciples through what sounds like an *ordinary* use of their senses of sight, hearing and touch. Barth is well aware that the New Testament details concerning Easter chronology and topography need not be taken literally. Luke's scheme of forty days may be interpreted typically, rather than as offering "precise chronological information as to the duration of the appearances." Likewise the conflict between the Galilean and Jerusalem traditions of Easter appearances should not lead us to attempt those "incongruous" "harmonizations to which the older commentators resorted" (CD III/2, 452). Must we then take *au pied de la lettre* all the vivid, physical details of the Easter stories found in Luke 24 and John 20–21?[8] These details suggest the anti-Docetic preoccupation of the two evangelists and their concern to stress three points: (a) the reality of the resurrection, (b) the continuity between the risen Lord and the earthly Jesus, and (c) the disciples' status as witnesses. When Jesus rose from the dead, it was no mere spirit that met the disciples but a person identical with the Jesus who had lived and died. Hence they could recognize him and testify to his new, risen existence. Moreover, it is at our peril that we deal with the Lucan and Johannine "realism" in isolation from the rest of the New Testament. For instance, neither in 1 Corinthians nor elsewhere in Paul's letters do we find any suggestion that the risen Jesus returned to such earthly activities as eating, drinking and being handled. As raised and exalted, he appeared to certain witnesses (1 Cor 15:5–8). Barth would be on much surer ground if he had invoked the divine initiative which effected these decisive encounters. It is fatal to allege that the objectivity of the Easter appearances stands or falls with an ordinary sense-perception of the risen Christ.

(3) *Cross and Resurrection.* During the 1920s Barth holds together Calvary and Easter almost to the point of identifying them. "Only in the cross of Christ," he declares, "can we comprehend the truth and meaning of his resurrection" (*Romans*, 150). Over this issue Barth shifts ground not by weakening the link between the crucifixion and the res-

urrection, but by choosing to speak of the resurrection as illuminating the crucifixion rather than vice versa. In *Credo* where he anticipates many lines later developed in *Church Dogmatics* he writes: "One cannot understand the cross of Christ otherwise than from his resurrection" (102). In fact, "the whole life and death of Jesus are undoubtedly interpreted in the light of the resurrection" (*ibid.*, 96). We face an irreversible sequence and may not go behind the resurrection to make the cross paramount. Jesus' death lacks any autonomous or absolute significance, and is to be properly understood in the light of Easter.

(4) *The Empty Tomb.* Notoriously the Barth of the 1920s professes little concern for Jesus' empty tomb. He does not bother to assert that the bones of Jesus lie somewhere in Palestine; the whole issue remains too trivial for him to commit himself to some position. "The tomb may prove to be a definitely closed or an open tomb; it is really a matter of indifference. What avails the tomb, proved to be this or that, at Jerusalem in the year A.D. 30?" (*Resurrection*, 142).

By the time Barth has come to write *Credo*, he has become convinced that to question or strike out the empty grave would be to tamper seriously with the apostolic witness (*Credo*, 100). Although "Christians do not believe in the empty tomb but in the living Christ," this does not imply "that we can believe in the living Christ without believing in the empty tomb," for it forms "an indispensable sign" which "obviates all possible misunderstanding" (CD III/2, 453). It precludes misinterpreting the existence of the risen Christ as something

> . . . purely beyond or inward. It distinguishes the confession that Jesus Christ lives from a mere manner of speaking on the part of believers. It is the negative presupposition of the concrete objectivity of his being (CD IV/1, 341).

Maintaining the empty tomb and with it bodily resurrection bears directly on what we hold about the personal existence of the risen Christ: "Unless Christ's resurrection was a resurrection of the body, we have no guarantee that it was the decisively acting subject Jesus himself, the man Jesus, who rose from the dead" (CD III/2, 448).

(5) *Resurrection and Second Coming.* The middle Barth's tendency to disengage the resurrection from time and place naturally involves a readiness to identify it with Christ's second coming. Differences of past, present and future are obliterated by using Kierkegaard's principle of

simultaneity. An eternal "now" absorbs the future and the past. The *parousia* ceases to be something truly future and turns into a timeless symbol for an immediate relationship to God which is always possible. The end of time is transmuted into the "beyond" of eternity (*Romans*, 116, 500). The ultimate in time becomes the ultimate in importance.

Although Barth subsequently shows himself still ready to describe the resurrection, "the outpouring of the Spirit and the final return of Jesus Christ" as "forms of one and the same event," he also maintains that "we must strongly distinguish" these three stages (CD IV/3, 294). The time of the Church constitutes an "interim period" in which we are still moving toward the final age of the second coming (*Credo*, 115, 117ff). He agrees that his earlier works fail to do justice to the movement toward that real end expressed by Romans 13:11f (CD II/1, 635). Like the resurrection this final episode, which will occur at the general resurrection of the dead, forms "a historical and therefore a temporal event" (CD III/2, 624). This reverses Barth's earlier position that "the resurrection of Christ, or his second coming, which is the same thing, is not a historical event."[9]

In his third theological period Barth cautions those who await the final *parousia* against grounding their hope in the limitations and contradictions of the present age. The New Testament does not look for Christ's return simply because of "the depth of human imperfection, corruption and need," or because of "the depth of the visible and palpable contradiction of the world," or because of "the depth of sorrow of creation also crying to heaven." New Testament hope expects the final removal of these evils, yet bases its longing only on "the fullness of Jesus Christ himself," on that "fullness of the love and power of God active in him." In these terms, Christ's final coming is "not something still lacking in his present action and revelation," but rather "the finality proper to it" (CD IV/1, 326f).

(6) *Reconciliation.* Thus far I have looked at five issues over which shifts of opinion may be detected in Barth's theology of the resurrection. Many of the points which came up—like the historical nature of the resurrection and the status of the empty tomb—will turn up again in this book. Let me now suggest where Barth's main contribution on the resurrection lies. The headings of reconciliation and revelation gather much of what he has to say.

First things first. For Barth our reconciliation with God has taken place. Like Karl Rahner[10] and unlike Bultmann[11] he understands it as an actuality, not a mere possibility offered to those who will appropriate it in faith. Humankind has in fact been changed by Christ's death and resurrection, which form "the basis of the alteration of the situation of the men of all times."

> In virtue of the divine right established in the death of Jesus Christ, in virtue of the justification which has come to them in his resurrection, they *are no longer* what they were but they *are already* what they are to be. They *are no longer* the enemies of God but his friends, his children (CD IV/1, 316; italics mine).

In explaining how this reconciliation was effected, Barth to an extent employs the so-called penal substitution view. Christ, the man-for-other-men, entered the heart of their alienation from God, took the place of those judged by God and became the object of divine anger. On Golgotha he carried man's sin and culpability for which he was condemned by God and punished by death.[12] God asserted his right against sinful men by judging them in the death of their representative. Hence

> . . . the death of Jesus Christ was . . . wholly and altogether the work of God to the extent that it is the judgment of death fulfilled on the representative of all other men appointed by God (CD IV/1, 300).

But in view of Jesus' act of obedience God acquitted and justified him by raising him from the dead. The resurrection constituted the Father's new verdict in vindicating the crucified Jesus and setting our justification in force. Since Jesus showed obedience as our representative, the broken communion between God and man was healed. God recognized Jesus' suffering death for us as our conversion, so that we were rescued from death to life.

> The sinful man who was condemned and punished by God on account of his sin is acquitted and justified by the same God, being invested with all the glory of one who is righteous, and therefore rescued from the death into which he had fallen. And this man was sinful in the sense that he was the bearer of our sin and took our place before God, and there accepted God's sentence and punishment for us. As our Head and Representative, he was sinful and died for sin. And as our Head and Lord he also rose from the dead, and beyond that sentence received God's justification.

In short, "man's justification in judgment" "has taken place in Jesus Christ" (CD II/2, 758, 762). Through the resurrection "the verdict of the Father," the "Yes of the reconciling will of God," has been both "effective and expressed" (CD IV/1, 297ff, 304).

Barth's attention to the reconciling force of Christ's resurrection merits endorsement, but the particular expression of this through the penal substitution theology requires relegation to the museum of theology. Barth realizes the difficulty of explaining how the culpability for personal sin may be transferred from the one who actually committed the sin to another. That Christ acted as the representative of other men lies beyond dispute. That he could literally carry the moral guilt of others remains unintelligible. [13]

If we part ways with Barth where he introduces the penal substitution theory, other aspects in his elaboration of the atonement deserve a sympathetic hearing. In part four of the *Church Dogmatics* he raises the question: Is there a positive aspect to the atonement? Can we pass beyond the negativity of divine self-humbling which Christ's death on the cross implied? Barth answers affirmatively, because the resurrection fulfills five conditions which would allow us to claim such a positive aspect for the atonement. (a) A new act of God must take place. This occurs at the resurrection in which the sovereign divine power dispenses with all human cooperation and manifests itself through what is clearly God's deed alone. (b) So far from forming the "noetic" converse of the crucifixion, this new act of God must be manifestly distinct from it. The resurrection fulfills this condition by following the crucifixion as a fresh divine intervention which remains irreducible either to the saving meaningfulness of the cross or to the disciples' realization of this meaningfulness. (c) Nevertheless, the new event must enjoy an inherent relationship to the cross. In freeing men for the future, the resurrection presupposes the role of Calvary which frees man from the past. The positive turning toward the future builds upon the negative turning away from the past. (d) God's new act must exhibit a spatio-temporal character as a specific, concrete event in history. With the resurrection we do not switch from the sphere of the historical to some timeless, non-historical realm. (e) This new act of God must form a unity with the cross, above all by being (like the cross) an event in the history of Jesus Christ (CD IV/1, 304–342).

Requirements (d) and (e) have already been critically examined at length in the discussion of the resurrection's historical character. In raising the issues covered by conditions (a) and (b), Barth has Bultmann's view of the resurrection very much in mind. Condition (c) recalls Aquinas' explanation that Christ's passion effected our salvation "by removing evils," while "the resurrection did so as the beginning and exemplar of all good things." Likewise, even though—unlike Barth—he does not develop a penal substitution theory, Aquinas expounds the crucifixion as a divine self-humbling. The resurrection constitutes a new act of God vindicating and exalting his Son who has humbled himself in obedience. Thus both Aquinas and Barth explain the unity of cross and resurrection by appealing to the divine activity.

Up to this point in the discussion of reconciliation our attention has been focused on the past, on what took place "back there" on Good Friday and Easter Sunday. But, as Barth clearly acknowledges, "Easter cannot just be regarded in retrospect" (CD I/2, 116). How is the reconciliation achieved through Christ's death and resurrection effectively and fully *made present for us today?* This question troubles Barth from the outset. In his *Epistle to the Romans* he replies by adopting Kierkegaard's principle of simultaneity. Through being simultaneously present to all times, eternity effectively abolishes the separation between the periods of past, present and future. In the *Church Dogmatics* he retains this principle to argue that the events of man's reconciliation belong to the perfect time of a transcendent world: "The Easter story . . . speaks of a present without any future, of an eternal presence of God in time" (CD I/2, 114). Barth also brings to bear the category of recollection in an attempt to bridge the gap between past and present. The resurrection is a remembered resurrection. Thus it is drawn into the present. But he seems aware of the fact that recollection as a human activity, "a mere backward look at a once for all happening," fails to explain sufficiently how the past reconciliation really affects the present (CD I/2, 116).

When we move to volume four of the *Church Dogmatics*, we find that Barth clearly recognizes that the *divine action* provides the bridge from past to present. It now seems to him insufficient to invoke either God's transcendent presence or such human acts as recollection and proclamation. "The eternal action of Jesus Christ grounded in his resurrection is itself the true and direct bridge from once to always, from himself in his time to us in our time" (CD IV/1, 315). The power of the resurrection meant not only that what Christ had done was fixed as the definitive reconciliation for all men of all times, but also that the reconciliation bears on us today.

> It is in the power of the event of the third day that the event of the first day—as something that happened there and then—is not something which belongs to the past, which can be present only by recollection, tradition and proclamation, but is as such a present event, the event which fills and determines the whole present (CD IV/1, 313).

In short, the bridge from the past event of reconciliation to us today is found in "the sovereign presence and action of the Resurrected himself" (CD IV/3, 286).

(7) *Revelation*.   Closely allied with Barth's interest in the atoning value of Christ's resurrection is his concern for its revelatory function. This theme runs through his treatment of the resurrection from the *Epistle to the Romans* down to the appearance of the last part of the *Church Dogmatics* in 1967 (IV/4). Other theologians may sidestep the revelatory value of Easter, but not Barth, nor for that matter Bultmann.

Barth points to the resurrection as the event in which Christ stands "wholly and unequivocally and irrevocably manifest" (CD III/2, 449). Without losing his divine being, God could take the form of a servant and humble himself in Christ through the crucifixion. The resurrection lifts the veil on the obscurity of Calvary. "The Easter time is simply the time of the revelation of the mystery of the preceding time of the life and death of the man Jesus." In the resurrection this man stands "manifested in the mode of God" (CD III/2, 445, 448).

Further, the resurrection discloses Christ as the representative man in his being-for-other-men. He can now be seen in relation to other men and the salvation-history of mankind. The Easter event constitutes the prism through which the apostles and their communities rightly acknowledge what Christ effects. "The Easter history opened their eyes to the nature of this man and his history, to the previously concealed character of this history as salvation-history" (CD III/2, 454). In an otherwise terribly wordy discussion on "The Glory of the Mediator" Barth expresses well the role of the resurrection in mediating a knowledge of who Christ is and what he does.

> In the event of his resurrection from the dead, his being and action as very God and very man emerged from the concealment of his particular existence as an inclusive being and action enfolding the world, the humanity distinct from himself and us all (CD IV/3, 283).

Ernest Hemingway remarks somewhere that praising one writer to another is like mentioning one general favorably to another general. "You learn not to do it the first time you make the mistake." Sad to say, something like this is true of some theologians. You learn to be careful in choosing the theologians you mention favorably to other theologians. Nowadays it is in many circles a "mistake" to praise Barth and his theology of the resurrection. It has become conventional to dismiss his contribution by pointing to his dubious claim on the "historical" nature of Easter. He attributes genuine historical character to the resurrection and yet denies historians the right to pronounce on the matter! Add too the sheer bulk of his writings on the resurrection and other themes. Before the *Church Dogmatics* we are like blind men around an elephant: they can size it up, but they cannot really take it in. Yet Karl Barth's statements on Christ's resurrection enjoy a permanent value. At very least they operate as a massive reminder that our theology will be drastically impoverished if we forget the function of the resurrection in the divine plan for reconciliation and revelation.

RUDOLF BULTMANN

Three pairs of words gather together the main lines of Bultmann's approach to Christ's resurrection: history and faith, science and myth, kerygma and eschatology. Let me explore in turn what these headings cover.

(1) *History and Faith.*   Bultmann's position on the resurrection is partly determined by his view that facts of past history (*Historie*) as such cannot and should not contribute to the decision of faith. Historical science may properly investigate and establish happenings of the past. But such objective, historical conclusions do not enter the sphere of faith, which looks to what is of ultimate significance for me and my existence. At the level of the existential-historical (*Geschichte*), faith offers me a new self-understanding here and now.

When applied to the resurrection, any appeal to objective, historical facts (for example, that Jesus appeared gloriously alive to the disciples, that his tomb was found to be empty or that the disciples testified to his resurrection) proves irrelevant for Christian faith. When he works as an historian in *The History of the Synoptic Tradition* (New York, 1968), Bultmann rejects the story of the empty tomb as "an apologetic legend" and "completely secondary" (290), but he allows for "the fundamental appearance to Peter." He agrees that "there was originally a genuine Easter story about Peter" (*ibid.*, 289–290), and even localizes the appearances (plural) in Galilee: "I have no doubt that the old tradition told of their [the disciples'] flight to Galilee, and placed the appearances of the risen Lord there" (*ibid.*, 285). Later on I will examine what Bultmann means by these admissions. Here I want only to note that for Bultmann, no matter what our historical conclusions about past happenings prove to be, they do not touch the resurrection and the decision of Easter faith: "The historical problem is not of interest to Christian belief in the resurrection" (*Kerygma and Myth*, 42).[13a]

Here Bultmann feels free to criticize Paul's appeal to witnesses (1 Cor 15:5–8) and the similar objective, historical understanding of the resurrection favored by Luke's Gospel and Acts. These New Testament authors pile up evidence from the past in a misguided attempt to compel faith. But the resurrection is no such "miraculous proof capable of demonstration," by which "the skeptic might be compelled to believe in Christ" (*ibid.*, 39). In 1 Corinthians 15:1–11 Paul was "betrayed by his apologetic" into a misguided "attempt to make the resurrection of Christ credible as an objective historical fact."[14]

Bultmann insists that when the resurrection is proclaimed, we are not asked to accept that something—namely, a miracle—once happened but that new life can happen for us now. Seen this way, "the resurrection is not an event of past history," some "fact of past history open to historical verification" (*ibid.*, 207). Rather it is "a reality that concerns our own existence" here and now[15]—as we shall see shortly, it is the "eschatological event par excellence" (*Kerygma and Myth*, 40).

(2) *Science and Myth.*   Bultmann has certain presuppositions about what Jesus' resurrection can or cannot be. He is sure that it "simply cannot be a visible fact in the realm of human history."[16] He writes of "the impossibility of establishing the objective historicity of the resurrection no matter how many witnesses are cited." He dismisses "an historical fact which involves a resurrection from the dead" as being "utterly inconceivable" (*Kerygma and Myth*, 39). Bultmann is convinced that corpses cannot come back to life or rise from the grave. Such resuscitations are impossible and hence incredible. So he speaks of "the incredibility of a mythical event like the return of a dead person into the life of this world" (*ibid.*, 39; trans. corrected).

John Macquarrie rightly asks about the source of Bultmann's conviction at this point. It does not come from Martin Heidegger, the philosopher on whom Bultmann relies. Heidegger's *Being and Time* (London, 1962) has nothing to say about the possibility or impossibility of resurrection. Macquarrie talks of a "hangover of liberal modernism."

> Bultmann has decided in advance that in this scientific age we cannot believe in miracles, and therefore we cannot believe in the resurrection as an objective event that once happened, even if we can believe in it in some other way.[17]

Macquarrie might have noted how Bultmann makes things easier for himself by parodying the nature of Jesus' resurrection. It is not the mere resuscitation of a corpse or "the return of a dead person into the life of this world." Rather than a "coming back" to this life, it is a passage to a new, transformed life in the other world. At the same time, Macquarrie does steer us toward the basic reason for Bultmann's assurance that "a resurrection from the dead" is "utterly inconceivable" as an historical fact. Bultmann bases his certainty on the notion that nowadays the natural sciences postulate a rigid uniformity in the laws of the universe. Hence theologians and historians, their thinking "shaped irrevocably by natural science" like all others (*Kerygma and Myth*, 3), must look on history as "a unity in the sense of a closed continuum of effects in which individual events are connected by the succession of cause and effect."[18] As Pannenberg and others have remarked, however, modern science does not rigidly espouse such a closed continuum which would necessarily exclude the possibility of such a uniquely new event as a final resurrection from the dead. I return to this point later.

Positively speaking, Bultmann takes the resurrection as "a mythical event pure and simple" (*Kerygma and Myth*, 38). His demythologizing program, so far from entailing the elimination of myth, calls for its translation and interpretation. Early Christians adopted mythical representations (a) to express their self-understanding with respect to the basis and limits of their existence, and (b) to express the significance of Christ for their new, authentic existence as believers. Thus Bultmann asks: What self-understanding is implied by the New Testament proclamation of the resurrection? What saving significance does that proclamation express? Ultimately it states the decisive meaning of the cross for human existence. The disciples knew the triumphant value of Christ's death on the cross (*Kerygma and Myth*, 39); he came alive for them, and they expressed the liberating power of the cross. Their proclamation of the resurrection does not ask us to accept some new, miraculous event which took place after the crucifixion, but to see the victorious value of the cross.[19] Thus Christ can come alive for us, if we share the disciples' understanding of existence and repeat their Easter faith.

(3) *Kerygma and Eschatology.* "Faith in the resurrection" is for Bultmann "really the same thing as faith in the saving efficacy of the cross" (*Kerygma and Myth*, 41)—that is to say, the same thing as believing in the cross as eschatological event. The "resurrection" of Christ has no independent status as a further event. Rather, it is the cross in its salvific meaning for me. The Church's kerygma challenges me: Am I willing to die with Christ? Am I ready to undergo crucifixion with him, make his cross my own, and realize the possibility of a new self-understanding created by the cross (*Kerygma and Myth*, 42)?

Alongside this cross-oriented version of the Church's Easter proclamation, Bultmann highlights *the presence of Christ* in the kerygma: "To believe in the Christ present in the kerygma is the meaning of the Easter faith." As "Jesus has risen in the kerygma," he "is really present in the kerygma," and it is "*his* word which involves the hearer in the kerygma."[20] This language of Bultmann has been notoriously liable to misunderstanding. (a) Is Jesus risen and does he "live" simply because and only insofar as he is proclaimed? If yes, his "resurrection" would coincide with sermons about him and he would be "present" only inasmuch as the saving message of his cross is proclaimed. (b) Or is Jesus proclaimed and present inasmuch as he is risen and lives?

Seemingly Bultmann wishes to maintain (b), but does so with two provisos. First, Christ is present only in the kerygma and in no other way: "Christ meets us in the preaching as one crucified and risen. He meets us in the word of preaching and nowhere else" (*Kerygma and Myth*, 41). Second, Bultmann refuses to go behind the kerygma to ask where Christ is when he is not being preached. Christ really encounters me but not as an objective, historical, and provable phenomenon. Although the kerygma and the faith it elicits do not create the risen Christ's existence, we are not allowed to ask about his existence apart from the kerygma and faith. It is the same with the existence of God: "That God cannot be seen apart from faith does not mean that he does not exist apart from it" (*ibid.*, 200f).

As we will see shortly, Bultmann's talk about Jesus being present in the kerygma seems almost equivalent to eternity being present in the kerygma. That rather leaves open the question: Is the risen Christ truly risen? Or is he eternal—one who lives from the resources of the eternal world?

Bultmann's high doctrine of the kerygma and Christ's presence in that kerygma carries with it a high doctrine of the Church: "The Easter faith is faith in the Church as bearer of the kerygma. It is equally the faith that Jesus is present in the kerygma" (*ibid.*, 103). In these terms resurrection faith directs itself toward the Church as much as toward the Christ who is present in the proclamation: "Faith in the Church as the bearer of the kerygma is the Easter faith which consists in the belief that Jesus Christ is present in the kerygma" (*ibid.*, 42).

This high version of the Church's kerygma also sets aside the ordinary categories of time that confine what is objectively historical. The salvation event evades such limits in two ways. (a) It is the always actualized, eschatological "now" which constantly faces me with the decision for or against faith. Through the kerygma the death of Jesus, an objective event in time which is verifiable historically, becomes an eschatological event which transcends historical limits:

The cross is not just an event of the past which can be contemplated, but is the eschatological event *in and beyond time*, insofar as it (understood in its significance, that is, for faith) is an *ever-present* reality (*ibid.*, 36; italics mine).

(b) This event also shows itself to be eschatological in that it brings to an end our old world of sin and death, our human time and our worldly efforts. It opens up the possibility of an existence beyond the world. This collapsing of the cross (and resurrection) into the present recalls the middle Barth's use of Kierkegaard's principle of simultaneity. An eternal and decisive "now" absorbs the past and the future.

BULTMANN AND BARTH

At this point it seems profitable to pause and take stock of Barth, Bultmann and the differences between them over the resurrection of Christ. Barth once compared Bultmann and himself to a whale and an elephant who look at each other. Out in the ocean the whale is sending a jet of water up into the air. On the shore the elephant is trumpeting loudly. The whale and the elephant can see and hear each other, but neither understands what the other is up to. The Barth-Bultmann debate on the resurrection went on for thirty years. Some issues and arguments came through clearly. It was not all a matter of spouting and trumpeting. In general Bultmann remained a lot closer to the positions held by Barth in the 1920s but modified by him after 1931.

Bultmann led off the debate with his mildly critical review of Barth's 1924 book, *The Resurrection of the Dead.*[21] In 1941 came Bultmann's essay "New Testament and Mythology," reproduced in the first volume of *Kerygma and Myth* from which I have been drawing. Barth criticized this essay in the 1948 volume of *Church Dogmatics* (CD III/2, 443ff). Bultmann reacted vigorously in a 1950 essay, "The Problem of Hermeneutics" (which later appeared in *Essays*, 234–261). Barth's long 1952 response, "Rudolf Bultmann—An Attempt To Understand Him," was included in the second volume of *Kerygma and Myth*, 82–132.[22] The 1953 volume of *Church Dogmatics* rounded off these decades of debates:

> The present situation in theology and also the peculiar themes of this book [on reconciliation] mean that throughout I have found myself in an intensive, although for the most part quiet, debate with Rudolf Bultmann. His name is not mentioned often. But his subject is always present (CD IV/1, ix).

The debate between Barth and Bultmann extended, of course, beyond Christ's resurrection. Furthermore, they shared some common ground. Let me sketch first the points of agreement.

(1) *Common Ground.* (a) To begin with, Barth was satisfied that Bultmann agreed on the central importance of Christ's resurrection: "We must at least give him [Bultmann] credit for emphasizing the central and indispensable function of the event of Easter for all that is thought and said in the New Testament." Barth went on to compare Bultmann favorably with W. G. Kümmel, who never mentioned the resurrection in his *Promise and Fulfillment* (Naperville & London, 1957) and with Oscar Cullmann. In Cullmann's *Christ and Time* (Philadelphia, 1964),

> . . . the resurrection comes in only at the end of the book and in a special connexion, without any real significance for the author's reconstruction of the New Testament conception of time and history (CD III/2, 443).

It is worth recalling Barth's appreciation of Bultmann, given that many exegetes and theologians continue to fall short like Kümmel and Cullmann. For diverse reasons they fail to recognize the central function of Easter for the New Testament and Christianity.

(b) Barth and Bultmann agreed that historical argument and conclusions should not and, indeed, could not support Easter faith. "Objective," historical investigation could never legitimate this faith and provide "security" through alleged proofs. The New Testament witnesses never offered such a legitimation. As Bultmann observed,

> . . . we cannot buttress our own faith in the resurrection by that of the first disciples and so eliminate the element of risk which faith in the resurrection always involves (*Kerygma and Myth*, I, 42).

We saw how Barth maintained that Paul and the other apostles, in proclaiming the Easter message, called for "a decision of faith," not "the acceptance of a well-attested historical report" which could be reliably established.

In a later chapter I come back to the issue of reasonable evidence in support of Easter faith. Here I wish only to note this. Barth and Bultmann both endorsed a "voluntarist" position which excluded any evaluation of historical or other evidence and emphasized the "risky" decision of the will to believe.

(c) Both writers insisted that the resurrection could not be rightly understood apart from the crucifixion. Bultmann declared: "The cross and the resurrection form an inseparable unity"; they "form a single, indivisible cosmic event" (*Kerygma and Myth*, I, 38f). Barth maintained the same inseparable unity, but his sense of the distinction between Christ's dying and rising was stronger. Hence "the *theologia resurrectionis* does not absorb the *theologia crucis*, nor vice versa" (CD IV/1, 304).

(d) Finally, with Barth as with Bultmann, there was a strong concern to elucidate the contemporary power and significance of the resurrection. We saw how Barth wrestled with the question of how the past reconciliation reached us here and now. Bultmann solved the issue in terms of the kerygma: "Through the word of preaching the cross and resurrection are made present" (*Kerygma and Myth*, I, 42).

(2) *The Differences.* (a) As I have indicated, in his final period Barth stressed the nature of the resurrection as a new act of God which followed on the crucifixion. Hence the resurrection was a distinct event in Jesus' history and not just the disclosure of the meaning of his cross. Here we run up against a decisive difference between the two antagonists.

Bultmann—like Barth in the 1920s—more or less identified resurrection with revelation, but then went further by reducing revelation to the Church's kerygma being announced here and now. Barth, even in that middle period, had distinguished revelation from the Christian kerygma in that the kerygma is "based on revelation." This makes the kerygma "preaching as distinct from mere protestation" (*Resurrection*, 155). Here in 1924 Barth had already touched upon what would in fact remain a key objection against Bultmann.

If Bultmann refused to go behind the Easter kerygma (and the faith to which it gives rise) to Jesus himself and the event of his resurrection, how could he distinguish this preaching from mere assertion? Yet Bultmann's collapsing of everything into the present kerygma was clear: "Christ meets us in the preaching as one crucified and risen. He meets us in the word of preaching and nowhere else. The faith of Easter is just this—faith in the word of preaching" (*Kerygma and Myth*, I, 41). Quite spontaneously the questions arise: Why accept this word of preaching? Did such events as Christ's crucifixion truly possess the significance the kerygma attributes to them? Surely we believe and find saving significance in his death only because we are convinced that it had in itself the significance for us attached to it by the proclamation? Bultmann did not deny an objective reality and significance which were independent of and prior to the Easter kerygma. But from a faith perspective he ruled that it is neither possible nor proper to go behind the word of preaching. In effect this was to dehistoricize the kerygma. He wanted us to accept the present significance of Christ in isolation from any past facts. He summoned people to Easter faith, but apart from the past event(s) which had first called that faith to life. The kerygma addresses us now, but Bultmann underplayed the fact that it also announces things which happened to and through Jesus Christ (1 Cor 15:3–5). He failed to see that the kerygma's existential significance *now* may not be separated from the reality of Jesus' history *then*.

The same problem really emerged from Bultmann's talk about the word of preaching offering us now "that which alone can illuminate our understanding of ourselves" (*Kerygma and Myth*, I, 42). But why should the kerygma and authentic self-understanding be linked to "Jesus is risen"? Why not to some other name and claim? So long as Bultmann imposed a veto against going behind the kerygma, no satisfactory answer could even be attempted.

(b) Bultmann's refusal to speak of Christ apart from the kerygma certainly invites the questions: Is it only the kerygma that is real? Does the risen Lord have no reality apart from the kerygma? And what is his presence in the kerygma? Bultmann, while dismissing as trivial speculation any discussion of how the risen Christ exists in himself, willy-nilly was forced to say something about Christ's presence in the kerygma. In *Kerygma and Myth* (I, 115) he called it a "sacramental happening," and in *Theology of the New Testament* he offered some explanation:

> . . . in the proclamation Christ is not in the same way present as a great historical person is present in his work and its historical after-effects. For what is here involved is not an influence that takes effect in the history of the human mind; what does take place is that a historical person and his fate are raised to the rank of the eschatological event (I, 305f).

Ultimately the difference here between Bultmann and Barth came to this. Bultmann declined to talk about the risen Christ's existence and presence apart from preaching and faith. Barth had no problem in acknowledging an objective reality: Jesus' presence and activity are not limited to the event of proclamation (CD IV/1, 548f). Hence Barth objected to Bultmann's position that "nothing can be said about the risen Christ as such. He is not allowed any life of his own after he rose from the dead." For Barth this was to "confine" wrongly "the real life" of Christ "to the kerygma and to faith" (*Kerygma and Myth*, II, 101).

(c) A third problematic area for Bultmann bore on the Easter faith of *the first disciples*. On the one hand, Bultmann maintained that "the faith of Easter" is "faith in the word of preaching." On the other hand, by definition the very first believers heard no Easter-proclamation to which they could respond in faith. For them there was no kerygma to find Christ present in.

What happened to those first disciples? Did they come to Easter faith through certain objective, historical events—namely, the appearances of the risen Lord? In *The History of the Synoptic Tradition* Bultmann gave no clear answer. It seems that he deemed the disciples' flight to Galilee to be historical, whereas the stories of the appearances reported by Matthew, Mark and Luke have a religious rather than an historical character. These legends do not tell us how Easter faith arose in and for the disciples. Did they overcome the scandal of the cross in their own minds and of their own accord come to faith? Did some event take place between God and the disciples to which Jesus' name got attached? In that case, as Barth commented, "the Easter history" would be "merely the first chapter in the history of faith, and the Easter time the first period in the age of faith" (CD III/2, 445). That view would transfer the event of the resurrection from Jesus to his disciples. Barth labeled it "a fundamental misunderstanding" to say that the resurrection "happened only in faith or in the form of the formation and development of faith" (CD IV/1, 336).

Barth himself was clear on how the Easter faith of the disciples first originated:

> This faith did not consist in a reassessment and reinterpretation *in meliorem partem* of the picture of the Crucified, but in an objective encounter with the Crucified and Risen (CD III/2, 449).

Through that encounter faith was "established, awakened and created by God" (*ibid.*, 445). Thus, on Christ's side, when risen from the dead he "appeared to his disciples prior to their faith in him" (CD IV/1, 342). On their side, the disciples' faith in the risen Lord sprang "from his historical manifestation, and from this as such" (CD III/2, 443).

Before moving on to list other differences between Barth and Bultmann in their interpretation of the resurrection, I think it worth remarking on some presuppositions behind the position of Bultmann just discussed under (a), (b) and (c). Bultmann professed to be interested in the present event of preaching, the revelation addressed to me here and now which invites my faith. Nevertheless, Bultmann relied on the truth of certain facts about the past. He supposed (a) that the present kerygma is identical with the New Testament kerygma, (b) that the One whom we meet as present in the word of preaching is Jesus Christ of whom the Gospels speak, and (c) that we repeat the original Easter faith of the disciples and enjoy the same possibility for authentic existence as they did. Bultmann's veto against going behind the present kerygma and introducing past facts could not be completely upheld—at least not at the level of his presuppositions.

(d) It does not seem necessary to struggle at length over other differences between Barth and Bultmann. It is enough to list them. Unlike Barth, Bultmann dismissed the empty tomb as "an apologetic legend" which could not serve as an indispensable sign of Christ's personal, bodily resurrection. Like the Barth of the 1920s but unlike the later Barth, Bultmann transmuted Christ's "second coming" into the "beyond" of eternity. He denied that the *parousia* is a separate event to come, a real end toward which we are moving in this interim period. Further, Barth highlighted an actual, objective reconciliation achieved in the past through Christ's dying and rising, whereas Bultmann spoke rather of the possibility of authentic existence offered through the word of preaching.

(e) A word about Bultmann's justified concern for human self-understanding. He appreciated the fact that the questions raised by our existence and our search for authentic life make us open to the Easter message. Barth complained that Bultmann reversed the New Testament order and took "affirmations about God's saving act and about man's being in Christ" to be "primarily" (but of course not simply) "statements about man's subjective experience" (*Kerygma and Myth*, II, 92). Yet if we ignore the subjective experience of human beings, how can we show God's saving act to be vitally significant for our lives? Bultmann's version of the resurrection was excessively subject-oriented. Nevertheless, he rightly acknowledged the human questioning which can and should make the Easter kerygma vitally significant. Here, as we shall see, Karl Rahner, Hans Küng and others can be associated with Bultmann through their interest in the conditions for the possibility of Easter faith.

Although Bultmann rightly explored our human openness to the Easter message, he failed—as we have seen—to safeguard the objective and bodily nature of the resurrection as event. His individualistic interpretation of the Easter message undercut the social dimension and public responsibility of Easter faith. He even asserted that "the chief aim of every genuine religion is to escape from the world" (*Kerygma and Myth*, I, 113). Barth's theology of the resurrection may have been overly objective, but it stood behind his sense of Christian responsibility in the world. Witness his support for the Confessing Church in its struggle against the neopaganism of the Nazis. The Barmen Declaration drew heavily on Barth when in 1934 it unequivocally maintained the Lordship of the risen Christ.

(f) Finally, a last reflection about Bultmann. A comparison with Melito of Sardis could help to place his views within the history of Christian thought. In the case of Melito we have an Easter homily but no theology of the resurrection. In the case of Bultmann we have an elaborate theology of the resurrection but—curiously—no published Easter homilies. His *This World and the Beyond* (London, 1960) contains twenty-one sermons but none of them centers on the resurrection. Nevertheless, it is reasonable to compare the Easter experience of being liberated and brought alive with Christ (as graphically described by Melito, Gregory of Nazianzus and other Church Fathers) with Bultmann's invitation to imitate the death and resurrection of Jesus in our lives: "To believe in the cross of Christ" is "to make the cross of Christ our own, to undergo crucifixion with him" (*Kerygma and Myth*, I, 36). Sinful human beings are asked "whether they are willing to understand themselves as men who are crucified and risen with Christ" (*ibid.*, 42).

Undoubtedly both Melito (in the later second century) and Bultmann (in the twentieth century) highlighted the paschal mystery being actualized in our midst and for our advantage. But the differences between the two are also striking. According to Bultmann, Christ is "risen into the kerygma" and "meets us in the word of preaching and nowhere else." Through faith the individual finds eschatological existence—beyond time and in an eternal now. Melito could have said that Christ "is risen into the liturgy," but never alleged that "outside the liturgy" it is impossible to meet Christ. Moreover, the risen Lord's redemptive, sacramental presence touched individuals within the community. Besides respecting the social nature of this presence, Melito did not take his appreciation for that redemptive power experienced here and now to the point of denying past and future and collapsing everything into a timeless, eternal now. The Christ of Melito's homily not only proclaims "I am the Christ," but also "It is I who destroyed death" and "I will raise you up with my right hand."

WOLFHART PANNENBERG

Wolfhart Pannenberg (b. 1928) has developed his thought on Christ's resurrection very much in opposition to the authoritarian approach of Barth and Bultmann which declined to verify claims through rational argument. To quote Bultmann:

The word of preaching confronts us as the word of God. It is not for
us to question its credentials. It is we who are questioned, we who
are asked whether we will believe the word or reject it (*Kerygma and
Myth*, I, 41).

For all their differences, both Barth and Bultmann agreed that Easter
faith could not and should not be supported by appeals to historical evidence or other such arguments. Pannenberg has always set his face
against such intellectual suicide. Let us see how he made his run at the
question of Jesus' resurrection in *Jesus—God and Man* (Philadelphia &
London, 1968; hereafter JGM).

(1) *Approaching the Resurrection.*   Pannenberg maintains strongly that to
accept Jesus' resurrection is to make a judgment on the basis of historical
evidence. He writes: "Whether or not a particular event happened two
thousand years ago is not made certain by faith but only by historical
research" (JGM, 99). He holds that historians, so often seen as a threat
to Christianity and its Easter faith, should pass judgment on the evidence for Jesus' resurrection.

Pannenberg requires only that historians refrain from approaching
the question of Jesus' resurrection with the prior conviction that the
dead cannot rise. To do that would be to rule out the resurrection in
advance. It would also betray a one-sided orientation toward the typical
at the expense of the historical, a conviction that such resurrection is
simply excluded by the rigid laws of nature. Against Bultmann it should
be pointed out that modern science has broken with a deterministic
world-view. The "laws of nature" leave open the possibility of unfamiliar, even unique events which are not determined totally by these
laws. Hence Pannenberg argues that it is up to the historian to investigate and settle claims about such events (JGM, 98).

In putting the case for the resurrection, Pannenberg looks to
scientific historical research. He parts company with those who allege
that the personal existence of the risen Lord can be verified through religious and sacramental experience (JGM, 27f, 113f). He suspects that
such appeals to experience remain open to delusion. Rational, objective
evidence offers the proper grounds for accepting or rejecting Jesus'
resurrection.

(2) *The Easter Appearances.*   For Pannenberg the appearances of the
risen Christ make the resurrection as reliably attested as any event in the
ancient world. Like Bultmann, Pannenberg interprets Paul's list of wit-

nesses in 1 Corinthians 15:5–8 as intended to provide proof for the fact of Jesus' resurrection. Unlike Bultmann, he respects the apostle's "intention of giving a convincing historical proof by the standards of that time," even if this was not being done "from the perspective of a historical inquiry that is supposedly disinterested" (*ibid.*, 89).

Pannenberg defends the discovery of the empty tomb as something historically factual: it served to confirm the visions of the risen Lord. "How could Jesus' disciples in Jerusalem have proclaimed his resurrection if they could be constantly refuted merely by viewing the grave in which his body was interred?" The Easter message "could not have been maintained in Jerusalem for a single day, for a single hour, if the emptiness of the tomb had not been established as a fact for all concerned" (JGM, 100).

(3) *Apocalyptic Expectation.* If we agree that the disciples truly saw Jesus risen from the dead, were they able to interpret this experience appropriately? Pannenberg notes how they understood and interpreted their visions through their prior apocalyptic view of history: at the end of time all things would be consummated in a general resurrection and judgment. The meaning of Jesus' definitive, glorious resurrection was instantly clear to the disciples: "If Jesus has been raised, then the end of the world has begun" (JGM, 67). Hence God, whose truth is to be known only through the whole of history, has been revealed. Christ's resurrection really anticipates the end of universal history and thus gives us access to that whole. Pannenberg writes:

> Only in connection with the end of the world that still remains to come can what has happened in Jesus through his resurrection from the dead possess and retain the character of revelation for us also (JGM, 107).

Pannenberg correctly points to the way in which their traditional expectation of a universal end showed the disciples the significance of their Easter visions and the resurrection of Christ which made those visions possible. In that way his resurrection "had its own meaning within its sphere in the history of traditions" (JGM, 73). Both then and now tradition and traditional beliefs deeply influence the interpretation of new events which are experienced. But the interpretation thus provided by tradition cannot be automatically justified. Pannenberg shows himself to be properly aware of the momentous importance of the point at stake:

Why the man Jesus can be the ultimate revelation of God, why in
him and only in him God is supposed to have appeared, remains incomprehensible apart from the horizon of the apocalyptic expectation
(JGM, 83).

How do we know that the fundamental elements of the disciples' apocalyptic expectation of the resurrection of the dead were true? Can it be
established that this expectation is still valid today?

Pannenberg sets about recommending the expectation of resurrection in three stages. First, an examination of our human activity shows
how it is determined by the fact that we anticipate a future fulfillment
which will give meaning to existence. Specifically, "the phenomenology
of *hope* indicates that it belongs to the essence of conscious human existence to hope beyond death" (*ibid.*, 85). All "hope for a coming fulfillment of existence seems to be foolish," if "death is the end" and
individuals have nothing "to be hoped for beyond death" (*ibid.*, 84). Second, hope for a fulfilled existence beyond death must involve the *whole*
human being:

> The concept of the undying continuation of the soul while the body
> perishes has become untenable today. The separation between body
> and soul that forms the basis of the concept is no longer tenable, at
> least in this form, in the light of contemporary anthropological in-
> sights (*ibid.*, 87).

Third, Pannenberg argues that it is reasonable to hold that *all* individuals will enjoy the common destiny of a fulfilled life beyond death (*ibid.*,
88).

What Pannenberg offers here is an updated version of the case for
resurrection in general which we have already seen coming from Clement, Justin, Athenagoras, Tertullian, Aquinas and others. At the same
time, Pannenberg goes beyond these predecessors in one important detail. He appreciates the decisive role played by a traditional expectation
of general resurrection when the disciples interpreted their visions of the
risen Christ. The tradition provided a context in which to interpret
these new experiences. The visions themselves modified the tradition
by indicating that one individual had been raised from the dead in anticipation of the final end.

How strong does Pannenberg believe his case for general resurrection to be? In the past many believers accepted such resurrection
as obviously true. The question arises: Can we take it to be true?
Pannenberg's answer is intriguing:

There is no answer to this question that can be formulated in a single sentence; it is answered at any particular time by theology as a whole, and not only by theology, but also by the way in which the faith of Christians, which is grounded upon the truth known in the past, stands the test today *in the decisions of life* (*ibid.*, 107; italics mine).

In other words, hope for a resurrected existence beyond death proves its meaning and truth through being acted upon and lived out.

(4) *The Resurrection as Historical.*   Pannenberg, as we have seen, interprets Jesus' resurrection above all in terms of eschatology and revelation. In that resurrection the end of all things became proleptically present and hence the meaning of history was disclosed. This universalizing perspective does not, however, weaken Pannenberg's insistence on the specificity of the resurrection as a particular event.

He describes historical events as "occurrences that actually happened at a definite time in the past." Both "the resurrection of Jesus" and "the appearances of the resurrected Jesus" fulfill this description, for they "really happened at a definite time in our world" (*ibid.*, 99). Pannenberg realizes that there is less difficulty about calling the Easter appearances historical. On those occasions the risen Christ "made himself known in the midst of our reality at a very definite time, in a limited number of events, and to men who are particularly designated" (*ibid.*). The *reality* of the resurrection itself, however, entails a new, transformed, post-mortem life which has no spatio-temporal location and which cannot be described directly but only symbolically through the apocalyptic metaphor of "rising from sleep." Yet the resurrection-*event*, that transition from being an earthly reality to being a risen reality, occurred "once at a definite time" (*ibid.*, 113) and in a definite place (Jerusalem). Hence Pannenberg will not tolerate a less historical qualification for the resurrection. "There is no justification," he writes, "for affirming Jesus' resurrection as an event that really happened, if it is not to be affirmed as an historical event as such" (*ibid.*, 99). Since the resurrection actually took place at a definite time in the past, it should be called historical.

(5) *A Query.*   The objectivity of the Easter experiences of Peter, Paul and the other witnesses listed in 1 Corinthians 15:5–8 is vigorously maintained by Pannenberg. They reliably report authentic visions of the risen Christ. Pannenberg, as we saw, does not accept—even as a secondary, confirmatory argument for the resurrection—the witness of

believers today who claim to encounter the risen Lord in prayer, preaching and the sacraments. If he lives now, he must have been raised from the dead back there and then.

Admittedly the Easter experiences of the apostolic witnesses involved, as I will argue in a later chapter, some element of sense perception when they saw the risen Christ. This is not the case with the faith experiences of believers now. Nevertheless, in numbers which go far beyond the few hundred witnesses cited by Paul, these contemporaries attest their encounters with the living Jesus. Can one justifiably accept as valid evidence the experiences of a limited number of persons from the past, while ruling out claims about the different but not totally different experiences of millions of men and women here and now?

Neither Melito of Sardis nor Bultmann put matters this way. But their attention to the redemptive and revealing presence of the risen Christ rested upon the validity of faith experience. They could talk as they did about Christ risen into the kerygma or present in the liturgy, since believers continue to encounter the Lord who lives now because he was once raised from the dead. Melito and Bultmann suggest to me that it is somewhat inconsistent on the part of Pannenberg to make so much of the apostolic Easter experiences while refusing to take into account—even as secondary confirmation—the faith experiences of millions of our contemporaries.

WILLI MARXSEN

Among the theologians and exegetes who have written on Christ's resurrection in the aftermath of Barth and Bultmann, no one stands further from Pannenberg than Willi Marxsen (b. 1919). Pannenberg is confident that historical research can and should be invoked to establish the basis of faith—namely, that the event of the resurrection truly took place. Marxsen, however, asserts that "the historian's answer to the question whether Jesus rose from the dead must be: 'I do not know; I am no longer able to discern.' "[23] According to Marxsen, even if the historian were able to answer this question positively, such "isolated talk about the reality of Jesus' resurrection" would remain a statement apart from faith, simply "the report of a somewhat unusual event" (*Resurrection*, 140). This is to separate resolutely the findings of historical research and the decision of faith. In that regard Marxsen differs markedly from Pannenberg and resembles Bultmann. But we shall see shortly how Marxsen's views also set him apart from Bultmann.

(1) *"Resurrection" and Faith.* Marxsen moves from the fact (noted centuries ago by Aquinas) that there were no eye-witnesses of the resurrection: "No individual of the primitive community ever claimed to have seen or experienced Jesus' resurrection as an event" (*Significance*, 24). "Jesus is risen" did not then directly report a direct, personal experience. Rather, according to Marxsen, it is a secondary, dispensable (*ibid.*, 32) reflection deduced from the primary experience of having found faith through "seeing" Jesus after his crucifixion (*ibid.*, 47). This secondary interpretation, "Jesus is risen," should not be turned into an event of history, but recognized for what it is—"one possible way of expressing the reality of having found faith" (*Resurrection*, 144), a way of expressing pictorially "the miraculous nature" of this faith (*ibid.*, 141, 156). Faith is the miracle for Marxsen, not the resurrection of Jesus himself.

Hearing all this, one might be tempted to parody St. Paul and exclaim: "Resurrection is swallowed up in faith. O resurrection, where is thy victory? O resurrection, where is thy sting?" But to continue with Marxsen's reconstruction.

After the crucifixion Peter was the first to believe, but it remains "completely unimportant *how* Peter arrived at his faith in Jesus after Good Friday" (*ibid.*, 126). All that matters for us is that he came to faith and discovered his mission. What triggered off Peter's faith and motivated him to take up the mission, even if it were an "appearance" of the risen Lord, is irrelevant for our faith now.

The faith of Peter and of all who came to faith after him coincides with the first article of the Creed and does not include any confession of Jesus crucified and risen. As Marxsen explains matters, "faith after Easter" was and is "no different in substance from that faith to which Jesus had already called men before Easter" (*ibid.*, 125f).

Instead of speaking of resurrection, Marxsen prefers to say, "the cause of Jesus continues" and "still he comes today." He writes:

> Jesus comes today and offers us what I have called his *cause*. . . . I take the risk of doing what he asks, contrary to all human reason—and then again, and yet again. And one day you discover that you are on the path through *this* life *to* life (*Resurrection*, 183f).

It is through the Church and its proclamation that Jesus still comes today. It does not preach the appearances of Jesus (*Significance*, 37) but rather his cause which can precipitate the faith that brings life.

(2) *Some Problems.* (a) Clearly the conviction that faith, by definition, has to be independent of reason is at work in the making of Marxsen's position. Rational evidence in general and historical arguments in par-

ticular can neither support nor endanger faith (*Resurrection*, 153). Faith is a risk "contrary to all human reason," and as such is neither verifiable nor falsifiable.

(b) Marxsen's version of faith carries with it a positivist view of history which reduces it to a concatenation of facts attested by sense experience. The "historical" remains strictly limited to what has actually occurred in a sense-perceptible way. Marxsen likewise restricts the notion of "event" to the strictly sense-perceptible sphere: " 'Event' is a historical category. To speak of an 'event' beyond the inherent human possibilities of perception is to speak loosely because categories are being shifted" (*Significance*, 22; see *ibid.*, 18).

The "spiritual perception" of faith does not provide access to any new, historical facts. It merely grasps "the significance" of phenomena like the ministry and message of Jesus which are "open to others as well" (*ibid.*, 21). Faith perceives a different meaning and gives a different interpretation to facts which are common property. In a word, Marxsen strongly maintains an old-fashioned distinction between fact and meaning.

(c) It is true but grossly insufficient to say that "the cause of Jesus goes on." Undoubtedly the teaching and example of the earthly Jesus continue to be effective. So too does the teaching of Socrates and the example of John Bunyan's pilgrim. We can take over Socrates' teaching without knowing who he was. We can imitate the example of Bunyan's pilgrim even though he never really existed. In the case of Jesus, we have someone who did not finish in death but continues with new life. Jesus is a living person *and hence* his cause goes on. Unless his resurrection truly happened, what basis have we for saying that he "comes today" with the same claim? Yet in all his talk about Jesus' coming again Marxsen never makes it clear that Jesus himself is personally present and that more is involved than simply an impersonal, disembodied cause.

(d) This last ambiguity feeds off Marxsen's assertion that "faith after Easter" was and remains "no different in substance from that faith to which Jesus had already called men before Easter." In other words, the crucifixion and resurrection do not enter into the confession of faith. Paul and the primitive tradition on which he drew may sum up the essence of Christianity as believing in the resurrection of the crucified Jesus (Rom 10:9; 1 Cor 15:3–5, 11; etc.). But Marxsen disregards this new content, and restricts faith to an obedient openness to the divine mercy which the earthly Jesus proclaimed. In this scheme of things the resurrection does not even function to ratify and vindicate the astonishing claims Jesus made during his ministry. Ultimately Marxsen reduces faith to commitment. He makes room for a "Jesuology" which undertakes a faithful discipleship in hearing the teaching and imitating the example of Jesus. He excludes any Christology which confesses that the crucified Jesus has been "made both Lord and Christ" (Acts 2:36) and "designated Son of God in power" by "his resurrection from the dead" (Rom 1:4).

This reductionism logically leaves out the Holy Spirit. Without the risen Christ there is no place for the Holy Spirit. It is only the cause of Jesus which goes on and not his Spirit. As we shall see, Marxsen exaggerates the importance of the Church as carrier of Jesus' cause. A kind of ecclesiology comes in to fill up the void left by the absence of any real Christology and Pneumatology.

(3) *Marxsen and Bultmann.*   To round out this presentation of Marxsen, it seems worthwhile comparing and contrasting his views with those of Bultmann. Despite some common elements, they diverge strikingly.

(a) Both authors agree that reason and historical investigation cannot vindicate faith and should not even try to do so. Both criticize and part company with the New Testament authorities where necessary. We have seen how Bultmann rejects Paul's appeal to the lists of those to whom the risen Christ had appeared (1 Cor 15:5–8). Marxsen does not feel bound by the fact that Paul and other early witnesses believe that God brought about as an actual occurrence the resurrection of Jesus (*Significance*, 17). Then both Bultmann and Marxsen endorse a high ecclesiology. Bultmann values the Church as the carrier of the Easter kerygma. For Marxsen the Church transmits Jesus' cause and seems to replace him. We read that "the whole richness of the anticipation of the *eschaton* which had taken place by means of and in Jesus now takes place by means of the Church, and in her" (*Significance*, 48). Marxsen goes so far as to say that the Church "now stands where Jesus stood. She summons and offers future salvation *now*." At once he qualifies this high vision of the Church by adding: "For it is not the Christian community itself who is acting, but in what it does and preaches, Jesus is alive with fullness of power, with a claim and with a promise" (*ibid.*). Even so it is by no means clear that Jesus is *personally* alive and present. Marxsen may mean only that the power, claim and promise of (the dead) Jesus remain fully alive in and through the preaching and activity of the community. Jesus lives and comes again merely in the sense that through the Church his "kerygma continues to be preached" (*ibid.*, 38) and so his purpose or cause "can still be experienced today" (*ibid.*, 50).

(b) At a superficial level it can be said that Marxsen agrees with Bultmann in arguing that the assertion of Jesus' resurrection involves a *reflection upon something else.* For Bultmann "resurrection" conveys the saving value of the cross. For Marxsen "resurrection" was a way of expressing the miraculous reality of having found faith through "seeing" Jesus after his crucifixion. However, where Bultmann maintains "resurrection" (albeit as a myth which should be reinterpreted for its existential significance), Marxsen is happy to drop talk of the resurrection as a secondary, dispensable reflection.

At bottom the radical difference consists in the fact that Bultmann proposes the crucified and risen Christ of the Church's kerygma, while Marxsen highlights the earthly Jesus whose kerygma continues to be preached despite the interruption of the crucifixion. Bultmann sees the Easter-kerygma as the constant factor, and rejects as theologically irrelevant any going back behind this kerygma. Marxsen criticizes Bultmann's unconcern with historical origins (*Significance*, 19), and returns to the historical Jesus' proclamation as the constant message to which nothing essentially new was added by Good Friday and any subsequent events. According to Bultmann, Christ "is risen in the Church's kerygma" and the meaning of Easter faith is to believe in Christ present in that kerygma. In Marxsen's terms, we do not believe in Christ but accept the cause of Jesus, who remains present in the sense that his kerygma "continues to be preached." Rather than speak of Christ's presence in the Church's kerygma, Marxsen talks of the presence of God in Jesus' kerygma which continues to be at work (*Significance*, 37). Marxsen's focus on the historical Jesus' kerygma robs the crucifixion of any real value. It becomes a temporary interruption in the preaching of Jesus' message. Bultmann, however, takes the cross to be "an ever-present reality," which offers us liberating power and challenges us to die with Christ.

Finally, Marxsen rightly affirms that the history of Jesus' ministry should not be let go. Bultmann wrongly depreciates the relevance for faith and theology of that history. Marxsen's conviction, however, leads him to another extreme. He believes that *any* resurrection theology will make the earthly Jesus "merely the precursor of the Risen One," so that "what Jesus did and brought would in that case have been no more than a prelude" to the real drama (*ibid.*, 45f). Against this, while insisting that the resurrection changes the human condition before God and does not merely restore the situation of the ministry, one should also insist that the ministry is essential for interpreting the resurrection of the crucified Jesus. The paschal mystery is the drama's climax. Yet what precedes Good Friday and Easter Sunday also forms a real act in the whole drama. In short, Marxsen is not justified in fearing that a resurrection theology necessarily deprives Jesus' ministry of real significance.

JÜRGEN MOLTMANN

I turn next to Jürgen Moltmann (b. 1926) whose *Theology of Hope* (German original 1964) initiated a new movement in theology which took issue with Bultmann over many points—not least his understanding and interpretation of Jesus' resurrection. Although Moltmann has also written elsewhere about the resurrection, I will draw mainly from his major treatment in *Theology of Hope* (New York & London, 1967; hereafter TH).

(1) *Resurrection as Promise.* Among other influences three writers led the young Moltmann to modify his essentially Barthian thought and move from a word of God theology ("God has spoken") to a word of promise theology centered around the eschatological promise which challenges our human hope. Gerhard von Rad's work on the Old Testament, presented as the history of divine promise which in its fulfillment evoked new, ever-increasing expectations, encouraged Moltmann to approach Christ's resurrection in a fresh way. A chapter on the Old Testament promise and history (TH, 95–138) preceded the discussion of "The Resurrection and the Future of Jesus Christ" (TH, 139–229). A few critics accused Moltmann of making Christ's resurrection a mere tailpiece to the history of Old Testament promise. They failed to recognize the importance of Moltmann's move: a genuinely theological method does not allow us to tackle the story of Good Friday and Easter Sunday without first taking account of what God had already promised, revealed and done through the history of the chosen people.

The New Testament scholar Ernst Käsemann fed Moltmann's new move by breaking with Bultmann's interpretation of eschatology as an other-worldly existence for the individual here and now. Under the banner of "apocalyptic, the mother of Christian theology," Käsemann highlighted the future and cosmic thrust of St. Paul's eschatological thinking. Pauline theology was oriented toward the world and its history and not specifically toward the individual.

In his *Das Prinzip Hoffnung* (Frankfort, 1959) Ernst Bloch provided Moltmann with a language of hope. His philosophy of hope also reminded Moltmann of Christian themes like promise, hope, future, mission and the category of the new.

Moltmann remained faithful to Barth by stressing the centrality of Jesus' resurrection: "A Christian faith that is not resurrection faith can . . . be neither Christian nor faith" (TH, 166). He made it clear that he did not intend either a kerygmatic centrality (the resurrection as proclaimed) or a sacramental centrality (the resurrection as shaping our liturgical life), but rather an historical centrality (the resurrection as an event which has happened to Jesus himself). He wrote: "Christianity stands or falls with the reality of the raising of Jesus from the dead by God" (TH, 165).

Moltmann holds together the crucifixion and the resurrection, but presents the resurrection as a distinct, new deed of God. Here he rejects not only Bultmann's reductionism (the resurrection being swallowed up by the crucifixion) but also the opposite form of reductionism (which highlights the resurrection at the expense of the crucifixion): "The resurrection can neither be reduced to the cross, as showing its meaning, nor can the cross be reduced to the resurrection, as its preliminary" (TH, 200). Neither form of reductionism can claim genuine support from the Pauline theology developed in 1 Corinthians, Romans, Galatians and other letters.

The three classical questions from Kant's *Critique of Pure Reason* ("What can I know? What ought I to do? What may I hope for?") stand behind an historical, ethical (or existential) and eschatological study of Christ's resurrection. Moltmann distinguishes but will not separate the three questions: "The question, 'What can I know of the historical facts?' cannot here be separated from the ethical and existential question, 'What am I to do?' and from the eschatological question, 'What may I hope for?' " (TH, 166).

In the event the third question dominates. Moltmann absolutizes the divine promise (disclosed in the resurrection) which opens up a new future in hope:

> . . . the event of the raising of Christ from the dead [the historical question] is an event which is understood *only* [italics mine] in the *modus* of promise. It has its time still ahead of it, is grasped as a "historic phenomenon" *only* [italics mine] in its relation to *its* future, and mediates to those who know it a future towards which they have to move [the ethical question] in history (TH, 190).

In these terms Christ's resurrection has its revealing and redeeming power, but *only* by way of promise. He is risen not so much into the kerygma which reveals to us the truth (Bultmann) nor into the liturgy which saves us (Melito of Sardis) but into God's future, that final future for all people and all things (TH, 212). We know the resurrection in the way it contradicts the God-forsaken, "negative present" (TH, 215) of our current experience and anticipates the future reality of the coming kingdom. Hence here and now "the resurrection of Christ does not mean a possibility *within* the world and its history" (italics mine), but only "a new possibility altogether for the world, for existence and for history" (TH, 179).

Within a few years of publishing *Theology of Hope* Moltmann qualified somewhat his sharp contrast between the negative present we experience and the positive future we expect. As we shall see, he began to speak of ways we *experience* Christ's resurrection here and now. Through "the Spirit of the resurrection" we experience faith, certainty, love and justification. Even in *Theology of Hope* he touched on "the tendency of the Spirit" who already in the present "quickens men in suffering and whose goal is the praise of the new creation" (TH, 216). The contrast between the negative present of experience and the positive future of hope was never total.

When handling the first or historical question about the resurrection ("What can I know of the historical facts?"), Moltmann does so from the standpoint of the third or eschatological question ("What may I hope for?"). Like Pannenberg he makes much of the fact that the appearances of the risen Christ were appropriated by the disciples inasmuch as they already hoped for a general resurrection of the dead: "The Easter appearances . . . were recognized and proclaimed within a horizon of apocalyptic expectation" (TH, 218). Moltmann's mindset comes through clearly. He does not primarily say that the Easter appearances communicated the high-point of God's *self-revelation* (reached with Christ's dying and rising), nor that they manifested the *redemption* effected through the events of Good Friday and Easter Sunday, nor that they gave rise to Christian *faith* and initiated the *kerygma*. The primary point about the appearances of the risen Christ is that the disciples understood and interpreted them through their hopes for a final future promised to the entire world. Hence knowing Christ's resurrection necessarily meant proclaiming it to the whole human race:

> If this event of the raising of Jesus can be rightly understood only in conjunction with his universal, eschatological future, then the only mode of communication appropriate to this event must be missionary proclamation to all peoples without distinction (TH, 188).

Of course, it is important for Moltmann that in the Easter appearances the controlling input came from the risen Jesus himself. He tells us that in these appearances

> . . . we have not merely dumb visions, but at the same time, and at bottom no doubt *first and foremost*, so-called auditions as well. This is

indicated by the fact that these visions were entirely a matter of vo-
catory visions (TH, 198; italics mine).

Later on I want to discuss a similar position endorsed by Hans Küng
(the apostles' experience of vocation). Here let me note simply that to
characterize the Easter encounters as "first and foremost" auditory experiences requires dealing with the fact that in 1 Corinthians 15:5–8 Paul
reports no word from the Risen Lord and that, in general, the New Testament represents those encounters much more as visual rather than as
auditory experiences. One is left wondering how to validate exegetically
Moltmann's statement. He comes across as very different from Pannenberg who, both in dealing with the appearances and with the discovery
of the empty tomb (which Moltmann passes over in silence), discusses
carefully the relevant New Testament passages.

All the same, what does Moltmann say about the activity of the
risen Jesus in his Easter appearances? First, the Lord who appears identifies himself with the crucified Jesus. We saw above how Moltmann
distinguishes the crucifixion and the resurrection. In fact when working
out the nature of the risen Christ's self-identification, he proposes that
the distinction between crucifixion and resurrection forms not only a
contradiction but even a total contradiction:

> The fundamental event in the Easter appearances . . . manifestly lies
> in the revelation of the identity and continuity of Jesus in the total
> contradiction of cross and resurrection, of god-forsakenness and the
> nearness of God (TH, 199).

(This dialectical language which surfaces strongly in Moltmann's *The
Crucified God* [London, 1974] recalls the middle Barth's penchant for af-
firmation and negation, thesis and antithesis, in speaking of God and
the divine revelation.)

Second, the risen Lord also identifies himself as one who is to come
(TH, 201). His future, Moltmann explains, promises "the kingdom of
God in a new totality of being" (TH, 203).

Third, the divine promise sets in force the apostolic mission: "The
pro-missio of the kingdom is the ground of the *missio* of love to the world"
(TH, 224). In view of what we will hear later from Jon Sobrino, it is
worth noting here how Moltmann describes the apostolic mission not
merely as Easter proclamation but also as a "*missio* of love" and "service
in the world": "The commission to apostolic service in the world was
held to be *the* word of the risen Lord" (TH, 202). Instead of merely waiting for "the coming lordship of the risen Christ" (TH, 329), all Chris-

tians are called to be "engaged in the apostolate of hope for the world" (TH, 328), offering "new impulses for the shaping of man's public, social and political life" (TH, 329). Here Moltmann shows himself decisively different from Bultmann who highlighted the Church's role as the bearer of the Easter kerygma which can bring the individual to a new self-understanding. For Moltmann the resurrection promise does not encourage a flight from the process of world history, but mobilizes the Christian community to engage itself in transforming the present because it looks for the universal future of God's kingdom.

(2) *The Fathers, Barth and Pannenberg.* In presenting Moltmann's interpretation of Christ's resurrection, I have also mentioned Bultmann, Melito of Sardis and others whose work can be usefully compared or contrasted with that of Moltmann. To place his contribution even more clearly, I wish to suggest briefly some ways in which he differs from the Fathers of the Church, Barth and Pannenberg. Then I can move to some reflections on analogy, causality and the nature of history. They too will help to situate and clarify Moltmann's theology of the resurrection.

My first chapter illustrated how the Fathers of the Church frequently organize their thinking and teaching on the resurrection around our hope to be raised from the dead. As Moltmann would do, they make much of the way Christ's resurrection promises us a share in his victory over death. But they do not have the resources of modern philosophy and biblical scholarship to construct a complete theology of hope. They live in a persecuted Church (Clement, Tertullian, Origen, etc.) or in a Church which has only recently become tolerated (Gregory of Nazianzus, etc.). We do not normally hear from them Moltmann's rhetoric about a resurrection hope which sets itself to transform the public, social and political life of the world. Their resurrection hope leads them to think much of life hereafter and to discuss problems about our risen existence (food, sex, the fate of those consumed by wild beasts and cannibals, etc.)—particular questions which Moltmann's general eschatology of hope leaves far behind. In sum, although the same powerful hope in the risen Christ and the resurrected world to come sets Moltmann together with many Fathers of the Church, they draw apart from him because their ancient world deeply differs from the late twentieth century in its resources, concerns and methods of argument.

At the University of Göttingen Moltmann absorbed the thought of Karl Barth and has remained faithful to much of what the mature Barth proposed about the resurrection. For instance, Moltmann understands the crucifixion and resurrection to be distinct events; he does not use the resources of reason to justify belief in the resurrection. At the same time, however, major differences turn up: for example, Moltmann makes nothing of the empty tomb which—as we saw—Barth called an "indispensable sign" for Easter faith.

The truly major contrast comes with Moltmann's emphatically futurist theology. The resurrection of the crucified Christ contains a promise "for his own and for the world" which has not yet been fulfilled. Hence "Christian hope expects from the future of Christ not only unveiling but also final fulfilment" (TH, 228), "the fulfilment of the lordship of the crucified one over all things" (TH, 229). Barth, however, interpreted the final *parousia* not as the real fulfillment of a promised lordship but rather as the unveiling of what "has already taken place once and for all" (*Dogmatics in Outline* [New York, 1949], 135). In other words, Christ's future coming will simply reveal to everyone the divine fullness which is already there (CD IV/1, 319). Whereas Moltmann insists that on the side of the risen Jesus the resurrection has set in train a dynamic process which has yet to be completed, Barth represents the final coming as the mere disclosure of what God has already accomplished through the events of Good Friday and Easter Sunday. Moltmann plays down all that Christ has made present for us today and interprets the resurrection primarily in terms of the future which has not yet come. Barth, however, speaks of eternity and presence rather than the future. "The *eternal* action of Jesus Christ" (CD IV/1, 315) means that the resurrection is not merely "something that happened there and then," but "is as such a *present* event, the event which fills and determines the whole *present*" (CD IV/1, 313; italics mine).

Above I have already called attention to one or two points of comparison and contrast between Moltmann and Pannenberg. In the next section of this chapter other such points will emerge. Here let me note two differences between them. Pannenberg moves with purpose to construct a *rational* case for maintaining the historical truth of Jesus' resurrection—something that Moltmann, like Barth, Bultmann and Marxsen, will not do. Second, Pannenberg "stations" himself in his scholar's study to reflect on the resurrection within the horizon of universal history. Moltmann, however, "stations" himself within the history of the divine promise which will finally transform "the negative, torturing and contradictory aspects of the world" (TH, 197). The evil and injustice we now suffer brand "the visible realm of present experience as a god-forsaken transient reality that is to be left behind" (TH, 18). Soon after the publication of *Theology of Hope* we find Moltmann modifying this totally bleak picture of present realities. But he continues to interpret human history as the history of suffering. It is within that horizon that he asks what the resurrection of the crucified Jesus might mean.

(3) *Analogy, Causality and History.* To do Moltmann's theology of the resurrection justice, we need to consider three further items which have already surfaced in this book.

(a) Chapter One illustrated the use of analogy by the Fathers of the Church. In presenting the resurrection, they introduced a variety of analogies from nature (the succession of the seasons, the legendary phoenix, etc.) and from the Bible (for example, the story of Jonah). Admittedly they were generally aiming to elucidate our coming resurrection rather than Christ's. But so too was Paul when he introduced some analogies from nature (1 Cor 15:35ff).

In this century Ernst Troeltsch has dominated and dictated the discussion of analogy's role in our understanding of history. It is with an eye on Troeltsch that Moltmann enunciates the principle:

> It is generally acknowledged that historical understanding nowadays is always analogical understanding and must therefore remain within the realm of what is understandable in terms of analogy. The omnipotence thus attaching to analogy implies . . . the basic similarity of all historical events, which is not, of course, identity . . . but presupposes that there is always a common core of similarity, on the basis of which the differences can be sensed and perceived (TH, 175–176).

This "presupposition of a fundamental similarity underlying all events" (TH, 176) raises "grave difficulties" (TH, 177) when we come to claims about Christ's resurrection, an event which is strikingly new and even unique. Moltmann realizes that dissimilarity forms the "other side of the analogical process" (TH, 178) and that therefore, absolutely speaking, analogical understanding does not rule out Christ's resurrection.

But where will Moltmann recognize pertinent analogies? Not in creation and ordinary human experience. Over this he disagrees with Pannenberg's claim that the principle of analogy allows for "what is dissimilar and individual, accidental and suddenly new" (TH, 178) emerging in history. Certainly Moltmann is right in holding that the resurrection of Christ is much more than just "a possible process in world history," something "accidentally new" thrown up in the ordinary flux of events (TH, 179f). But do we not find some (at least remote) analogies to the resurrection in our regular experiences of nature (for instance, spring following winter) or in remarkable events of "ordinary" history like a shattered nation rebuilding and coming to new strength after a catastrophic defeat in war? Moltmann outlaws introducing such analogies. There is "no basis" (TH, 197) for using these comparisons between Christ's resurrection and either "that which can be experienced any time and anywhere" (TH, 180) or "the history we know" (TH, 197). This view entails a radical separation between the order of creation (the realm of our ordinary experience and history) and the order of final redemption (promised through the resurrection of the crucified Jesus). According to Moltmann, the first order does not yield any analogies which illuminate the second.

Apparently his assertion that for the resurrection "there are no analogies in the history we know" (TH, 197) also covers the special history of God's people in the Old Testament. Unlike those who composed and celebrated the liturgy of the early Church, he draws no analogy between the events of the exodus (see also 1 Cor 5:7) and the events of Christ's crucifixion and resurrection from the dead. This leaves out that elaborate comparison between the night of the resurrection and the night of deliverance from Egypt developed by the *Exultet* or Paschal Proclamation.

Initially Moltmann proposes simply an eschatological analogy. It is the future kingdom of God which can help us grasp the meaning of the first Easter, or rather vice versa. He writes: "The resurrection of Christ does not offer itself as an analogy to that which can be experienced any time and anywhere, but as an analogy to what is to come to all" (TH, 180). At first sight, this statement has a certain appeal. It respects the "enormous" nature of the resurrection as the beginning of the end of the world. At the same time, however, such an eschatological comparison offers little help to those seeking some minimal understanding of Jesus' victory over death. It "explains" what is unclear (the resurrection) through what is even more unclear (the *eschaton*)—a case of *ignotum per ignotius*.

Fairly soon after the appearance of *Theology of Hope* Moltmann began recognizing some analogies to Jesus' resurrection in what we experience here and now.

> Only from the history of its [the resurrection's] effect in the believers and in the church can the historian arrive at some understanding of this event. . . . If in the history of death there are no analogies to Jesus' resurrection, there are at least analogies in the category of the Spirit and his effects. For us today, the experiential form of the resurrection is "the Spirit of the resurrection" or "the power of the resurrection." It is the justification of the godless in a world of

unrighteousness, the experience of faith, certainty in the midst of un-
certainty, the experience of love in the midst of death (*The Future of
Hope*, ed. F. Herzog [New York, 1970] 163).

Moltmann gave some ground here, but restricted the use of analogy to
the order of (Christian) redemption. It was *only* from the history of the
resurrection's effect "in the believers and in the church" that he believed
the historian could "arrive at some understanding of this event." Moltmann continued to rule out analogies drawn from ordinary experience
and general history (the order of creation).

   Later we will find Karl Rahner appealing to our experience of the
Spirit to illuminate the apostles' encounters with the risen Lord. On
"the experience of love" as a means of interpreting the resurrection,
however, there is practically nothing developed in the entire Christian
tradition. Chapter Eight of this book will explore the resurrection as a
mystery of love.

   (b) Earlier in this chapter I reported Bultmann's belief that modern
science postulates a rigid uniformity and Pannenberg's justified rejection of this belief. Moltmann raises the same issue:

> In face of the positivistic and mechanistic definition of the nature of
> history as a self-contained system of cause and effect, the assertion of
> a raising of Jesus by God appears as a myth concerning a supernatural
> incursion which is contradicted by all our experience of the world
> (TH, 177).

Moltmann's answer leaves us with a dichotomy between (scientific) reason and faith: "The reality of the resurrection cannot be comprehended
by the historical means of the modern age" (*ibid.*). He would have done
better to have pointed out that the mechanistic cause-effect understanding no longer obtains. Both in the physical sciences and in the human
sciences the guiding model is now the notion of probability which does
not necessarily exclude even startling novelty. In other words, within
the framework of understanding which has emerged in these disciplines
in the last fifty years, an event such as the resurrection may be highly
improbable but not *a priori* impossible.

   Chapter Seven of this book will return to this question: "What does
it mean to say that God intervened to cause the resurrection of Jesus
from the dead?"

   (c) The nature and contribution of historical knowledge surfaced
in my discussion of Barth, Bultmann, Marxsen and Pannenberg. For
Moltmann the Easter texts in the New Testament report such "a dif-

ferent experience of history" (TH, 175) and of what is divinely possible
that we cannot align this with the modern, human understanding of history and of what is historically possible (TH, 177). Hence, instead of
trying to slot the resurrection into some pre-existing concept of history,
he takes a God- and future-centered view of the resurrection as *the* his-
tory-making event and proposes a new understanding of history on that
basis. "By the raising of Christ," he explains, "we do not mean a possible
process in world history, but the eschatological process to which world
history is subjected" (TH, 179f).

This goes beyond Pannenberg, who may emphasize the way
Christ's resurrection really anticipates the end of history but maintains
a certain intellectual autonomy for the notion of universal history. In
Moltmann's approach eschatology swallows up history. One is left in a
quandary trying to think about the past and present course of history.
If the resurrection subjects world history to an eschatological process,
what can one say about that process before the *eschaton* arrives? At best
we can only hope to make some provisional, fragmentary guesses about
what has happened and is happening.

To fill out this sampling of twentieth-century theological reflection
on Christ's resurrection, I want to take up next the views of Rahner,
Küng and Sobrino.

3

Rahner, Küng and Sobrino

To complete this sampling of twentieth-century theology of the resurrection I plan to discuss the work of Karl Rahner (1904–1984), Hans Küng (b. 1928) and Jon Sobrino (b. 1938). Their approaches to Easter are, respectively, theological, apologetical and practical. The question of hope in the face of death gives shape to Rahner's theological interest in the resurrection. Küng tackles the question of truth and wishes to justify intellectually Christian belief in Jesus risen from the dead. Sobrino writes for those who suffer oppression and presents the resurrection as an active message of liberation. Other points of divergence and convergence should emerge in the course of this chapter.

KARL RAHNER

Notoriously Rahner weaves his reflections on the resurrection (or whatever else is under discussion) into a tightly meshed, unified pattern. To clarify matters, however, we can distinguish three major concerns of his resurrection theology: its starting point, the nature and justification of Easter faith and the redemptive impact of Christ's resurrection.

(1) *The Starting Point.* Like Bultmann, Moltmann and Pannenberg, Rahner knows that the human situation rightly enters into the making of a resurrection theology. In Rahner's case this means elaborating an understanding of death—of death itself and not just of all the painful sufferings which might precede death. "The correct starting-point for a genuine theology of Easter," Rahner maintains, is "a true theology of death."[1] Certainly some reflection on death is needed if we wish to grasp the inner link between Jesus' crucifixion and resurrection. What then does Rahner's theology of death offer?

77

He endorses what he learned from Martin Heidegger and what we find in Heidegger's *Being and Time* about human existence as "being-towards-death." The coming event of death casts its shadow over one's entire life; it is not merely something which becomes present only at the end. Rahner writes:

> Knowledge, even if mostly an implicit knowledge, of the inevitability of death, though not of its when and where, intrinsically determines the whole of life. In this knowledge death is always already present in human life.[2]

Rahner values the positive side of actual death, despite the painful indignity of that climactic event. On the one hand, as a consequence and expression of our sinful state, death violates human integrity and looks like an empty and futile disaster. Yet, on the other hand, it is

> . . . an active consummation from within brought about by the person himself, a maturing self-realization which embodies the result of what a man has made of himself during life, the achievement of total personal self-possession, a real effectuation of self, the fullness of freely produced personal reality (*ibid.*, 60 = ETh, 331).

In this way "death is the event in which the very man himself becomes his definitive self" (*ibid.*, 58 = ETh, 329). In this event "the fundamental decision which a man has made in regard to God, the world and himself, and which dominates his whole life, receives its definitive character" (*ibid.*, 61 = ETh, 333).

In the case of Christ his utter obedience to the divine will not only enhanced the positive aspects of death (as complete fulfillment) but also transformed the negative side of death (as an experience of weakness, emptiness and evil). What had been "the manifestation of sin" became the contradiction of sin, the manifestation of a "yes" to the will of the Father. Death turned into life, something entirely different from what it appeared to be.[3] Had Christ not died, the world would have been a different place. As it was, in his death "his human reality and grace" became existential determinants of "the whole cosmos" (*ibid.*, 66). How does Rahner ground or at least clarify this claim?

To understand and interpret Jesus' life and death, Rahner draws on Heidegger's account of death—or rather on his description of the life-long phenomenon of human dying. Death itself, precisely as such, is not a moment in life and so lies beyond the scope of any phenomenological description. For Heidegger "Being" manifests itself through the interpretive "mission" of "being-there," *Dasein*, man. As such, however, *Dasein* exists only as "Being-in-the-world." At death *Dasein* ceases to be *there* in the world, and nothing meaningful can be added. Thus Heidegger's phenomenology offers no possibility for describing actual death (or, for that matter, resurrection).

Hence when Rahner comes to the death of Jesus, he has no Heideggerian framework to use and switches somewhat toward the traditional (scholastic) version of death as the separation of body and soul. In this life our body is our presence to the world, but greatly limits that presence. Through death the human spirit, far from becoming an isolated, "other-worldly" unit, breaks through to an intimate union with the material cosmos as a whole. Rahner puts it as follows:

> . . . in death, and only in death . . . man enters into an open, unrestricted relationship to the cosmos as a whole. . . . He is integrated, as a constant and determining factor, into the world as a whole, through his own total reality achieved in his life and death. . . . Because death *in some way* opens to man the real ontological relationship of his soul to the world as a whole, it is through his death that man *in some way* introduces as his contribution the result of his life into the radical, real ground of the unity of the world (*ibid.*, 63; italics mine).

Earlier in *On the Theology of Death* Rahner does not use this more tentative language ("in some way"), but speaks more immediately of the possibility of a "direct influence" on the entire universe.

> The individual person, once rendered pancosmic through death, by this real ontological and open relation to the whole cosmos, might come to have a direct influence within the world (*ibid.*, 22f).

In a unique way the death of Christ himself actualized this possibility. He became an all-cosmic presence, the very heart of the universe.

> When the vessel of his body was shattered in death, Christ was poured out over all the cosmos; he became actually, in his very humanity, what he had always been according to his dignity, the heart of the universe, the innermost center of creation (*ibid.*, 66).

This thoroughly positive interpretation of Jesus' death stands in sharp contrast with the negative interpretation offered by Barth (Chapter Two). By defining Good Friday so positively Rahner can more easily hold together Jesus' death and resurrection. Yet one should also bring out some difficulties Rahner's position needs to face.

Rahner stresses so much the (redemptive) influence over all creation which resulted from the death on the cross that he seems to leave little room for the actual resurrection to effect anything. If in death Jesus has become the heart of the world and through his grace already determines the whole of the universe, what more can his resurrection achieve? Rahner, however, does picture the resurrection as doing something new and specific. It is the event in which "God irrevocably adopts the creature as his own reality." The man Christ is divinized and transfigured in such a way that his resurrection is the "final beginning of the glorification and divinization of the *whole* reality" (ThI vol. 4, 128f).

Here Rahner appears to respect the "contribution" of the resurrection. Nevertheless, he undercuts this admission by asserting that "Good Friday and Easter can be seen as two aspects of a strictly unitary event." If "the resurrection of Christ is not another event *after* his passion and death," what is it? Rahner calls it "the manifestation of what happened in the death of Christ" (*ibid.*, 128).

These last words have inevitably reminded commentators of Bultmann's view that "resurrection" reveals and expresses the meaningfulness of the cross. Yet Rahner stood apart from any such impoverishing reductionism. First, he never claimed that the resurrection was *merely* or *only* the manifestation of what happened in and through the crucifixion. On any showing, the resurrection *also* served to manifest what had truly happened on Good Friday. The language Rahner used allows us to urge this distinction in his favor: among other things the resurrection of Jesus *also* revealed the true meaning of his crucifixion.

Second, as I said when discussing Barth, both Rahner and Barth differ from Bultmann in maintaining that the dying and rising of Christ *actually* changed the situation of human beings and their world. That comes through clearly from Rahner's language about God irrevocably adopting "the creature as his own reality" and beginning "the glorification and divinization" of the world.

Third, Rahner himself modified or at least clarified what he intended when he talked of the crucifixion and resurrection as "a strictly unitary event." In "Resurrection" (SM vol. 5) he continued to talk of "a single event" but with two "inseparably interconnected phases." He wrote: "Jesus' resurrection is an element in a single event in which the death is the first phase which goes to constitute the actual resurrection itself." Rahner refused to reduce the resurrection to a mere "mythical expression" of the meaningfulness of the cross, speaking rather in factual terms of Easter Sunday as the goal and fulfillment which also conditions and interprets Good Friday:

With Jesus . . . the resurrection must be the goal and fulfilment precisely of his death, and both factors of the one occurrence must mutually condition and interpret one another (332 = ETh, 1441).

The more troublesome difficulty has been that in Rahner's interpretation the resurrection seems to be swallowed up—not so much by his theology of death and the cross, but by an all-inclusive theology of the *incarnation*. Considering the incarnation "as a formally salvific act," he thinks that in virtue of "its inmost essence" "the one event composed of death and resurrection" is *already* "implied and accepted" (ThI vol. 4, 130). If this already happened with the incarnation, what specific contribution to salvation was actually left to be accomplished by the death and resurrection? I will return to this question later.

(2) *Justifying Easter Faith.* Rahner takes a clear and helpful stand on the making of Easter faith. Two elements intertwine in bringing people to believe in Jesus as risen from the dead: the witness of the first disciples and our own primordial orientation toward a risen existence beyond death. I will draw here on Rahner's *Foundations of Christian Faith* (New York, 1978; hereafter *Foundations*).

Unlike Pannenberg, Rahner does not take it upon himself to establish the sheer historicity either of the Easter appearances or of the empty tomb. He leaves these matters to exegetes. Yet he is concerned to explore the disciples' experience of the risen Lord and to stress its "peculiar," in fact "strictly *sui generis*" nature (*Foundations*, 277).

Here Rahner excludes two common misconceptions. We should not understand the first disciples to have enjoyed

> . . . an almost solid sense experience. There is no such sense experience of someone who has really reached fulfillment, even presupposing that he must indeed have freely "manifested" himself. For this manifestation to imply such a sense experience, everything would have to belong to the realm of normal and profane sense experience (*ibid.*, 276; translation corrected).

As having "really reached fulfillment," the risen Christ is glorified and transformed into his final, eschatological state. Rahner is *not* saying that such an eschatological reality from the "other" realm can never in any way be manifested in and through our sense experience. (After all a risen body may be matter finally and fully spiritualized, yet it remains in some sense truly material and therefore can impinge on our world.) But

Rahner is saying that by definition a glorified being cannot enter in a massive, grossly material way into our world of normal sense experience. If the risen Christ had entered or did enter our world in that way, he would "fit into" space and time and hence could be weighed, measured, finger-printed, and subjected to various laboratory tests. That would mean that he was an ordinary, earthly being (subjected to the normal limits of space and time), and no longer a glorified and eschatologically transformed being. By definition a "solid" sense experience of the risen Christ was (and is) excluded.

Rahner also warns against comparing the Easter experiences of the first disciples "too closely" with "mystical visions of an imaginative kind" which happened "in later times" (*ibid.*). This careful language allows only for some comparison to be drawn. Like mystical visions these Easter encounters were not everyday, mundane experiences, but extraordinary episodes which produced deep joy and a certainty that what had been experienced was real and objective in the sense of being given "from without." Why does Rahner refuse to press the comparison? It is not an "apologetic" caution which knows that mystical visions and Easter encounters can be thoroughly self-authenticating for the persons concerned, but which recognizes that both kinds of experience remain open to the charge of being no more than pious hallucinations. Nor is Rahner's reason the fact that the New Testament reports not only Easter appearances to single individuals (Peter, Paul, Mary Magdalene and James), but also such appearances to *groups* of disciples (the Twelve, the five hundred, etc.). Rahner might have pointed out that accounts from elsewhere of genuine mystical visions can parallel somewhat the appearances to individuals but offer little help for interpreting the appearances to groups.

Rahner has three reasons for maintaining "the peculiar nature" of the Easter appearances. (a) First, the disciples themselves, while conscious of the fact that, "while given from 'without' " like authentic visionary experiences, those appearances were "different" (*ibid.*, 277). Here Rahner finds ample backing from the New Testament which presents a fairly wide range of visionary experiences, but reports the Easter appearances quite differently. Unlike the angelic communications to Joseph (Matt 1:20–21; 2:13, 19–20), none of the Easter appearances is said to occur during sleep in a dream. They do not take place by night, as do several "revelations" mentioned in Acts (16:9–10; 18:9; 23:11; 27:23). Nor can these appearances be likened to Peter's vision of the sheet let down from heaven. Even though that experience occurs by day and when he is awake, unlike the Easter appearances it happens in ecstasy (Acts 10:9–16). To sum up. The New Testament, while calling certain phenomena "visions" (2 Cor 12:1; Luke 24:23; etc.), apart from one passage (Acts 26:19), never uses that term of a resurrection appearance. What is more important than terminology, however, is the fact that—except for Luke's triple version of the appearance to Paul (Acts 9:3ff; 22:6ff; 26:12ff)—we would never think of classifying the Easter encounter as "mystical visions of an imaginative kind." Whatever one says about the consciousness of the first disciples themselves, the New Testament texts consistently present the Easter appearances as quite different from the familiar kinds of visionary experience.

(b) Rahner points out that the New Testament presents the Easter experiences as something irrepeatable and "reserved to a definite phase in salvation history," and hence "not to be expected indefinitely" (*ibid.*, 277). Presumably he has in mind here passages like 1 Corinthians 15:8 ("last of all he appeared also to me") and John 20:29 (which implies that only the Easter witnesses "saw and believed," whereas all later disciples would believe, even though they had never seen). Whatever the specific details of the appearances to Peter, Paul and the other basic witnesses, those experiences ended. This sets them apart from experiences of "mysticism which can be stimulated and repeated" (*ibid.*). As a widespread and seemingly universal religious phenomenon, mysticism is simply not confined to a particular period in salvation history, and hence does not offer a close analogy to the distinctive Easter experiences.

(c) Rahner adds a third consideration which sets the appearances of the risen Christ apart from the visions of Teresa of Avila, John of the Cross and other such classical mystics.

> The theology of mysticism . . . denies to the mystics to whom Jesus "appears" the character of being resurrection witnesses, and denies to their visions any equality with the appearances of the risen Christ to the apostles. . . . Our faith remains tied to the apostolic witnesses (*ibid.*, 274).

In the history of Christianity the great mystics have attracted much attention as teachers of prayer and leaders of religious reform. But neither they themselves nor their leading commentators (like Evelyn Underhill or Allison Peers) have ever tried to lend legitimacy to their function for the Church by claiming that mystics take their place with the first disciples in witnessing to the truth of Jesus' resurrection from the dead. How then does Easter faith depend upon Peter, Paul and the other apostolic witnesses?

Rahner carefully distinguishes between their role for us and the function of ordinary, "secular" testimony. Someone could assure me that at midday last New Year's Day he saw a middle-aged man dive into the Tiber from the Ponte Cavour. Even though I was away in another part of the city at the time, I could accept this evidence as "credible" and have "faith" in this testimony, because I could "evaluate the credibility of the witness from similar experiences" I have already had myself (*ibid.*, 275). In Rome and in Paris I could, for example, have actually seen people take such plunges at high noon on New Year's Day. However, in the case of the first disciples' witness to the Easter appearances, I simply have never had such an experience. I was not there to enjoy an appearance of the risen Christ in the period following his resurrection. My history has stationed me in a different place and time. From my own particular experience I do not know what it is like to share in the origins of Christianity and see the risen Lord.

Yet we today, Rahner argues, "do not stand simply and absolutely outside the experience of the apostolic witnesses," separated by an historical gulf which nothing can ever bridge. At the primordial level we share with them (and indeed all human beings) the same "transcendental hope in resurrection," an implicit orientation toward a total and lasting fulfillment of our existence (*ibid.*). Like Joseph Maréchal, J.B. Lotz and others, Rahner finds this dynamic openness implicitly present in every exercise of human knowledge and freedom.

Easter faith emerges through the interplay of three forces: the historical witness coming from the first disciples, our primordial (transcendental) hope in resurrection and the interior help of the Holy Spirit. Because of our transcendental hope, the apostolic witness to Jesus' resurrection does not bring us "something which is totally unexpected and which lies totally outside the horizon of our experience" (*ibid.*). For our knowledge of the first Easter we depend upon the first disciples. But their historical witness to Jesus as risen and alive reaches those who implicitly already experience a thrust toward the full and permanent life of resurrection. These historical and transcendental elements intermesh in the formation and legitimation of Easter faith.[4]

Not only our transcendental hope (which we share with all human beings) but also the "experience of the powerful Spirit" (*ibid.*, 276) sets us together with the first disciples. Christologically their experience differed from ours; the Easter appearances of the risen Lord were as such "peculiar," "strictly *sui generis*" experiences (*ibid.*, 277). Pneumatologically their experiences are similar to ours; the same Holy Spirit touches our lives powerfully and interiorly as happened to those first witnesses.

(3) *Resurrection as Transformation*.   When Rahner remarks that the resurrection "can be adequately understood only in reference to the absolute mystery of the Incarnation,"[5] it is too easy to detect here the principle "in my beginning was my end" and imagine that he alleges that the successive phases of Christ's life, death and resurrection were truly, if latently, already present and operative in the primary event of the incarnation. When we read that "in virtue of the inmost essence of the incarnation, seen itself as a formally salvific act, the one event composed of death and resurrection is implied and accepted" (ThI vol. 4, 130), it can sound as if everything was over at the incarnation. It may seem that everything was included in that event and nothing remained except for the truth to be disclosed.

Nevertheless, even in his earlier writings (before Rahner came to a stronger appreciation of the redemptive impact of the resurrection), the notion of the incarnation does not swallow up what is to come. Rather it initiates a dynamic movement which would remain incomplete, if not meaningless, but for Good Friday and Easter Sunday: "The incarnation itself is a divine movement which is fully deployed only in the death and resurrection of Jesus Christ" ("Salvation," SM vol. 5, 428 = ETh, 1522). In these terms Rahner presents the reality and meaning of the resurrection as the culmination and proper completion of what began when the Word became flesh. This dynamic unified movement from the incarnation to the resurrection forms the great, efficacious sign of God's will to save and divinize the world.

Hence Rahner does acknowledge specific salvific effects in the resurrection—first as the climactic event through which God definitively accepts and divinizes a created humanity: "The resurrection of Christ . . . is the event in which God irrevocably adopts the creature as his own reality" (ThI vol. 4, 128). Second, this act entails a radical transformation that affects the whole world.

> The world is such a unity, physically, spiritually and morally, that the decision of the man Christ, as a real component of the physical world, as a member of the biological family of humanity . . . as a member of the human community in its history of light and shadow, is ontologically, and not merely by a juridical disposition of God, the irreversible and embryonically *final beginning of the glorification and divinization of the whole reality (ibid.*, 129; italics mine).

Third, what we meet in the risen Christ is the redemptive "significance of his temporal life," now "accepted by God, set free to work, and actually effective" (*ibid.*, 131). The exalted Lord provides "the permanent

and ever-active access to God"—a process which "has already begun but
is still reaching completion in us" (*ibid.*, 132f), as we move through the
life of grace to glory.

Fourth, besides its saving, transformative effect, the resurrection is
also the climax of revelation. Through this event God "communicates
himself to the world in the Son whom the resurrection definitively identifies and acknowledges" ("Resurrection," SM vol. 5, 331 = ETh,
1440). It is only to be expected that Rahner would bring together both
the salvific and the revelatory force of the resurrection. Redemptive
grace and revelation form the two faces of the one process which Rahner
likes to call the divine self-communication.

All this by no means exhausts what Rahner has to say about
Christ's resurrection. But to continue this sketch of Roman Catholic approaches to Easter, I take up now Hans Küng.

HANS KÜNG

Convenience suggests drawing from Küng's *On Being a Christian*
(London, 1976; hereafter OBC) and highlighting certain items in his discussion of the resurrection. The section on Jesus' resurrection in *Eternal
Life?* (London, 1984) largely repeats what already turned up in OBC.
Four headings can introduce Küng's treatment: some preliminaries, his
success as apologist, the resurrection itself, and the appearances of the
risen Lord.

(1) *Some Preliminaries.* (a) Küng observes the danger of exemplifying
Ludwig Feuerbach's view that belief in the resurrection is simply the
projection of our hunger for eternal life.

> We must not confirm Feuerbach's suspicion that we are *merely* proj-
> ecting our own needs: that the resurrection is *nothing more* than the
> satisfaction of man's longing for a direct assurance of his personal im-
> mortality (OBC, 343; italics mine).

This is carefully chosen language which implicitly admits that we have
our need and our longing for personal immortality. Here a certain convergence with Rahner's transcendental hope shows up—at least in this
sense: we have some kind of desire or thrust toward a personal existence
which will never end. It is this dynamic openness to eternal life which
makes the question of Jesus' resurrection critically important to us.

(b) Another preliminary point looks less well made. Küng writes:

If . . . we want to believe in some sort of resurrection not only halfheartedly, with a bad conscience, but honestly and with conviction, the difficulties must be faced squarely and without prejudices of faith or unbelief (*ibid.*, 346; see *Eternal Life?* 125).

This quotation illustrates nicely a distinctive character of this apologist: the division of people into two classes—those of whom we must disapprove because they believe "only halfheartedly, with a bad conscience," and those who join Küng himself in facing difficulties "squarely" and believing "honestly and with conviction." But my misgivings do not concern his apologetical style but rather something else, the appeal to put aside "prejudices of faith or unbelief."

Perhaps Küng wishes only to contrast an irrational approach with a reasonable one and to invite his readers to join him on the side of reason. Nevertheless, what he says sounds ominously like a plea to suspend temporarily one's faith (or lack of faith), so as to reflect on the resurrection from some neutral, impartial point of view. I am left baffled by the implication that we can find such an "objective" ground on which to assess the arguments for and against the resurrection of Christ. In his now classic *Truth and Method* (London, 1975) Hans-Georg Gadamer demonstrates the futility of searching for such an allegedly neutral position. Like many others he recommends rather an awareness of "one's own bias (*Voreingenommenheit*)" and a "conscious assimilation of one's own fore-meanings (*Vormeinungen*) and prejudices" (*Truth*, 238).

Let me hasten to add that in places Küng accepts the role of "prejudgment." He concludes, for example, his section on "historical criticism" by noting: "Christian faith can open new depths to the scientific scholar, perhaps the decisive depth. Right from the outset an absolutely presuppositionless science of history is impossible" (OBC, 157). The problem is that Küng appears to move between two irreconcilable positions. *Either* one can agree with Gadamer (and many others) on the role of legitimate "prejudices," "fore-meanings" and "bias." *Or* one can revive the widely discredited attempt to tackle "without the prejudices of faith or unbelief" the issues concerning the historical origins of Christianity and, specifically, the resurrection itself. But one cannot do both.

Perhaps Küng intends only to put aside *false and unproductive* prejudices *before* examining the evidence for and the difficulties against Christ's resurrection. In that case, he should heed Gadamer's warning that the interpreter

is not able to separate *in advance* the productive prejudices that make understanding possible from the prejudices that hinder understanding and lead to misunderstandings. This separation, rather, must take place in the understanding itself (*Truth*, 263; italics mine).

(c) A third matter of method, the role of the imagination, invites some comment. In places Küng wishes to exclude the imagination from participating in theological reflection on the Easter mystery. He insists that resurrection entails a radical transformation into a life which is "utterly different" and simply unimaginable:

> Here there is nothing to be depicted, imagined, objectified. . . . Neither sight nor imagination can help us here, they can only mislead us. The reality of the resurrection itself therefore is completely intangible and unimaginable.

Nevertheless, Küng also allows that in dealing with Christ's resurrection we use "pictorial," metaphorical and imaginative language—"symbols" which do not convey "direct knowledge" of something which remains in itself "unimaginable" (OBC, 350; see *ibid.*, 379). Presumably this language and these symbols yield some *indirect* knowledge of the resurrection. But this implication remains undeveloped.[6]

Here Küng leaves his readers a long way from Gadamer's position. That philosopher wishes the imagination to be "in free harmony" with the understanding (*Truth*, 43), and devotes the first part of *Truth and Method* to the question: How does truth emerge from the experience of art?

Undoubtedly the imagination can lead us at times into a mess. That happens when we use images in misguided attempts to describe directly and "explain" at length otherworldly realities. (Is it only this that Küng wishes to warn his readers against?) All the same, there is at least some value to be found in the view with which William Blake so identified himself—that truth is perceptible to the imagination rather than to the mind. After the period of the Church Fathers theologians have, of course, monotonously neglected art and the imagination as guides to religious truth. But—to parody Ludwig Wittgenstein—what we can in no sense imagine, we must confine to silence and non-belief.

Apropos of the resurrection it is not too wildly wrong to ask: How does the truth of the risen Lord emerge in the experience of Christian art and imagination? It could well be that the eye of the artist and our common fantasy offer considerable help here. The hints of the imagination—so often taken up into the Church's liturgy—may be worth more than the self-imposed silence of theologians. Clement of Rome and other such Fathers realized how such hints can illuminate the mystery of the risen Lord.

(2) *Küng the Apologist.*   During the history of Christianity many apologists (like Augustine and William Paley) have argued from observable effects (in the origins and life of the Church) to their only plausible cause (Jesus' resurrection from the dead). Küng handles this effect-cause argument with admirable skill. He does so first by comparing Jesus with three others who initiated religious movements.

> We are faced with the *historical enigma of the emergence . . . of Christianity.* How different this was from the gradual, peaceful propagation of the teachings of the successful sages, Buddha and Confucius; how different also from the largely violent propagation of the teachings of the victorious Muhammed. And all of this was within the lifetime of the founders. How different, after a complete failure and a shameful death, were the spontaneous emergence and almost explosive propagation of this message and community in the very name of the defeated teacher (OBC, 345).

In the case of all three founders time was on their side. Buddhism originated with Gautama (c. 563–c. 483 B.C.), who spent most of his long life teaching the way of enlightenment. The Chinese sage Confucius (c. 550–478 B.C.) also spent many years spreading his wisdom and attracting disciples, until he died and was buried with great pomp outside Kufow. A wealthy wife and then military victories helped Muhammed (c. 570–632) to gather and propagate his teaching. As the recognized prophet of Arabia, he died in Medina and was buried there. In these three instances we can point to various publicly verifiable causes which furthered the spread, respectively, of Buddhism, Confucianism and Islam: the long careers of the founders, financial resources and success in battle. In the case of Christianity the founder had none of these advantages: his public career was extremely short (at most just three or four years); he lacked military and financial support. Add too the way Jesus' life ended in humiliating failure and disgraceful death on the cross. After all this the subsequent, "almost explosive propagation" of his "message and community" in his very name remains an "historical enigma," unless we admit a proportionate cause (the resurrection).

Küng moves against those who deny Jesus' resurrection by explaining away the claim as resulting naturally from the psychological state and religious convictions of the disciples. Is this explanation historically plausible? Some of Jesus' disciples came to think of him in Messianic terms, but it is doubtful that they understood and accepted what he said about himself as suffering Son of Man. Then he was executed on the charge of being a Messianic pretender (Mark 15:26 etc.). What options were available for these disciples? They could have modified their belief

in him and interpreted him as another martyred prophet like John the
Baptist and others before him. In Küng's words:

> Would it not have been very much simpler for the primitive com-
> munity to proclaim Jesus . . . merely as one of those *martyr-prophets*
> who were persecuted and killed but were justified before God [the
> English translation omits this clause], whose tombs for that very rea-
> son were being reconstructed and cared for at the time of Jesus and
> who were venerated as intercessors? (OBC, 371).

Instead the first disciples preached Jesus as risen from the dead. How
does one account for that proclamation if no resurrection had taken
place?

Here Küng's argument could be tightened somewhat. To be crucified was not only to suffer a most cruel and humiliating form of execution, but also to die under a religious curse (Gal 3:13) and outside "the
camp" of God's covenanted people (Heb 13:12–13). In other words, crucifixion was seen as the death of a criminal and godless man who died
away from God's presence and in the place and company of irreligious
men. To honor anyone who perished in that way was an awful and profound scandal (1 Cor 1:23). Given that crucifixion was such a disgrace,
could Jesus' disciples have proclaimed him even as a martyred prophet?

In fact they began preaching the crucified Jesus as the divinely endorsed Messiah risen from the dead to bring salvation to all. Like others
Küng points out that the notion of a Messiah who failed, suffered, died
and rose from the grave was simply foreign to pre-Christian Judaism:
"The idea of a resurrection of the Messiah—still more of a failed Messiah—was an absolute novelty in the Jewish tradition" (OBC, 372).
Since their previous religious beliefs could not have led Jesus' disciples
to make such startlingly new claims about him, what triggered off this
religious novelty? Where did it come from, if not from Jesus' resurrection itself?

(3) *The Resurrection Itself.* In the last chapter I noted how the overly
subjective perspectives of Bultmann and Marxsen are scored with the
shadows of problems. Küng's objective line shines out clearly: "Easter
is an event primarily for Jesus himself: Jesus lives again *through God—
for their* [the disciples'] *faith*" (*ibid.*, 352). Küng obviously wishes to maintain an objective position which refuses to merge Jesus' resurrection
with the rise of faith after the crucifixion. In the first instance the resurrection personally affected Jesus himself in his being brought to new

life. Secondarily, this event triggered off a fresh relationship of faith for the disciples.

Apropos of Jesus' corpse, Küng takes the empty tomb to be unlikely and, indeed, unnecessary:

> There can be identity of the person even without continuity between the earthly and the "heavenly," "spiritual" body. . . . The corporality of the resurrection does not require the tomb to be empty (*ibid.*, 366).

Here Küng defends a corporeal resurrection, but dispenses with any *bodily* continuity between the earthly and risen existence of Jesus. The totally new "spiritual" body comes into existence without any continuity with the former, earthly body, and yet without imperilling the genuinely personal identity of Jesus. In his risen state he is identical with, and no mere substitute for, the person who died on the cross and was buried. Küng seems to locate Jesus' continuity simply at the level of soul or spirit. The new, "heavenly" body totally replaces the one which ended in the tomb.

In Küng's statement "can" and "require" are telltale words. As such he speaks at the level of principle—of what God *could* do. In theory the resurrection of Jesus, Küng argues, does not require an empty tomb; his personal identity could be preserved without the corpse being transformed and taken up into his new, "spiritual" existence. To an almost painful degree, Aquinas and other medieval theologians often took a similar tack in arguing from principles (whether real or merely alleged) to facts. Both in the medieval past and today, however, it would seem to me much sounder to establish and accept facts and then try to make sense of them rather than begin with general principles—in this case principles about continuity between something we know by experience (our earthly existence) and something of which we have no direct experience ("heavenly" existence). Later I wish to argue that a reasonable case can be made for the particular fact in question—namely, Jesus' empty tomb. Then I can reflect on its general theological significance.

(4) *The Easter Appearances.* As Rahner does, Küng maintains unambiguously the non-repeatable, *sui generis* nature of Jesus' Easter encounters with the first disciples. Their unique experiences gave them the unique, once-and-for-all role of becoming the foundational witnesses to Jesus' resurrection.

> These experiences of the first witnesses were—like those of the prophets—unique vocations. And we cannot expect a religious en-

lightenment and awakening which for us would be a repetition of those unique experiences of the first disciples. We are *thrown back on the testimony of the first, foundational witnesses* (*ibid.*, 379).

Küng holds firm to the New Testament record of *multiple appearances* (to individuals and to groups). He sets his face against those who allege that Easter faith began merely with some experience on the part of Peter: "A reduction of all the appearances . . . to the one appearance to Peter, as if the former were merely to confirm the latter, is not justified" (*ibid.*, 348f). In Chapter Two we saw Marxsen claiming that Peter was the first to believe, even if it remains completely irrelevant how this happened. In my *Interpreting Jesus* (120–24) I evaluated Edward Schillebeeckx's theory about Peter's deep sense of forgiveness playing a decisive role in the conversion of the first Christian community. Earlier in this century Adolf von Harnack and others turned Peter's "vision" of the risen Lord into the exclusive basis for Christian faith.[7] Küng disagrees with that kind of reductionism which devalues the testimony coming from the Twelve, Paul and the others to whom the risen Lord appeared.

Here and there Küng's own interpretation of the Easter appearances has suffered at the hands of translators. For instance, *Signposts for the Future* (New York, 1978) has him telling us of the first believers "who regarded their faith as something that really happened to them" (21). However, the original text, *20 Thesen zum Christsein* (Munich, 1975), speaks of the first witness "*die ihren Glauben auf einem wirklichen Widerfahrnis gegründet sahen* (who saw their faith as grounded on a real occurrence)" (38). This "real occurrence," which grounded the new, post-Easter faith of the disciples consisted in their "true encounters with the crucified Jesus, now raised up," "their quite definite experiences of him as raised from the dead" (OBC, 373, 375). Küng is *not* saying that after being shattered by the death of their master, the disciples found that a new faith "really happened to them." Rather "true encounters" with the risen Lord triggered the new faith which made them "his witnesses and apostles" (*ibid.*, 373).

In explaining the risen Lord's appearances to the first disciples, Küng introduces a comparison with the calls of Old Testament prophets: "*The appearances involve vocation*. . . . These can be best understood if *compared with the callings of Old Testament prophets*" (*ibid.*, 376). The point turns up again in *Eternal Life?* where he describes the appearances as "calls to proclamation akin to those of the prophets" (134). Obviously this classical comparison between the New Testament apostles and the Old Testament prophets stands up in various ways. Paul (Gal 1:11–16, especially 15–16) apparently thought of his apostolic vocation as being "akin" to those of Jeremiah (1:5) and Isaiah (49:1). Moreover, in fairness to Küng it should be noted that he thinks in terms of an analogy, not a strict parallel.

There are, however, a number of differences which seriously limit the value of the comparison. Primarily the Old Testament prophets hear the word of God both at the time of their original callings and later. Only secondarily do they see visions. It is exactly the opposite with the Easter witnesses. The New Testament portrays them much more as having seen the risen Lord rather than as having heard his voice or word. Later I will need to reflect on the nature of the apostolic experience. Here I want only to remark that Peter, Paul and the other Easter witnesses, unlike their alleged counterparts in the Old Testament, were much more "seers" than "hearers." Second, the word of God comes directly to individuals like Amos, Isaiah and Ezekiel; the Scriptures report experiences happening only to individuals who find themselves driven to convey certain messages to the people at large. In the case of the Easter appearances, however, not only individuals but also groups (above all the Twelve) encountered the risen Lord. The *collective* experience and witness also belong to the essential Easter story in a way which the case of the classical prophets does not parallel.

Third, all of the Easter witnesses except Paul have an experience of *recognition*. They recognize the risen One whom they meet as personally identical with the Jesus whom they have previously seen, heard, touched and followed during his earthly life. The classical prophets know, of course, that the God who calls them has been the God of Abraham, Isaac and Jacob. But there is no question of Amos, Isaiah and Jeremiah recognizing someone whom they themselves have previously known as living on this earth. The prophetic "recognition" of the Deity whose word comes to them is quite different from the recognition of the risen Christ on the part of his first disciples. Fourth, Amos and other classical prophets find themselves called unexpectedly and without any apparent preparation (see, for example, Amos 3:8; 7:14f). In the case of the Twelve and some other Easter witnesses, their association with Jesus during his lifetime formed a period of training. Even if they were not ready for his death and resurrection, in the long run their memory of experiences from the ministry fed into and supported the post-Easter mission. Their time with the earthly Jesus had formed a kind of "novitiate" for those destined to become apostolic witnesses to the resurrection—a "novitiate" which is not paralleled in the case of Amos and other classical prophets.

In sum, Küng's comparison between the Old Testament prophets

and the official witnesses to the resurrection, while not valueless, remains limited and does not illuminate very much the apostolic experiences of the risen Lord.

JON SOBRINO

While acknowledging the relevance of other works by Sobrino, I
wish to discuss only *Christology at the Crossroads* (New York, 1978). In
any case, that book contains the most extensive treatment of the resurrection he has so far provided.

(1) *Approaching the Resurrection.* Sobrino states clearly his conviction
about "the hermeneutic locale for understanding the resurrection of Jesus" being found not merely in our being-toward-death (Rahner) but in
the whole "history of suffering." Within that history "the questioning
search for justice," by asking about the final future of victims and their
murderers, puts us in a position to understand and interpret matters:
"Basic discussion about Jesus' resurrection . . . has to do with the
triumph of justice. Who will be victorious, the oppressor or the op-
pressed?" (*ibid.*, 244). This question, which opens the way for interpreting the resurrection, expresses itself as a hope. Unlike Rahner,
however, Sobrino speaks of a hope which faces not only death but also
injustice: "The first hermeneutical condition for understanding the resurrection of Jesus . . . is a hope *against* death and injustice" (*ibid.*, 380).
    Like Pannenberg and Moltmann, Sobrino tackles a classic diffi-
culty raised by historical positivism against Jesus' resurrection—the
supposition of analogy: "On the epistemological level our knowledge of
history is analogical. This means that we come to understand the new
on the basis of the old." Hence, as the purported resurrection claims that
something has taken place which does not correspond to the old but is
extraordinarily new, from this historical point of view we can neither
understand the claim nor accept it. Sobrino's reply is not completely
satisfactory: "The analogical supposition that the new is to be known on
the basis of the old is wholly gratuitous, if not false. . . . Human beings
can be defined as open to novelty and the future" (*ibid.*, 249).
    Unlike Pannenberg, Sobrino does not appreciate that the principle
of analogy should not produce a one-sided orientation toward typical
events, at the expense of unfamiliar and even unique claims. Analogy
allows for what is different, perhaps even strikingly different. It makes
room for novelty as well as claiming some measure of similarity. In fact,

Sobrino himself reaches for the principle of analogy when comparing and contrasting the divine omnipotence shown, respectively, in creation and in the new creation which is resurrection:

> God's omnipotence in the resurrection cannot be known solely through analogy with his omnipotence at the creation. In the latter instance he demonstrates his power over *nothingness*. In the case of the resurrection, however, he must overcome not only nothingness but also the death that is caused by *injustice* and *evil* (*ibid.*, 261).

If "God's omnipotence in the resurrection cannot be known solely through analogy with his omnipotence at the creation," it means that it can be known at least partly through that analogy. Sobrino should not have labeled the analogical supposition as "gratuitous, if not false" but have agreed that "the new is to be known *at least partly* on the basis of the old." This is precisely his own approach when he suggests, or at any rate implies, that the new creation of resurrection is to be known at least partly on the basis of the old (the original creation).

(2) *The Events Themselves*. What then does Sobrino say about the events of Good Friday, Easter Sunday and their aftermath? First, he states very well the personal *and theological* crisis into which the crucifixion plunged the disciples. After identifying himself with the divine cause, Jesus was not rescued from the human *and religious* disgrace of his death.

> The cross posed a fundamental crisis . . . [which] was not merely anthropological but also theological. It was not just that the disciples were disillusioned and frightened into disloyalty. They simply could not see how they could relate Jesus to God when God left him to die on the cross (*ibid.*, 264f).

But after that come those "novel" and "privileged" experiences when the risen Lord disclosed his presence and made himself known to the disciples (*ibid.*, 275f). (Without laboring the point, Sobrino lines up here with Küng, Rahner and all those who acknowledge the special, irrepeatable nature of those Easter appearances.) Thanks to the appearances (which revealed to them the resurrection), "the disciples experienced the fact that God had not abandoned Jesus on the cross after all" (*ibid.*, 269).

Like Küng and others, Sobrino holds that we can set about verifying historically the Easter encounters—"the time and place where the disciples claim to have experienced apparitions, and the credibility of the disciples" (*ibid.*, 252). Then, unlike Küng but like Moltmann (and for that matter Rahner), Sobrino emphasizes the "unfinished" nature of the resurrection as a redeeming and revealing reality:

> It [the resurrection] is still in the process of fulfillment insofar as its saving efficacy is concerned. In its historical structure . . . the revelation of God effected in Christ's resurrection is a promise . . . a possibility *for* the world and *for* history (*ibid.*, 252).

Very much along the same lines as Moltmann, Sobrino plays down what Christ's resurrection has already changed and speaks only of "a possibility for" the world and its history. Like Moltmann, he tends to absolutize the lasting role of divine promise and human hope in shedding light on the world and its history. "Even after Jesus' resurrection," he writes, "history can *only* be grasped by way of hope" (*ibid.*, 251).

As Moltmann had done in *Theology of Hope*, Sobrino notes how the risen Lord's appearances triggered off a mission of proclamation and transformation:

> All the accounts of Jesus' appearances stress a mission. Jesus does not appear simply to show himself to people. His appearances are always bound up with a vocation to a mission. . . . This mission should not be restricted to proclaiming what happened to Jesus. . . . It also has to do with the transformation of the world (*ibid.*, 254).

This talk about "all the accounts" stressing a mission and the appearances being "always bound up with a vocation to a mission" fails to do justice to the Emmaus story (Luke 24:13–35), which—so far from *stressing* a mission—simply highlights the movement of the two disciples toward their recognition of the risen Lord "in the breaking of the bread." At the same time, Sobrino wisely contents himself with simply observing the "vocation to a mission" as essentially involved in the appearances. He avoids the exegetical difficulties which we saw to be created by Moltmann's assertion about the Easter encounters being "first and foremost" auditory experiences.

On the active mission of a hope which seeks to transform the world, Sobrino begins reasonably but ends by making some excessive claims:

> The resurrection sets in motion a life of service designed to implement in reality the eschatological ideals of justice, peace and human solidarity. It is the earnest attempt to make those ideals real that enables us to comprehend what happened in Jesus' resurrection. . . . *It is possible* to verify the truth of what happened in the

resurrection *only* through a transforming praxis based on the ideals of the resurrection. . . . The resurrection *can* be understood *only* through a praxis that seeks to transform the world (*ibid.*, 255; italics mine).

Some of this may seem attractive after Küng and others who seek to understand Jesus' resurrection—either largely or even wholly—by simply discussing it in a rational, academic way. Certainly a serious attempt to implement justice, peace and human solidarity will also help us to grasp what happened in Jesus' resurrection. Nevertheless, have those who make only a half-hearted attempt to practice the ideals no chance whatsoever of appreciating anything about the resurrection? Can those whose praxis does not seek to "transform the world" never hope in any way to understand and verify the truth of the resurrection? It would be different if Sobrino had qualified his assertions as follows:

It is possible to verify *fully* the truth of what happened in the resurrection only through a transforming praxis. The resurrection can be *properly* understood only through a praxis that seeks to transform the world.

As it is, the claims for a transforming praxis as the *only* way of understanding and verifying the resurrection absolutizes the role of "doing the truth." It would mean that we can know reality only by changing it. Beyond doubt, transforming praxis offers one criterion for verifying claims, but it should not be turned into an exclusive test. The practical approach of Sobrino adds something to Rahner's philosophico-theological interpretation of the resurrection and Küng's apologetical defense, but transforming praxis cannot become an absolute alternative.

This chapter could go on elaborating points of convergence and divergence. Rahner, Küng and Sobrino, for example, do not integrate the empty tomb into their vision of Jesus' resurrection. But to link the first part of this book with my own synthesis in the second part, I can sum up the findings under the following headings:

(a) the resurrection as real event (Origen, Aquinas, Barth, Pannenberg, Küng and many others);
(b) Easter faith (Barth, Bultmann, Marxsen and Rahner);
(c) the Easter revelation (Barth and Pannenberg);
(d) redemption through the resurrection (the early Church's liturgy, Fathers of the Church, Aquinas, Barth and Rahner);

(e) Easter promise and hope (the Fathers, Aquinas, Moltmann and Sobrino);

(f) Easter and love (no special development);

(g) communicating the resurrection (Bultmann?).

Let me take up in turn themes (a) through (g).

4

The Resurrection as Event

In his *Jesus* (Philadelphia, 1949) Martin Dibelius states the first basic issue to be faced once we move beyond the events of Jesus' crucifixion and burial:

> The New Testament narratives show that . . . the disciples . . . fled (Mark 14:50), and gave up Jesus' cause for lost (Luke 24:19–21). Something must have happened in between, which in a short time not only produced a complete reversal of their attitude but also enabled them to engage in renewed activity and to found the primitive Christian community. This "something" is the historical kernel of the Easter faith (141).

As we shall see later in this chapter, a few writers like Rudolf Pesch, at least the Pesch of 1973–80, would find this statement too strong and would question the "complete reversal" of attitude. They see the disciples moving more smoothly from the period of Jesus' ministry to the foundation of the primitive Christian community. Others like myself find that Dibelius has glossed over certain elements which make the emergence of the primitive community even more startling. It understates matters to speak of the disciples as "giving up Jesus' cause" and then "engaging in renewed activity." After a brief ministry in which he lacked the worldly resources available to other religious founders, Jesus died a shameful and scandalous death. Then, despite the crucifixion, the disciples began to propagate Christianity dynamically in the name of the one who had failed so disgracefully. In the last chapter I explained and expanded this line of argument which comes from Hans Küng[1] and tries to do full justice to the quite extraordinary reversal of attitude on the part of the disciples.

Allowing for such qualifications, we may properly use Dibelius' classic statement of the question. What was the "something" which happened after the events of the first Good Friday? Was it Jesus' personal resurrection from the dead, his own passage to a new, transformed and final mode of life? Or was the "something" much less than that—a resuscitation of Jesus who had not suffered brain death, a borrowing from stories about dying and rising gods, a new consciousness on the part of the disciples, or a case of simple hallucination? I take up in turn these four counter-explanations before exploring matters more positively.

FOUR COUNTER-EXPLANATIONS

In Chapter Two I criticized the views of Bultmann and Marxsen which jeopardize and reduce the event of Jesus' own resurrection. But the subtle positions of those two scholars do not often reach the wider public, at least not to the extent sometimes achieved by the four theories I want to consider now.

(1) *Buried Alive.* The ingenious "swoon theory" which H.E.G. Paulus floated in the last century comes to this. Jesus did not die on the cross but was taken down alive, buried, revived in the tomb, somehow got out and so "appeared" to his followers. This hypothesis of a revival in the tomb turns up in works by Duncan Derrett, Robert Graves, D.H. Lawrence, George Moore, Barbara Thiering, and in a Moslem story about Jesus escaping to Kashmir where he eventually died in extreme old age. Some variants on this "happy ending" to the passion narrative have Jesus going away to live with Mary Magdalene, as in *The Holy Blood and the Holy Grail* by Baigent, Leigh and Lincoln.

Against these different versions of the "swoon theory" it must be said that their major source, the New Testament itself, contains not a shred of hard evidence in their favor. The Gospels, St. Paul and the primitive Christian kerygma (which gets quoted in 1 Corinthians 15:3b–5, the early speeches in Acts and elsewhere in the New Testament) agree that Jesus genuinely died by crucifixion and was buried as a dead man (for instance, 1 Cor 15:4; Mark 15:37, 32–47). Other ancient sources corroborate this. The Jewish historian Flavius Josephus (c. 37–c. 100), in his *Antiquities* 18:63–64 reports that Jesus was crucified on the orders of Pilate. It appears that some Christian or Christians revised this passage in Josephus by adding material in praise of Jesus, but at least the information about his execution seems to go back to Josephus himself. In his *Annals* 15:44 (written in A.D. 112–113), the Roman historian Tacitus explains that the name "Christians" came from the founder of their sect,

Christ, who was executed by the "procurator" Pontius Pilate during the reign of the Emperor Tiberius. In an obscure passage the Babylonian Talmud (*Sanhedrin* 43a) writes of "Yeshu," who led some Israelites astray by his magic but was then "hanged on the eve of Passover." These extra-biblical, Roman and Jewish sources show little historical knowledge, but they indicate no doubt whatsoever that Jesus genuinely died by execution. Like the passion narratives in the Gospels, these other documents contain not the slightest hint that Jesus was or could have been still alive when the executioners had finished with him.

In the nineteenth century David Friedrich Strauss (1808–1874) cast many doubts on the Gospel story but even so had no truck with the swoon theory. He put his finger on another knockdown difficulty against any hypothesis of a half-dead Jesus reviving in the tomb and then returning to his followers:

> It is impossible that a being who had stolen half dead out of the sepulchre, who crept about weak and ill, wanting medical treatment, who required bandaging, strengthening and indulgence . . . could have given the disciples the impression that he was a Conqueror over death and the grace, the Prince of Life, an impression which lay at the bottom of their future ministry. Such a resuscitation . . . could by no possibility have changed their sorrow into enthusiasm, have elevated their reverence into worship.[2]

Add too the fact that neither the New Testament nor any other source provides evidence for the existence and activity of a Jesus who was revived from apparent death. In *Anastasis* (Shipston-on-Stour, 1982) Derrett admits as much when he writes of "the loud silence of the gospels and epistles" about Jesus' brief life after his revival from clinical death (71). For "loud silence" read "no evidence at all."

At the end of the day, the "swoon theory" reduces the origin of Christianity not only to a banal story about a bungled execution but also to a gross act of misrepresentation. In place of Jesus' true resurrection from the dead, we are told that he had an incredibly lucky revival from apparent death, an escape which his disciples later misrepresented when they claimed that he had been "raised from the dead, never again to revert to corruption" (Acts 13:34). The "swoon theory," by granting Jesus only a temporary respite from death after an extraordinarily unpleasant brush with crucifixion, makes the New Testament's language about his glorious, new incorruptible existence (for instance, 1 Cor 15:20ff; Luke 24:26; 1 Tim 3:16; Heb 2:9; 1 Pet 1:11) simply incomprehensible or else a bold lie.

(2) *Dying and Rising Gods.* Chapter One recalled Celsus, the second-century critic who used alleged parallels from Greek mythology and religion to argue that the stories about Jesus' resurrection were not unique. Celsus anticipated claims made around the turn of this century by some members of the History of Religions School and popular but unscientific writers like Sir James Frazer (1854–1941).[3] They spread the notion that the Christian claims about Jesus were only another version of ancient stories about dying and rising gods or heroes. Deities like Dionysus, Isis and Osiris were believed to embody new life and fruitfulness which succeeded the decay and death of winter. Could the springtime feast of Jesus' resurrection be modeled on and derived from such sacred legends? A 1984 British television program, entitled "Jesus the Evidence," favorably entertained that question. In its third part, which went out at prime time on Easter Sunday, the program began by showing a group of people joyfully celebrating, and then commented:

> This is the annual discovery of the resurrection of the Lord. Not Jesus. Not the Christian Lord—but Adonis, a pagan Lord. . . . His annual resurrection was evident all round. Life for everyone would continue. It was a festival that enthralled our ancestors. Such cycles of death and resurrection were common in ancient religions. What does this mean for the death and resurrection of Jesus?

Even with the best will in the world, it is hard to see much of a parallel and connection between the cult of Adonis and the resurrection of Jesus. Both were/are spring festivals for a community celebrating some kind of new life given through one name (Jesus or Adonis). Adonis may have been credited with returning to life on the third day after his death.[4] But there any similarity stops. In classical mythology Adonis was a beautiful youth beloved by Aphrodite. While hunting a boar, he was gored to death, but each year was permitted to return from the underworld to his mistress for six months. It is not hard to pile up the differences between the story of this vegetation deity and the case of Jesus.

Unlike Jesus, there is no reason to believe that Adonis ever existed historically. In the legend he died by accident, not the disgraceful death of one condemned to be crucified as a blasphemer and threat to national security. Those who venerated Adonis never alleged that he died "for us and for our sins," nor did they hope for an afterlife through union with him. Any blessings such vegetation cults were thought to bring concerned health and prosperity to be experienced here and now in this world. The worshipers never claimed that Adonis returned transformed and glorious from the underworld. In this life he already was extraordinarily beautiful. Above all, his return was a cyclic, vegetation myth, an annual affair of nature, not a once-and-for-all, final resurrection from the dead.

One could go on adding other items to illustrate how dubious any connection is between the Adonis legend and the Christian message about Jesus' resurrection. Adonis was not credited with having been the pre-existent Son of God sent into this world (see, for example, Gal 4:4). He was deemed to have been born on this earth, a man from a mythical, primal period who received a kind of immortality after his death. Further, there is no evidence that in the crucial first two decades (A.D. 30–50) Christianity borrowed from the cult of Adonis or any other vegetation deity. It would in any case have been difficult to do so at the very beginning of the Christian movement: from first-century Palestine there is hardly the slightest trace of any cults of dying and rising gods. Finally, Adonis was honored in an agricultural feast which celebrated new organic life (*bios*) and tolerated sexual license. On all three scores this feast differed from the Christian Easter. Because he died and rose at the time of the Passover and the commemoration of the people's exodus from Egypt, Jesus' resurrection had an historical setting; it promised believers eternal life (*zōē*), not mere deliverance from biological death. Far from being encouraged by the resurrection celebration, the sexual aberrations of early Christians were rebuked as being inconsistent with that feast and its implications (for example, 1 Cor 6:9–20).

In brief, any link between the cult of such vegetation deities as Adonis and Jesus' resurrection will work only if one maximizes the resemblances, ignores the radical differences and glosses over the sheer lack of historical connection.[5] As regards possible historical connections, let me remind readers that I am *not* dealing with second-century Christianity (which had contacts with the cults of dying and rising gods and heroes), but with the first two decades when the proclamation of Jesus' resurrection got going (A.D. 30–50).

(3) *Merely a Change in the Disciples.* In *On the Trial of Jesus* (Berlin, 1961) Paul Winter expresses movingly the view that "resurrection" was an event which affected (and continues to affect) the disciples, not Jesus himself. The "something" which happened after his death and burial was only a change in them, not a new, transformed life for Jesus.

> Crucified, dead and buried, he yet rose in the hearts of his disciples who had loved him and felt he was near. Tried by the world, condemned by authority, buried by the Churches that profess his name,

he is rising again, today and tomorrow, in the hearts of men who love
him and feel: he is near (149).

In these terms, "resurrection" was not a fact about Jesus himself but
simply a fact about his disciples, past and present. After the crucifixion
a new beginning was to be found only with those disciples, not with
Jesus. Something happened to the original (and later) disciples, not to
the dead Jesus himself.

Where Winter emphasizes the affection and devotion of Jesus' followers, others highlight their new insight and consciousness. In his *Systematic Theology: A Historicist Perspective* (New York, 1968) Gordon
Kaufman conflates final resurrection with the resuscitation of a corpse
to propose a similar under-interpretation of the Easter event. It dawned
on the disciples "that God really had broken into history through Jesus
of Nazareth, and still was breaking into history in the community of the
church." Hence,

> . . . the theologically important element in their new-found com-
> munal faith was their consciousness of the *continuing activity of "the
> God and Father of . . . Jesus Christ"* (Rom 15:6) *in their historical existence,*
> not the resuscitation [*sic*] of their former friend and leader (428–429).

Thus "the resurrection was preeminently an event in the *history of meaning*" (*ibid.*, 433). After Jesus' death the "real meaning of human existence
first became sharp and clear and certain" to his disciples, and thus
through them became "an effective power within history" (*ibid.*, 434).
In brief, "resurrection" describes a change in the disciples, not something which happened to Jesus himself.

In her correspondence with Thomas Merton, Rosemary Ruether
proposed a similar under-interpretation of what occurred after Jesus
"got strung up like a common criminal and his followers cut the scene
like rabbits." They turned "the denouement itself into salvation" by
starting "a seminal idea [about creation and an historical *kairos*] that con-
tinually lights up reality in new ways."[6] Here again the "something"
which happened after the crucifixion gets reduced to being *merely* a discovery of meaning, an insight, a new consciousness, a transforming
change in the disciples themselves. The event lay totally on their side
and in no way affected the dead Jesus.[6a]

The basic problem with any such "change of heart" or "new insight" version is that it must deny that the first Christians and New Testament authors mean what they again and again say. There are
kerygmatic/credal fragments which pre-date the writing of the New

Testament: for example, "he was raised" (1 Cor 15:4), "God raised up Jesus" (Acts 2:23f, 32), and "the Lord has risen indeed" (Luke 24:34). There are many affirmations by Paul about Christ's own resurrection (for example, Rom 14:9; 1 Cor 15:12ff); the four Gospels and other New Testament books (for example 1 Pet 1:3) write repeatedly about Jesus' resurrection. The "new insight" theory, however, supposes that in these and many other instances early Christians, although appearing to claim some new fact *about Jesus* (his personal resurrection from death to new life), were really using a deceptive form of discourse and talking only about some new, seminal idea which now possessed their hearts and minds. This "explanation" entails the conclusion that the basic Easter message of the first Christians has been fundamentally misunderstood for many centuries. Their assertive propositions about Jesus' personal resurrection from the dead—so it is claimed—expressed a hidden meaning which one can now see to have differed drastically from the conventional sense of the words they used. They were speaking only of themselves, never of a new event affecting Jesus himself.

This position is quite implausible. When Paul quotes an early Christian formulation about "Jesus Christ and God the Father, who raised him from the dead" (Gal 1:1), the ordinary conventions covering the use of language indicate that this confession primarily concerned Jesus and offered some factual information about what happened to Jesus himself after his death. A new event, distinct from and subsequent to the crucifixion, brought Jesus from the condition of death to that of a new and lasting life. To allege that the true primary referent in the proposition "the Father raised Jesus from the dead" was not Jesus but his disciples is to open up an extraordinary gap between what Paul (and other New Testament witnesses) wrote and what they meant. They wrote "the Father raised Jesus from the dead," but—in defiance of general usage and public conventions governing the recognition of words— they primarily meant "the Father raised us to a new life of faith."

In dealing with other ancient texts (for example, those coming from Julius Caesar, Cicero, Josephus, Philo, Plutarch and Tacitus), no one would attribute to them such arbitrary "liberty" in switching the referent and expressing a hidden meaning which differs from the conventional sense of words they used. Here the differences between secular and religious classics from the ancient world are irrelevant. The question is one of very basic grammar and meaning. The New Testament authors introduced Jesus as the object ("God raised Jesus") or subject ("Jesus was raised" or "Jesus rose from the dead") in their fundamental claims about the resurrection. Did they write down the name "Jesus" but secretly mean some other object or subject ("the disciples") in these sentences? Are we to imagine that the New Testament authors were deliberately deceptive in their use of language? Or were they remarkably incompetent? These are the only plausible alternatives open to us if we wish to maintain that their assertions about Jesus' resurrection were "merely" assertions about themselves.

In *Reason, Truth and God* (London, 1969), when he discusses Matthew Arnold's version of Christianity, Renford Bambrough puts his finger on the motive which often seems to lie behind the reductionism of various "new insight" theories.

> What he [Arnold] does say is that what is usually thought to be meant by the propositions of the Christian religion is unverified and unverifiable, and that therefore those propositions must mean something else that he *can* believe. This is a gross *non sequitur*, but it is not a rare aberration, not an idiosyncratic lapse on the part of Arnold. It is a common response to the predicament that Arnold found himself in (79).

A passing remark by Kaufman hints at such an Arnold-style desire to find a more believable meaning in the New Testament propositions about Jesus' resurrection: "Contemporary belief, of course, will not necessarily involve the conviction that the crucified Jesus became personally alive again" (*Systematic Theology*, 426).

A non-believing friend of mine, a philosopher who recognizes but does not accept the real New Testament claims about Jesus' resurrection, finds a "patronizing" attitude in the exponents of the "new insight" theory. He compares it to the attitude of a few anthropologists: "These people can't possibly mean *that* by what they are saying. They must mean something else." My friend puts it this way: "The supporters of the 'new insight' theory know better than the New Testament authors what those authors meant when they wrote what they did."

This may be too severe. At any rate one can spot a startling difference between modern reductionists and traditional skeptics like Celsus, Porphyry and David Hume. Those skeptics acknowledged the *meaning* of the New Testament assertions, but in the name of reason and common sense they rejected the *truth* of Jesus' resurrection. The reductionists, however, tamper with the meaning of those assertions and then accept the truth which they have fashioned for themselves.

In the end, perhaps the problem comes to this. The exponents of the "new insight" thesis fail to distinguish between people holding something to be true and the effects of this claim on those who make it. In speaking of his resurrection Jesus' followers primarily claimed a new fact about Jesus himself. Holding his resurrection to be true had deep, transforming effects on them. These effects depended, however, on the fact that they held something to be true: namely, that Jesus himself had passed from the state of death to a new and final life.

Or perhaps the problem concerns very simply the activity of God. The New Testament proclaims that Jesus was (i) crucified by men and then (ii) raised by God. Some at least of the defenders of the "new insight" theory seem reluctant to admit that God could and does intervene in such "special" ways. Hence the New Testament *must* mean something else, something which they can believe. Yet their way of dealing with (ii) does clear violence to the New Testament claim.

(4) *Hallucination.* A number of writers, including at least one of those who espouse the "new insight" thesis, have maintained that the disciples hallucinated the risen Christ's appearances. Some of those who take this view realize that the shocking disgrace of Jesus' crucifixion was so radical that it required more than ordinary spiritual reflection to overcome the scandal of the cross and bring the disciples to discover the meaning of what had happened. Whether for this or different reasons, Celsus in the second century and D.F. Strauss in the nineteenth century and several contemporary authors have suggested that hallucinations triggered off the new consciousness and changed attitudes of the disciples. Thus Kaufman, while doing his best to offset the negative connotations of the term "hallucination" (*ibid.*, 423, fn. 24; 424, fn. 29), assures us that "these alleged appearances [of the risen Christ] were in fact a series of hallucinations produced by the wishful thinking of Jesus' former disciples" (*ibid.*, 422). Like some others, Joel Carmichael alleges that these hallucinations or merely subjective visions began with Peter (*The Death of Jesus* [New York, 1962], 210, 215). By a kind of chain reaction the hallucinations then spread to the other disciples, who were all "surely temperamental by nature" (*ibid.*, 218):

> After the first vision [= Peter's] the mere multiplication of visions afterwards is still easier to imagine, considering the well-known contagiousness of collective visions, hallucinations and so on (*ibid.*, 217).

In *Jesus the Evidence* (London, 1984) Ian Wilson adds his own twist to the hypothesis of hallucination:

> . . . it is possible that he [Jesus] prepared his disciples for his resurrection using the technique that modern hypnotists call posthypnotic suggestion. By this means he would have effectively

conditioned them to hallucinate his appearances in response to certain
pre-arranged cues (the breaking of the bread?), for a predetermined
period after his death (141).

Wilson supports his theory by gratuitously attributing the use of hyp-
nosis to Jesus and mentioning a modern experiment in post-hypnotic
suggestion on one volunteer who "was known to be a good hypnotic subject" (*ibid.*, 141f).

Those who support the hallucination hypothesis run into several
major difficulties. First, wishful thinking on the part of Jesus' disciples
fails to account psychologically for the first appearances. What the Gospels record seems credible; the crisis of Jesus' arrest and disgraceful
death left his disciples crushed. When Jesus appeared, they doubted and
were reluctant to accept his real, risen presence (Matt 28:17; Luke
24:36ff; John 20:24f). Only by ignoring the evidence can we imagine
them anxiously awaiting his return from the dead and out of their imagination hallucinating his appearances. The appearances, once they began, would have generated such a desire to see him again and again. But
such an attitude did not exist after Jesus' crucifixion and prior to his first
post-resurrection appearance(s). The hallucination hypothesis offers a
psychological explanation, but cannot produce the historical evidence
in support of such an explanation.

Second, we rightly discard hypotheses which attribute some hal-
lucinatory experience to Peter which then sets off a quick chain-reaction
among people supposedly prone to visions—"temperamental by nature"
(Carmichael) and "good hypnotic subjects" (Wilson). As we saw in
Chapter One, Origen long ago pointed out that there is no evidence that
Jesus' followers were by disposition visionaries. Further, the chain-reaction claim fails to account for the appearances to Paul near Damascus,
which took place several years after the appearance to Peter (that prob-
ably occurred in Galilee and certainly nowhere near Damascus). Paul
poses a peculiar difficulty for Wilson. Since that apostle enjoyed no contact with Jesus during the ministry, he simply could not have been "effectively conditioned to hallucinate" an appearance "in response to
certain pre-arranged cues."

Third, the religious novelty in what the disciples claimed about Jesus is not accounted for by the hallucination hypothesis which interprets
matters on the basis of what the disciples already believed and expected
before Jesus died. This hypothesis cannot explain the remarkably new
thing which they began to do by proclaiming the resurrection of a crucified Messiah. In the section on Hans Küng in Chapter Three we saw
the degree of religious novelty involved in that Easter proclamation.

Add too the quite new element entailed in claiming the final resurrection of one individual before the end of the world. In *Resurrection* Pheme Perkins describes very well the variety of views about resurrection and immortality which existed in first-century Judaism (37–56). Despite all the variety, however, no one expected that one person would or could enjoy final resurrection before the world ended and the dead rose for a general judgment. Hence hallucinating disciples projecting their prior beliefs could not have claimed that Jesus had been raised and glorified in anticipation of a universal resurrection of the dead which was still to come (for example, 1 Cor 15:20). There was no such prior belief to be projected.

KNOWING JESUS TO BE RISEN

If we agree that Jesus truly died by crucifixion, that the early Christians did not borrow some legend about a dying and rising god, that in preaching the resurrection they were primarily asserting some new fact about Jesus himself and that they did not hallucinate his appearances, what should be taken up next? We have the early Christian message: Jesus was raised from the dead (for example, Acts 5:30) and lives (for example, Luke 24:5; Rom 6:9f; 14:9) as the beginning of the divine renewal of all things (1 Cor 15:20, 23; Col 1:18). How did the early Christians know or claim to know about Jesus' resurrection?

To express the greatness of the prophet Elijah a biblical legend speaks of him as going to God without passing through death. Elisha witnesses his master's assumption into heaven (2 Kings 2:11f). Dio Cassius (56.46f; 59.11) reports how sycophants would maintain that they had seen the soul of a dead Roman emperor ascend into divine glory. Our New Testament sources, however, never allege that anyone witnessed the actual event of Jesus' resurrection. Around the middle of the second century the apocryphal Gospel of Peter did so (9.35–11.45). Western painters have often followed suit by portraying Jesus as rising from the dead and the guards (Matt 27:65–28:4, 11–15) as terrified witnesses of the very act of resurrection. But neither Paul nor our canonical Gospels make such a claim. How then did the first Christians come to know of Jesus' resurrection?

(1) *The Disciples Already Prepared.* Some have argued that by the time Jesus died and was buried, his first disciples were already fully prepared to acknowledge that he would rise from the dead. Their religious beliefs,

human resources and psychological state were such that they required
no fresh influences "from outside" to become aware of Jesus' resurrection. The conditions for the possibility of knowing and accepting their
master to be risen and exalted were all already given by the time of his
burial. Nothing new needed to happen before they recognized his resurrection.

Almost an entire issue of the *Theologische Quartalschrift* (153 [1973],
201–283) was dedicated to Rudolf Pesch's original presentation on the
rise of the disciples' Easter faith and various reactions to his interpretation. In essence, he denied the historicity of the Easter appearances
and maintained that the disciples simply applied to the case of Jesus a
prior Jewish tradition about the martyrdom and resurrection of godly
persons, especially eschatological prophets. To know that Jesus had
risen the disciples needed no further information or input after the crucifixion. However, the existence of such a prior tradition is quite un-
certain. For that and other reasons, in a 1980 lecture which became a
chapter in the *Festschrift* for F.-X. Durrwell's seventieth birthday, Pesch
withdrew his earlier hypothesis and accepted the visions of the risen Jesus as real events in history through which the disciples knew of their
Lord's resurrection and exaltation.[6b]

In his *Jesus* (New York, 1979) Edward Schillebeeckx made much of
pre-crucifixion factors in the genesis of the disciples' Easter faith.

> After the first shock of his dying, the memory of Jesus' life and es-
> pecially of the Last Supper must have played a vital role in the process
> of their conversion to faith in Jesus as the Christ, the one imbued to
> the full with God's Spirit (313).

Furthermore, Schillebeeckx argued that Mark deliberately exaggerated
the degree to which the disciples abandoned the cause of Jesus (*ibid.*,
323–327). This was to maintain more continuity between (a) the pre-
Easter and (b) the post-Easter faith of the disciples, and hence leave less
need for a new influence to bring them to (b). Nevertheless, as we shall
see, Schillebeeckx did allow for some fresh factor intervening to gen-
erate their resurrection faith.

All in all, the notion of a smooth, even a fairly smooth, transition
between (a) and (b) is not persuasive. Before they met Jesus, the first
disciples evidently believed in Yahweh. During the ministry at least
some of them accepted Jesus as messianic agent of divine salvation. But
even those do not seem to have been prepared for Jesus' arrest and disgraceful crucifixion. Contemporary Judaism had no concept of a dying
and rising Messiah, nor any notion of one person enjoying a final, glo-

rious resurrection from the dead even though the end of the world had not yet occurred. It looks reasonable to suppose that the disciples were deeply affected by the arrest, conviction and crucifixion of Jesus—both psychologically and theologically. God had let their master die in an utterly shameful and scandalous fashion. Any faith they had in Jesus was destroyed.

At this point it is worth recalling that some authors, while recognizing the profound break the disciples suffered at Jesus' death, allege that the psychodynamics of sorrow and guilt can explain how Peter and the others came to grasp that Jesus now lived in glory and would return to judge the world. In *Kyrios Christos* (Nashville, 1970) Wilhelm Bousset suggests how the change came after all the hopes of the disciples had been shattered:

> It is a psychological law that such a disappointment of the most ardent hopes by brutal reality causes, or at least can cause, after a period of discouragement, a swing to the other extreme, in which the human soul, with a defiant "nevertheless," rises victorious to an outlook which makes the impossible possible (50).

In the very same paragraph in which he criticizes those who "hazard some rather questionable historical guesses about the psychological development" of the first disciples, James Mackey proposes or at least implies that "a period of quiet reflection" could have led these disciples to develop what he calls "the myth of the man Jesus."

> We are all surely familiar with the way in which faith can edge through our blindness or stubbornness, or recover again after a shock, with nothing more than a period of quiet reflection to facilitate such enrichment of our lives. Many of us indeed can think of an example of how the tragic death of a good man in pursuit of a good cause first shocked us into near despair, but then, without the help of any subsequent event, itself overcame the shock it had caused and ended by proving even more inspiring to us than was the man's life (*Jesus the Man and the Myth* [London, 1979], 115–116).

Of course, Mackey clearly throws doubt on the fact that the first Christians asserted that Jesus rose from the dead in a new event subsequent to the crucifixion. But my point here is simply to note how the psychodynamics of grief and guilt are once again invoked, in order to explain their new claim, "the myth of the man Jesus." There is some family resemblance between Bousset's "swing" in the human soul and the "inspiring" results from Mackey's "period of quiet reflection."

In "The Apocalyptic Myth and the Death of Christ" Barnabas Lindars tentatively puts forward something similar. After the shock and tragedy of the crucifixion, a "process of reflection" could have led the disciples to the conviction that Jesus was exalted and risen into glory (*Bulletin of the John Rylands Library*, 57 [1975], 384). Lindars adds: "The third day is really just about long enough for this process of reflection to have taken place and to have led to a deep conviction" (*ibid.*). One wonders how two good nights' sleep could have been enough to cope and deal in this way with the horror of Jesus' crucifixion. But the real response to Bousset, Mackey and Lindars is to take up the two dramatic causes repeatedly named by the New Testament as the catalysts which let the disciples know about the resurrection and so brought about a profound change in them: the appearances of the risen Jesus and the discovery of the empty tomb. They were convinced he was risen from the dead not because of quiet mental reflection or anything else than the evidence of their senses. Some of them saw him alive and all of them could verify his empty tomb. Let us turn now to the Easter appearances and the discovery of the empty tomb.

(2) *The Appearances.*   The early Christian kerygma (for example, 1 Cor 15:5–7; Luke 24:34), Paul (1 Cor 9:1; 15:8; Gal 1:12, 16), the four Gospels (Matt 28; Luke 24; John 20 and 21; and, by implication, Mark 16:7), Acts (for example, 1:3; 10:40f; 13:31) and the appendix to Mark (16:9–20) attest that the risen Jesus appeared both to various individuals and to groups of witnesses, above all "the twelve," or "the eleven" as Luke 24:33 more accurately calls them after Judas' defection. These appearances of the living Jesus were the primary way the disciples came to know that he was risen from the dead.

Back in Chapter Two we saw how Bultmann attributed little or no theological importance to the appearances and the origins of faith in the risen Christ. Even if the Easter vision of Peter originated resurrection and messianic faith, for Bultmann it really did not matter how that vision was produced and what guaranteed its reliability. All of this was part of Bultmann's general emancipation of faith from history and reduction of the historical continuity between the earthly Jesus and the kerygmatic Christ.

Here I wish to pursue two recent underinterpretations of the Easter appearances. Then I will move to deal directly and positively with those appearances.

(a) In their 1984 television program mentioned above, Helmut

Koester and others tampered with the credibility of the Easter appearances by relating them to other religious phenomena and claims.

> We know that stories [about the appearance of Jesus to the apostles and many others] were in circulation very very early because they're described in the earliest part of the New Testament, the Letters of Paul written about 50 A.D. [= principally, 1 Cor 15:5–8]. There is nothing very unusual about appearance stories in which divine beings appear in glory, surrounded by blinding light to give commands. There are numerous examples in the Old Testament, the New Testament, and in the literature of other religions of the time. The Old Testament, for example, cites several appearances of God to the prophets Isaiah and Ezekiel. In Egyptian stories of the time, the goddess Isis was also reported to have appeared to mere mortals. In Greece, numerous witnesses . . . testified to having seen the god Asclepius healing men and predicting the future (from the transcript of "Jesus the Evidence").

There is much here to combat and repudiate. First of all, it is certainly stretching language to say that Paul's letters "describe" appearances of the risen Jesus (see 1 Cor 9:1; 15:5–8; Gal 1:12, 16). They assert these appearances without describing them. Second, Koester ignores the fact that in at least two places the New Testament has preserved kerygmatic and credal material about the appearances which *predate* Paul's letters (1 Cor 15:5 and possibly 1 Cor 15:7; Luke 24:34). But it is the proposal to understand the Easter encounters on the model of "appearance stories in which divine beings appear in glory, surrounded by blinding light to give commands" which is much more misleading and deserves detailed rebuttal.

In Matthew, Luke and John the risen Lord's divinity emerges (for example, Matt 28:9; John 20:28) and he gives commands (for example, Luke 24:49; Matt 28:18–20). But nowhere according to the Easter texts does he "appear in glory, surrounded by blinding light." Mark 16:7 ("he is going before you to Galilee; there you will see him") does not suggest such a glorious, luminous appearance. What Paul reports about the Easter appearances contains nothing about glory and blinding light (1 Cor 9:1; 15:5–8; Gal 1:12, 16). Acts is the only New Testament book which associates "light from heaven" (Acts 9:3; see 22:6, 9, 11; 26:13) with a post-resurrection encounter. As Luke tells the story, strictly speaking there is no appearance of the risen Lord to Saul/Paul, but only a voice which identifies itself as "Jesus" (Acts 9:5 parr.). So much for the proposal to read the post-resurrection encounters as appearances of a divine being "in glory, surrounded by blinding light to give commands." Behind Koester's proposal is a 1982 article by James Robinson which I discuss at length in an appendix to this book.

Even if the post-resurrection encounters do not fit this pattern, are there "numerous examples" elsewhere in the New Testament of divine beings appearing "in glory, surrounded by blinding light to give commands"? I can only think of very few examples which literally fulfill this definition (Matt 28:2–7; Luke 2:8–14; Rev 1:10ff). In the transfiguration story Jesus does not appear to Peter, James and John; he is already with them as they go up the mountain. He becomes transfigured and glorious but does not himself issue any commands (Mark 9:2–8 par). The New Testament often enough speaks of "commands" coming from heaven but they do so normally *without* a scenario of "glory" and "blinding light." At the transfiguration there is simply a voice "out of the cloud" which declares: "This is my beloved Son; listen to him" (Mark 9:7 par). The angel Gabriel brings a divine message to Mary but the annunciation story lacks any elements of "glory" and "blinding light" (Luke 1:26–38). In Matthew's infancy narratives "an angel of the Lord" three times "appears" to bring Joseph certain commands but does so "in a dream" without any associated elements of luminous glory (Matt 1:20f; 2:13, 19f).

What of Koester's claim that the Old Testament contains "numerous examples" of divine beings appearing "in glory, surrounded by blinding light to give commands"? He refers us to the classical prophets and, in particular, to Isaiah and Ezekiel. In the case of these two prophets we do come across such visions in "glory" (for example, Isaiah 6:1ff). But Koester here ignores something which emerged during the presentation of Küng's views in Chapter Three. Unlike the apostolic witnesses to the risen Christ, the Old Testament prophets were not primarily "visionaries" but rather "hearers" of the divine word. Their characteristic experiences of God are represented as verbal and aural rather than as visual. The mode of hearing expresses a different relationship from that of seeing. The prophetic experiences do not yield a close analogy to what the New Testament reports about the apostolic experiences of the risen Lord.

Koester turns quite preposterous when he alleges a parallel between the stories of the risen Jesus' appearances and "appearance stories" in "the literature of other religions of the time." He mentions Asclepius (better called Aesculapius) and Isis, the principal goddess of ancient Egypt who was supposed to have been decapitated by one of her sons. Isis was not a historical person like Jesus of Nazareth. There was no question of her having risen from the dead after a public execution. The evidence for her having appeared to "mere mortals" fails to match the evidence for the appearances of the risen Jesus. Koester has no useful parallel in Egyptian stories about Isis, still less in the case of Aesculapius. That god of medicine in Greek mythology never existed as an historical person on earth, and never underwent death by public execution. Far from being credited with appearing by day as risen from the dead like Jesus, Aesculapius was credited with appearing in dreams or by night to heal and predict the future. Instead of healing the sick or predicting the future, the risen Jesus of Matthew, Luke and John does other such things as initiating the mission, giving (John) or promising (Luke) the Holy Spirit, and opening the minds of the disciples to the meaning of the Scriptures (Luke). The huge gap between the stories about Aesculapius and those about Jesus rules out any useful and illuminating parallel.

(b) Where Koester wants to relativize the witness to the risen Jesus' appearances by linking them with a broad range of supposedly similar phenomena, Schillebeeckx examines the appearances largely within the story of Jesus and Christianity. Nevertheless, in his own way he relativizes the special character of those appearances by presenting them as the first instance of experiences available to all later Christians. This interpretation, as we shall see, does not correspond with the New Testament claims, nor, as we saw in Chapter Three, is it endorsed by Küng, Rahner and Sobrino. Despite their differences, all three recognize the unique, unrepeatable nature of the Easter appearances.

In *Jesus* Schillebeeckx expounded the Easter experience of Peter and the other disciples as follows. Through the real but invisible influence of the risen Lord they underwent a deep forgiveness and conversion which they expressed in the model of "appearances." But their talk of "appearances" was only a way of articulating what the invisible Jesus had done for them after his resurrection and did not refer to genuinely historical events (354–390).[7]

In his *Interim Report on the Books "Jesus" and "Christ"* (New York, 1982) Schillebeeckx conceded that when the first Christians spoke of "appearances," this "need not be a pure model; it can also imply an historical event" (147, fn. 43; see 148, fn. 46). Even before the publication of this *Interim Report* he explained that he did not deny that the disciples to whom Jesus "appeared" had enjoyed some kind of sense experience (*Christ* [New York, 1980], 529). When they experienced him as alive, they may have seen him alive, even if this was not necessarily so (*Interim Report*, 75).

For Schillebeeckx the Easter experience of the disciples was essentially a matter of forgiveness and conversion, a "renewal of life and the experience of Jesus' spiritual presence" (*ibid.*, 78). But obviously this "experience of the new (spiritual) presence of the risen Jesus in the gathered community" (*ibid.*, 80) can be shared by any of his followers anywhere and at any time. Peter and the other Easter witnesses were only chronologically the first to experience "Jesus' new saving presence in the midst of his people on earth" (*ibid.*, 81). All later Christians can gather together to know the same forgiveness and conversion through the same, new presence of the risen Lord. There is no very significant difference between the disciples' Easter experience and subsequent experiences of the risen Lord (*Jesus*, 346, 647).

Schillebeeckx names *only one* special aspect of the *first* apostles' Easter experience: the fact that they had known Jesus before his death, "a circumstance that gave them a unique privilege" (*ibid.*). The disciples who were with Jesus during his ministry recognized the risen Christ as being identical with the master whom they had known and followed: "It is the Lord" (John 21:7). No later group or individual believer, not even Paul, could duplicate this aspect of those first post-resurrection meetings with Christ. Peter, Mary Magdalene and other disciples served as bridge persons who linked the period of Jesus' ministry with the post-Easter situation. In that way their experience of the risen Lord was unique and unrepeatable. But much more should be added about their "once only" experience and its aftermath.

Peter, Paul and other apostolic witnesses who meet the risen Christ have the mission to testify to that experience and found the Church. These witnesses have seen for themselves and believed. In proclaiming the good news and gathering together those who have not seen and yet are ready to believe, these original witnesses do not need to rely on the experience and testimony of others. Their function for Christianity differs from that of any subsequent believers, inasmuch as they alone have the once-and-for-all task of inaugurating the mission and founding the Church. Others will bear the responsibility to continue that mission and keep the Church in existence. But the coming-into-being of the mission and of the Church cannot be duplicated. The way in which that unique function rests upon some difference in their respective experiences is expressed by John's classic distinction between those who have seen and believed and those who are "blessed" because they "have not seen and yet believe" (John 20:29).

St. Paul also draws attention to some real difference between the fundamental post-resurrection encounters and all later experiences of the risen Lord. "Last of all," he recalls, Christ "appeared also to me" (1 Cor 15:8). This episode constituted Paul's apostolic calling and the basis for his mission (1 Cor 9:1; Gal 1:11ff). Other Christians share with him the gift of the Holy Spirit and life "in Christ," but they did not and do not experience that fundamental meeting with the risen Lord which made Paul a founding father of the Church. He never remarks to his readers: "Christ has appeared" or "Christ will appear to you."

This is not to say that Christians other than the resurrection witnesses were thought to have no access to the risen Jesus. He remained present through word and sacrament (Luke 24:30ff), in the community (Matt 18:20), in his body (1 Cor 12:27), through persons who suffer (Matt 25:31–46) and through his Spirit (2 Cor 3:17). Nevertheless, the risen Lord did not appear to all those Christians and make them normative witnesses to his resurrection and authoritative founders of the Christian Church.

Here one should be clear about the theological implications of Schillebeeckx's position. Once the special nature of the Easter appearances gets left behind, the apostolic witnesses cease to be normative interpreters of the risen Jesus and authoritative founders of the Christian Church. It is difficult to see why their experience of him should remain a lasting criterion for believers and why their conversion should be the norm for Christian conversion. Schillebeeckx himself seems to draw this conclusion by remarking that it is only "for the knowledge [but not for any normative interpretation?] of Jesus in whom we believe" that we depend on these witnesses. They "have no [other] advantage over us than that they were there at the time" (*Interim Report*, p. 7).

(c) Having criticized Koester and Schillebeeckx, how would I report and assess the appearances of the risen Jesus?

In the New Testament these appearances turn up in the resurrection kerygma (for example, 1 Cor 15:3–5; Luke 24:34) and in the appearance stories of Matthew, Luke and John. Where once it was common enough to maintain that the stories developed out of the kerygma, contemporary exegesis respects their relatively independent status. Pheme Perkins puts it as follows:

> The kerygmatic proclamation of 1 Cor 15:3–5 is not a summary of a resurrection narrative. Nor are the narratives simply [an] imaginative expansion of the kerygma (*Resurrection*, 113f).

These sources diverge on secondary matters. Who was the first to see the risen Lord? Mary Magdalene (John 20:14–18) or Peter (1 Cor 15:5; Luke 24:34)? Where did the appearances take place—in Galilee (Mark 16:7) or in and around Jerusalem (Luke 24)? Yet the resurrection kerygma, Paul and the evangelists agree on the primary fact of appearances to certain individuals and to groups, in particular "the Twelve" (1 Cor 15:5).

What does the New Testament indicate about these appearances? As raised from the dead and enjoying a new, transformed and final life, Jesus is no longer subject to the limitations of the material universe, exists apart from this world, and "lives to God" (Rom 6:10). He freely emerged from the "other" world to enter into contact with people in this world, revealing himself to them, calling them to faith and mission, and did so in a way which involved some kind of external perception. Paul understands and interprets his encounter with the risen Jesus as entailing revelation and a call to faith and mission (1 Cor 9:1; 15:8–11; Gal 1:1, 12, 15f). Paul's language suggests some analogy to the vocations of Old Testament prophets (Isaiah 6:1, 5; 49:1; Jer 1:5). The problem is with the extramental perception. Did the Easter appearances involve a vision in space? Was there someone "out there" to be seen?

In reporting or referring to the encounters with the risen Christ, the New Testament heavily privileges the language of sight. He "appeared" (for example, 1 Cor 15:5–8; Luke 24:34) and they "saw him (for example, 1 Cor 9:1; Matt 28:17; John 20:18, 20).[8] Occasionally in New Testament Greek "see (*horaō*)" can be used of intellectual perception, just as blindness is a metaphor for incomprehension. Thus "for those outside everything is in parables, so that they may indeed see but not perceive, and may indeed hear but not understand" (Mark 4:11f). But normally "seeing" and "appearing" include some visual component (for example, Mark 9:4; Luke 5:12; John 1:29; Acts 2:3).[9] Further, instances like Mark 4:11f deal with the intellectual perception of some *truth* or the failure to comprehend some truth. One can "see" truth in a purely interior, non-corporeal way. But with the Easter encounters we are dealing with a bodily resurrected *person* appearing to other persons who exist within our space/time world and see him. In that case it would be difficult to imagine how a purely spiritual, interior seeing could be reconciled with the New Testament terminology of the appearances. This is not to allege that when the risen Jesus appeared, he was an exterior object to be perceived by any who happened to be present, irrespective of their private dispositions. (I return to this point shortly.) Nor do I deny the fact that in general Paul and the evangelists show little interest in describing and explaining the nature of the appearances. I wish only to point out that some visual component seems implied by the New Testament language for the encounters with the risen Jesus.

There can be no doubt about the curious "ordinariness" of the Easter appearances as reported by the Gospels and Paul. Unlike other communications from the divine world, they do not take place during ecstasy (Acts 10:9ff; 2 Cor 12:2–4; Rev 1:10ff), nor in a dream (Matt 1:20; 2:12f, 18f, 22), nor by night (Acts 16:9; 18:9; 23:11; 27:33). The appearances occur under "normal" circumstances and without the traits of apocalyptic glory which we find elsewhere (Mark 9:2–8; Matt 28:3f). The one exception is Paul's experience on the Damascus Road as reported by Acts (9:1–9; 22:6–11; 26:12–18), in which he sees "a light from heaven, brighter than the sun" (Acts 26:13). But there is no mention of this phenomenon when Paul himself writes of his encounter with the risen Christ (1 Cor 9:1; 15:8; Gal 1:12, 16). It is hard to see what justifies R. Fuller and H. Grass in holding that a "light appearance" is not only the type of appearance to Paul but even that this is normative for the tradition generally.[10]

At least from the second century on, some critics have cast doubt on the appearances by noting their non-public character. Celsus and Porphyry, for instance, argued that if the risen Christ truly appeared risen from the dead, he should have made himself known to his Jewish opponents, to Pilate and Herod, and even better to the members of the Roman Senate. Reimarus found the lack of such public appearances to be irreconcilable with Jesus' alleged mission to call all people to a new faith:

> Even if we had no other scruples concerning the resurrection of Jesus, the one that he did not appear publicly would be sufficient in itself to overthrow any plausibility; for it can never be reconciled with the purpose for which Jesus is supposed to have come into the world.[11]

In responding to Celsus, Origen argued that the risen Christ could not be perceived in an ordinary way as if he were just another object in this world. The resurrection brought the new revelation of Christ's divinity, something which was not to be seen with the eyes of the old creation. Origen's sense of the new conditions for the communication between the sender/revealer (the risen Christ) and the receivers (the apostolic witnesses) deserves to be developed.

The resurrected Christ himself constitutes the beginning of the end of the world (1 Cor 15:20, 23), the realized presence of the new creation. Through his risen bodiliness matter has been elevated to a final destiny which goes far beyond the bodiliness we experience in this world. "Exalted at the right hand of God" (Acts 2:33), Christ is revealed as sharing in the divine mystery and not to be manipulated, weighed, measured or in other ways treated like an ordinary object in this world. He appears where and to whom he wills and disappears when he wills (for example, Luke 24:31).

Those who accept this new state of the risen Christ should find little difficulty in acknowledging what it entails: graced powers of perception on the part of those who saw him. Here 1 John's words about the final vision of God could be reversed and applied: "When he appears we shall be like him, for we shall see him as he is" (3:2). To see the risen Christ required a transforming grace for the recipients of that experience. To see him they needed to be first made in some sense like him, a grace which was not given either to the guards at the tomb (Matt 28:4, 11) or to Saul's companions on the road to Damascus (Acts 9:7 par).

This graced perception of the risen Christ involved both *preparation* and *collaboration*. Earlier I criticized those like the Pesch of 1973–80 who maintained that by the time the passion came the original disciples were already fully prepared for Easter faith. Nevertheless, one should not go to the other extreme and insinuate a complete discontinuity. Their association with him during the ministry in some way prepared such disciples as Peter and Mary Magdalene for their special, personal experience of the risen Jesus. Paul misunderstood the righteousness given through faith in Christ and persecuted the early Church. Yet his faultless rectitude in keeping the law (Phil 3:6) also served as a kind of preparation for his seeing the risen Christ, a preparation which evidently was not verified in the case of Caiaphas, Pilate, Herod Antipas and the members of the Roman Senate.

The appearances of the risen Christ also invited a collaboration which did not leave the disciples in the state of purely passive observers (if there could be such a state). They were not coerced into meeting him, recognizing him and accepting his resurrection. In Matthew's account the eleven freely kept the rendezvous on the mountain in Galilee (27:7, 10, 16). Even so, when Jesus appeared, some remained doubtful. They had to allow those doubts to be dealt with when Jesus came up and commissioned them (Matt 28:17–20). Luke's Emmaus story portrays a gradual entering into the experience of the risen Lord which brought the two disciples to invite him to stay with them. It was then they finally recognized him in the breaking of the bread (Luke 24:13–35). In John's account Mary Magdalene first "turned" around physically (20:14) and then, when called by name, "turned to" the risen Jesus and acknowledged him (20:16). This second "turning" fairly clearly indicates Mary's spiritual collaboration in the meeting.

To be sure, much more needs to be said exegetically and historically about these episodes from Matthew, Luke and John. My point here is simply to note how these three Gospels, for all their differences, converge in recalling that the encounters with the risen Lord invited the disciples to collaborate freely. The appearances were deeply self-involving experiences through which the disciples became dedicated witnesses (Acts 2:32; 3:15; 4:20; 5:32; 10:41; 13:31). From what we know of Caiaphas, Herod, Pilate and the members of the Roman Senate at that time, one would not imagine them to be ready for such generous and even heroic participation in a personal experience of the risen Lord.

The next chapter will face the question which has doubtless entered the reader's mind: Why believe that Peter, Mary Magdalene, Paul and the other Easter witnesses genuinely saw Jesus when risen from the dead? Before taking up that issue, we should spend a little time on the secondary cause which brought the first Christians to know about Jesus' resurrection, the discovery of his empty tomb. "Secondary" indicates here the order of importance, not necessarily the chronological order of events. The discovery of the empty tomb may have preceded in time the first appearance of the risen Jesus.

(3) *The Empty Tomb.* Apropos of this tradition, the 1984 program, "Jesus the Evidence," admitted the existence of very strong evidence in support of the conclusion that the Church of the Holy Sepulchre in Jerusalem does enclose the actual tomb of Jesus. It allowed too that the Gospel stories about women finding Jesus' grave to be open and empty are "unique to Christianity."

(a) Then that program fell into a contradiction about the role of the empty tomb for faith. We were first told that "to most Christians, the empty tomb is proof that Jesus did physically rise from the dead." Then we heard that "most Christians readily accept that belief in the physical resurrection is not a question of [open to?] proof and never will be. His resurrection . . . is one of the great mysteries of their faith." If "most Christians readily accept" that belief in Jesus' physical resurrection is not open to proof, how can they hold the empty tomb to be "proof that Jesus did physically rise from the dead"?

The New Testament is aware that by itself the empty tomb does not prove Jesus' resurrection. In John's Gospel Mary Magdalene thinks rather that the corpse has been shifted to some other place: "They have taken the Lord out of the tomb, and we do not know where they have laid him" (John 20:2; see 20:13, 15). The only scientific way of establishing what "most Christians" think about the function of the empty tomb would be to take some surveys among them. One of the graffiti which turns up on city walls in the spring could well indicate what very many people hold: "There will be no Easter this year. They have found the body." This suggests what I have heard over and over again in different parts of the world: ordinary believers' faith in Jesus' resurrection does involve his grave being empty. They would not believe in his resurrection from the dead unless that tomb had been found open and the corpse gone. They take the empty grave to be implied in what they confess in the Creed (he "rose again in accordance with the Scriptures"). But, as I said, the only appropriate way of finding out what "most Christians" hold about the empty tomb would be through properly conducted surveys, which in this matter have not yet been done. Hopefully the majority of Christians would prefer to speak of Jesus' *bodily* resurrection rather than his *physical* resurrection, as the program "Jesus the Evidence" did. Here "physical" can too easily suggest that the resurrection was merely a case of the reanimation of Jesus' corpse and ignores the glorious transformation stressed by Paul in 1 Corinthians 15:42ff. "Bodily" expresses the personal reality of Jesus' resurrection, while allowing more easily for his new, transformed existence. Yet, once again, only a scientific survey could establish the language "most Christians" prefer to use.

Here I do not wish to introduce and dwell upon the beliefs of contemporary Christians. The question rather is the one posed by "Jesus the Evidence": "Are the Gospels' blunt assertions that the tomb was empty reliable?" The program began by raising a difficulty advanced as long ago as Celsus and Porphyry:

> All four Gospels contain remarkable discrepancies. In Mark's Gospel, the earliest, the women see a young man in a white robe. In Luke's Gospel they see two men in brilliant clothes. In Matthew's Gospel they see one angel. And in John's Gospel, the latest [= the last], Mary Magdalene sees two angels. It is as if each successive Gospel writer has embellished the earlier story.

Embellishment is hardly the right word here. The four Gospels maintain an "angelic" element in their empty tomb narratives. Exegetes agree that Mark's "young man" is to be understood as an angel. Likewise Luke's "two men in brilliant clothes" are angelic beings. John's two angels do not announce Jesus' resurrection but rather act as guards of honor who courteously question Mary about the reason for her distress (John 20:13). Successive embellishment hardly fits the movement from Mark to John. By announcing Jesus' resurrection Mark's angel does something much more significant than the Johannine guard of honor. "Differences" rather than "embellishments" describes better the various ways the four evangelists handle the angelic tradition in their Easter narratives. All Gospels agree in reporting that one or more women found Jesus' tomb to be open and empty. There are no "remarkable discrepancies" about that central datum in their tomb stories.

The program "Jesus the Evidence" brought up another common

objection, the silence of the first Christian author: "Paul's letters were written twenty to thirty years before the Gospels, yet nowhere does he mention the empty tomb—a striking omission." The implication is that the story of women discovering the tomb to be open and empty was fabricated between the time of Paul's letters and the writing of the first Gospel (Mark). Yet Paul, it should be remarked, "omits" (= does not mention) many things about Jesus: his parables, his works of healing, the details of his passion and even the very place of the crucifixion, Jerusalem. Paul does report the kerygmatic statement about Jesus being buried (1 Cor 15:4) and interprets baptism as also entailing a sacramental participation in that burial (Rom 6:4). When Paul reaffirms the early Christian proclamation about Jesus being raised (1 Cor 15:4), most exegetes have agreed that Paul means a resurrection from the grave. He could not imagine a resurrection which did not involve an empty tomb. Paul's own reflections on the risen body (1 Cor 15:35ff) would be ruled out, if Jesus' corpse had remained in the grave. The apostle understands resurrection to reverse death and entombment. One can also appreciate why the kerygma cited and expanded by Paul fails to announce the discovery of the empty tomb. By itself such a discovery does not establish Jesus' resurrection in the way the appearances do (1 Cor 15:5–8). In short Paul's "striking omission" fails to take on any decisive significance.

(b) At this point it could be worth recalling some of the many recent and contemporary exegetes and theologians who defend the essential reliability of the empty tomb story: Berten, Blank, Blinzler, Brown, von Campenhausen, Delorme, Fitzmyer, Fuller, Grundmann, Jeremias, Künneth, Léon-Dufour, Martini, Moule, Murphy-O'Connor, Mussner, Nauck, Pannenberg, Rengstorf, Rückstuhl, Schenke, Schmitt, Schubert, Schweizer, Seidensticker, Strobel, Stuhlmacher, Trilling, Vögtle and Wilckens. These scholars support the truth of the empty tomb traditions with different degrees of intensity and, sometimes, for differing reasons. But they converge in maintaining a kernel of reliable history in the narrative of the empty tomb. Schillebeeckx, after drifting away toward denial in *Jesus*, admits in *Interim Report* that the historicity of the empty tomb is difficult to deny (88).

Notoriously the evangelists do not agree about secondary details, which concern principally the women and the angel(s). The four Gospels offer differing answers to such questions as: How many women went to the tomb? Why did they go there? How many angels intervened? Where were they? What did they do and say? What emotions did the women show in the face of the angelic presence and message? What did the women do afterward? Yet the four evangelists, Mark (followed by Matthew and Luke) and John, agree on the primary datum.

To her astonishment, at least one woman (Mary Magdalene) found Jesus' tomb to be open and empty two days after his death and burial. Is this tradition historically reliable?

(c) If we examine first the various arguments brought against the essential historical truth of the empty tomb, only one argument (to which I will come shortly) has any plausibility. On the flimsy basis of Acts 13:27–29, some have claimed that the Jewish or Roman authorities buried Jesus in a common grave or at least a grave unknown to his followers. But the vague language of this passage in Acts ("they asked Pilate to have him killed . . . they took him down from the tree and laid him in a tomb") should be read in the light of the passion story which has already been told by the author of Acts and which ends with a burial by Joseph of Arimathea in a tomb that was known to some female followers of Jesus (Luke 23:50–56).

Matthew reports that the Jewish authorities spread the story that the tomb of Jesus was empty because the disciples had stolen the body (Matt 28:11–15) and proclaimed his resurrection, a counter-explanation repeated in the second century by Justin's opponents in his *Dialogue with Trypho* and in the eighteenth century by Reimarus. But what we know of the moral character of the first Christians rules out any such massive and deliberate fraud on their part.

Other opponents of the empty tomb story have postulated some kind of mistake on the part of the women. At the beginning of this century Kirsopp Lake suggested that the women went to the wrong tomb which happened to be empty and where they met a young man who told them that Jesus' corpse was not there ("he is not here"). They fled, thinking they had seen an angel who had told them of the resurrection. But exegetes commonly agree that in Mark (the earliest Gospel) the evangelist genuinely intends an angel when he introduces "a young man sitting on the right side, dressed in a white robe" (Mark 16:5). The message, "He has risen, he is not here; see the place where they laid him" (Mark 16:6), may not be divided in the trivial way Kirsopp Lake proposed.

Some have hypothesized that after the first burial Joseph of Arimathea returned and removed the body to another place. When the women visited the original tomb, they found it empty and imagined that Jesus had risen from the dead. Apart from the fact that the Gospels nowhere hint that Joseph returned as claimed, there is no evidence that—in defiance of legal sanctions—corpses were ever transferred in this way. Moreover, could or would Joseph of Arimathea have remained silent when the Christians began to proclaim Jesus' resurrection if he knew the real facts?

Chapter One of this book mentioned the counter-story reported by Tertullian. Before the women arrived on Easter Sunday morning, a local gardener had removed the corpse to stop the disciples trampling down his vegetables when they came to visit Jesus' tomb. In his first Jesus-book Malcolm Muggeridge advanced the theory that, hearing of Jesus' kingship and hoping for some gain, grave-robbers stole the corpse. It has been suggested that Jesus' body disappeared because it fell down a crack opened by an earthquake. The prize for sheer silliness must go to the theory that the corpse had decomposed with unique speed. When the women arrived on the third day, there were simply no remains to be found![12]

Practically the only argument against the historicity of the empty tomb which merits some attention is the view that takes the tomb stories to be "a particular form in which the resurrection was preached,"[13] secondary, "legendary elaborations of the message of the resurrection."[14] Put more precisely, this argument holds that Mark 16:1–8 and the subsequent empty tomb stories neither convey nor intend to convey any factual information about the state of Jesus' tomb, since they were simply imaginative ways of announcing the resurrection and entirely derivative from the mainline proclamation of the resurrection of the crucified Jesus and his subsequent appearances (1 Cor 15:3–8). The elaboration is usually supposed to have taken place over ten or fifteen years, between the appearances reported by 1 Corinthians 15:5–8 and the writing of Mark's Gospel.[15]

In her *Resurrection*, however, Perkins shows the flimsiness of the hypothesis that the traditions of the risen Jesus' appearances naturally produced empty tomb stories. Careful exegesis indicates that the two traditions (appearance stories and empty tomb stories) have independent origins. The differences between the two traditions are such that it is hard to see the first producing the second (84, 90, 94).

Major elements found in 1 Corinthians 15:3b–8 simply do not turn up in Mark 16:1–8: the appeal to Scriptures (1 Cor 15:3, 4), the atoning death "for our sins" (1 Cor 15:3), the title "Christ" which has become a second name for Jesus (1 Cor 15:3), and the appearances to "more than five hundred brethren," to James, to "all the apostles" and to Paul (1 Cor 15:6–8). Mark's empty tomb story promises appearances only to the disciples and Peter (Mark 16:7). Mark's story contains some major items of which 1 Corinthians 15:3b–8 knows nothing at all: the discovery of the empty tomb by three women, the interpreting angel and the promise of appearances *in Galilee*. Even a cursory comparison between 1 Corinthians 15:3b–8 and Mark 16:1–8 illustrates the dubiousness of the thesis that appearance traditions produced empty tomb stories.

(d) On the positive side, there is a reasonable case to be made for the basic reliability of the empty tomb story. Both the tradition behind the Synoptic Gospels and that which entered John's Gospel testified to one (Mary Magdalene) or more women finding Jesus' grave to be open and the body missing. Early polemic against the message of his resurrection supposed that the tomb was known to be empty. Naturally the opponents of the Christian movement explained away the missing body as a plain case of theft (Matt 28:11–15). What was in dispute was not whether the tomb was empty but why it was empty. We have no early evidence that anyone, either Christian or non-Christian, ever alleged that Jesus' tomb still contained his remains.

Furthermore, the central place of women in the empty tomb stories speaks for their historical reliability. Women were central: Mary Magdalene (John 20:1–2) and perhaps other women (Mark 16:1–8 par) to their astonishment found Jesus' tomb to be empty on that first Easter Sunday. If these stories had simply been legends created by early Christians, they would have attributed the discovery of the empty tomb to male disciples rather than women. In first-century Palestine women were, for all intents and purposes, disqualified as valid witnesses.[15a] The natural thing for someone making up a legend about the empty tomb would have been to have ascribed the discovery to men, not women. Legend-makers do not normally invent positively unhelpful material.

All in all, accepting the empty tomb puts us in better agreement with the known data. But did or does the empty tomb taken simply by itself establish the resurrection of Jesus? Of course not. As we saw above, New Testament Christians were well aware that an empty grave did not point straight to the resurrection and could be explained in other ways. In John's account Mary Magdalene discovered the tomb to be empty and immediately thought of grave-robbers: "They have taken the Lord out of the tomb, and we do not know where they have laid him" (John 20:2). It was the appearances which primarily established Jesus' resurrection. The empty tomb confirmed what the early Christians knew from the witnesses to the appearances (see, for instance, Luke 24:34; John 20:18).

In this chapter I have been concerned to sketch the kind of case which can be made for the historicity of Jesus' empty tomb. Much more can and should be added. A real empty tomb obviously excludes the view that the "resurrection" merely expressed the new consciousness to which the disciples came after Jesus' death and burial. Moreover, a rich symbolism for redemption emerges here. For instance, whereas graves naturally symbolize death, the open and empty tomb of Jesus expresses the fullness of new, risen life. Chapter Seven will take up this theme.

This present chapter lingered over two points: the claim the first Christians made about Jesus' personal resurrection and the two main ways they came to know about this event (the appearances of the risen Jesus and, secondarily, the discovery of his empty tomb). Much else could be added: for example, on the differences between the language of Jesus' resurrection and exaltation on which I wrote in *What Are They Saying About the Resurrection?* (63–66). In *Resurrection* (for example, 236–246) Perkins demonstrates that the New Testament traditions of Christ's resurrection did not develop from those of his exaltation; if anything, it was vice versa.

But it is high time to move to the key question which has doubtless been plaguing many readers: Why can and should we believe that the "something" which happened after Jesus' crucifixion and burial was in fact his personal resurrection from the dead?

5

Believing in the Risen Christ

In *Jesus the Evidence* Ian Wilson agrees that "the belief that Jesus had risen from the grave . . . caught on very soon after the crucifixion and spread like wildfire" (142). "The hypothesis" that Jesus' personal resurrection from the dead lay behind this belief, however, is "impossible to prove" and, therefore, can be "set aside" (*ibid.*, 141).

Wilson betrays here a hardy prejudice about the nature of evidence. If we do not or cannot assemble full "scientific" evidence to demonstrate some thesis to disengaged and allegedly "neutral" observers, we should set that thesis aside. Wilson could be making the standard impossibly high about many deeply cherished and reasonable beliefs on which people build their lives. Now that he is long dead, I doubt, for instance, if I could ever prove that I am the son of the man I have always taken to be my father. After all my mother could have had a secret lover; I have no way of disproving that absolutely. Nevertheless, the convergent signs make it reasonable for me to continue identifying myself as the child of the two parents who raised me as their son. I would be weirdly misguided if I set aside that belief simply because it is impossible to prove it absolutely. To lack coercive evidence which might fully and publicly prove this or some other such belief is not necessarily to have no evidence at all.

But is it a reasonable and responsible act to believe in Jesus Christ as truly risen from the dead? Can such faith be rationally justified in any way? This question has already surfaced in earlier chapters. For all their differences, Barth and Bultmann agreed that historical argument cannot and should not support Easter faith. Marxsen also argued that historical research has nothing to do with the decision of faith. Yet Pannenberg has maintained that the evidence of history can verify claims about Jesus' resurrection from the dead. In his own way Küng also acts as rational apologist for Easter faith.

128

An empirical approach to this issue could take the form of collecting and examining cases of persons who moved from non-belief to belief in Christ's resurrection. What tests worked for them? What evidence counted? How did they come to make the move? Was it reasonable for them to have done so?

As far as I know, no such case-research has ever been undertaken. It would seem to be a difficult project to complete. Many people do not put the question of faith explicitly in terms of accepting the proposition "He rose again," but rather as a matter of believing in God, committing their lives to Jesus (whose attractive teaching and evident holiness have touched their hearts and minds), and through baptism joining the community Jesus brought into being. Admittedly to believe in the God of creation and new creation implies resurrection. Jesus' dedication to his mission brought him to crucifixion and then resurrection from the dead. In celebrating baptism and the Eucharist, the Church remembers the death and resurrection of the risen Lord. In these terms Jesus' resurrection enters deeply into any conversion to God, Jesus and the Church community. Nevertheless, few people appear to focus and articulate the step of faith precisely and clearly as coming to accept Jesus as risen from the dead. This could complicate an empirical, case-study approach to Easter faith.

How then might we justify the option of those who "have not seen and yet believe" (John 20:29) in the risen Jesus? While granting the essential roles of divine grace and human freedom, can we in any way establish the reasonableness of Easter faith? What public tests and other evidence are available and appropriate for accepting Christ's resurrection and knowing it to have truly happened?

Before taking up a position here on the validation of Easter faith, I need first to say something about Christian faith in general.

FAITH

It still seems to me reasonable to describe human and, specifically, Christian faith in terms of three distinguishable, if inseparable, dimensions of one act: confession, commitment, and confidence or trust. Through confession, believers assent with their minds to certain truths about God. The consent of their will means that they freely commit themselves to act in certain ways. Their confidence entails actively and imaginatively anticipating a future fulfillment and entrusting it to God. Chapter 5 of my *Fundamental Theology* developed such an analysis of

faith. Here I wish to presuppose that analysis and add some further reflections.

(1) *Story.* The element of story comes across as important for confession. At least in part, faith involves assenting to and through a story.
Deuteronomy presents the proper response to God as telling a story
with *gratitude.*

> A wandering Aramean was my father; and he went down into Egypt
> and sojourned there, few in number; and there he became a nation,
> great, mighty, and populous. And the Egyptians treated us harshly,
> and afflicted us, and laid upon us hard bondage. Then we cried to
> the Lord the God of our fathers, and the Lord heard our voice, and
> saw our affliction, our toil, and our oppression; and the Lord brought
> us out of Egypt with a mighty hand and an outstretched arm, with
> great terror, with signs and wonders; and he brought us into this place
> and gave us this land, a land flowing with milk and honey (Deut 26:5–
> 9).

The early Christians did justice to their Easter confession of faith not
only by transmitting it in brief formulae (1 Cor 15:3b–5, etc.), but also
by expressing it in the form the Easter story took in Peter's speech on
the day of Pentecost:

> Men of Israel, hear these words: Jesus of Nazareth, a man attested to
> you by God by mighty words and wonders and signs which God did
> through him in your midst, as you yourselves know—this Jesus, de-
> livered up according to the definite plan and foreknowledge of God,
> you crucified and killed by the hands of lawless men. But God raised
> him up, having loosed the pangs of death, because it was not possible
> for him to be held by it. . . . This Jesus God raised up, and of that
> we all are witnesses (Acts 2:22–24, 32).

Here I am not concerned to discuss whether, even in part, Peter deliv-
ered his missionary speeches reported by Acts. My point is merely to
note the narrative form. Early Christians confessed the Easter story by
telling it with gratitude.

Recognizing the value of narrative invites a certain adaptation of
Thomas Aquinas' lapidary version of faith, "to think [*cogitare*] with assent" (*Summa theol.* 2a 2ae, 2.1). Setting aside for the moment the fact
that this version makes faith primarily (or even exclusively?) an act of
knowledge, I suggest we can usefully modify Aquinas' words and say,
"to tell a story [*narrare*] with assent." In these terms Christian faith

would then involve telling the resurrection story with conviction (confession), dramatizing the story in one's own life (commitment) and putting one's trust in this story for the future (confidence).

(2) *Reason and Truth.* (a) A little later in this chapter I plan to criticize a one-sidedly rationalist approach to Christ's resurrection. Before doing so I would like to recall various forms of "reason." When taken together, they obviously display a certain analogy to the tridimensional account of faith I have just been summarizing.

Like Sherlock Holmes, *logical* reason searches for and pieces together the clues available here and now that can show us what happened back there and then. This reason guides much work in biblical exegesis as it attempts to observe the laws of its discipline. Gathering and examining the data on the resurrection, it asks: What clues indicate the personal contributions to the Easter story made by Paul and the evangelists, the input from the Christian communities during the previous decades, and the details which derive from the very events themselves of the crucifixion, burial and resurrection of Jesus? This logical reason as such creates nothing new and does not take personal decisions when it puts together and assesses the data.

In G.K. Chesterton's detective stories Father Brown symbolizes *practical* reason or the intellect as guiding human decisions. By intuitively weighing the evidence, he succeeds in identifying the culprit. Whether it happens in this more intuitive fashion or by slowly evaluating many facts, practical reason ends by choosing some course of action. It synthesizes the data to reach a personal decision. It brings us to a commitment.

Finally, there is *creative* reason or the intellect as producing new ideas and hypotheses. Imagination plays a role here by enabling us to deal inventively with the present and leap forward to the future. Artists who succeed in breaking through to fresh forms and new insights symbolize this function of reason. They illustrate creativity in the pursuit of truth. In *The Principles of Art* (Oxford, 1938) R.G. Collingwood remarked: "Art is not indifferent to truth; it is essentially the pursuit of truth" (288). John Henry Newman belongs here with his insistence that the reasonableness of faith entails its being credible for our imagination.

Even more than practical reason, creative reason eludes the grasp of logical reason. Creative reason, by enlarging and reordering our sense of reality, goes beyond the hard, prosaic data that engage logical reason which wants everything to be patently intelligible. Nevertheless, it would be false to represent these three functions of reason as if they were independent entities rigidly separated from each other. After all it is the one human being who can think logically, choose decisively and respond imaginatively. Presumably Sherlock Holmes, Father Brown and John Henry Newman could communicate with each other. But the link between the logical, practical and creative reason transcends any mere association between three separate agents. It is located within the dynamic unity of the one acting subject. In their function and interaction these three forms of reason show some resemblance to faith's assent to truth, commitment to action, and imaginative anticipation of the future.

(b) The different dimensions of *truth* offer a further chance of elucidating my tripartite version of faith. The believer takes up the truth of the Easter story in three ways: as something to be known and accepted, as something to be done, and as something to put one's confidence in. The resurrection of Jesus is not only a truth which can be, at least minimally, described as his passage through death to a new, transformed existence. This truth also involves something to be done and something which opens up the future in trust. In other words, our judgments about Jesus' resurrection can correspond to the facts. Yet the truth of this resurrection is pragmatic and imaginative as well. The truth of Easter faith not only entails but also goes beyond a confessing assent to an event which once happened.

Thus far I have brought in the notions of story, reason and truth to enrich my presentation of faith. Before examining the Easter faith, I wish to add a word about a problem created or at any rate expressed by ordinary speech.

(3) *Oversimplification.* The tendency to oversimplify faith is deeply embedded in much ordinary speech. Saying "I believe that Jesus rose from the dead" can sound like saying "I think that it is (most) probable that he did so," or "I am (extremely) inclined to accept his resurrection." Following this line would reduce Easter faith (in the direction of Aquinas' general notion of faith), and make it simply as such "thinking about Jesus' resurrection with assent." Faith's "object" would then be a fact to be affirmed (with certainty? with high probability?) by the intellect, and faith itself cut down to the element of confession.

The commitment and confidence of which Paul wrote in Romans[1] do not enter this concept of faith. They are seen as moral consequences of resurrection faith, not as its integral constituents. They become a matter of living by or acting on one's belief, in such a way that those who believe in Jesus' resurrection will at least sometimes or in some circumstances act and trust differently from those who do not.

Besides failing to measure up to the fuller New Testament account of faith, any view which takes belief in the resurrection merely as an intellectual assent to a fact will have trouble showing that it is (a) a divine gift, and (b) a reasonable, free and obligatory human act. All theories, of course, have to face great difficulty in maintaining the Christian claim that faith is at the same time a gift from God and a human act. Over and above *that* difficulty, however, the view which maximizes intellectual assent can hardly account for the free and obligatory nature of faith. If believing simply means intellectually assenting to truth, it does not appear to be under our voluntary control. We could not freely decide to believe because we think we should do so. The evidence presented to our reason would automatically lead us to "think about Jesus' resurrection with assent."

EASTER FAITH

What does the making and living of Easter faith require now? Can we describe and even justify the option of those who "have not seen and yet believe" (John 20:29) in the risen Jesus? Let me make my run at an answer by first excluding two approaches which one could label "rationalist" and "fideist."

(1) *The "Rationalists."* One fairly widespread attitude toward Jesus' resurrection reduces matters to such questions as: Could we or how could we establish reasonably the truth of this claim? What public checks and evidence are available for accepting this resurrection and knowing it to have truly happened?

One great merit of this "rationalist" mentality has been to promote more willingness to reflect on some necessary questions. What counts as reasonable and relevant evidence for the truth of Jesus' resurrection? What standards should we expect this evidence to reach and how should we interpret it?

This approach, however, has frequently failed through reducing evidence to *historical* evidence from the past and then restricting its sources of evidence to the New Testament, the early Church and its environment. But, as we shall see, the evidence to be considered goes beyond some relevant historical data from the first century. It also includes, for example, personal checks and the confirmation of personal experience. The question of Jesus' resurrection cannot be solved by historical evidence alone.

A "rationalist" approach to the case for Jesus' resurrection, even one which finishes with a favorable verdict like Frank Morison's *Who Moved the Stone?* (London, 1930), risks forgetting that this is not just a matter from the past to be investigated and established (or refuted) to one's intellectual satisfaction. Accepting the truth of the resurrection and believing in the risen Christ is much more than a merely mental exercise about past claims and past facts. Easter faith goes beyond assenting to the testimony of the Easter witnesses and confessing ("On the third day he rose again") to call for commitment ("We believe in one Lord, Jesus Christ") and confidence ("We look for the resurrection of the dead and the life of the world to come").

Even the sentence "He rose again," which looks like an assertive proposition or factual description and could be simply that in ordinary language usage, is here used in an "extraordinary" way, so that it *also* affirms an intention about the present and expresses a hope for the future. A merely "rationalist" discussion of Jesus' resurrection can slip over the fact that a sentence ("He rose again") which simply looks like a statement *also* functions as something else. It has the force of the commitment and confidence which the Nicene Creed elsewhere makes explicit ("We believe in one Lord, Jesus Christ" and "We look for the resurrection of the dead").

(2) *The "Fideists."*   That broad and varied group whom we can typify as "fideists" know that "other-worldly" facts like the risen existence of Jesus ultimately count through being related to experienced reality and entering our personal existence here and now. In faithfully accepting and integrating Jesus' resurrection into their lives, they recognize the divine power which makes this possible. In brief, the personal experience which supports commitment to and confidence in Christ becomes the major or even the sole justification for Easter faith. This is the spirit of those who maintain that for those who believe no reasoned legitimation of faith is necessary, whereas for those who do not believe no such legitimation is possible.

The strain of fideism runs from the sophisticated theologies of Barth (despite his sometimes extreme antipathy to an anthropological approach), Bultmann and Marxsen to simple Christians who sing in chorus:

He lives, he lives,
Christ Jesus lives today:
He walks with me and talks with me
Along life's narrow way.

He lives, he lives,
Salvation to impart;
You ask me how I know he lives. . . .
He lives within my heart!

Over various issues Barth and Bultmann turned away from Adolf von Harnack (1851–1930), but they continued to endorse their teacher's conviction that historical evidence could not and should not validate faith. In his *What Is Christianity?* (New York and London, 1901) von Harnack disqualified claims about the appearances of the risen Jesus and the discovery of the empty tomb, and identified Easter faith as a God-given and freely accepted belief in two things: Jesus as living Lord and life eternal for us.

> . . . how is the Easter faith to be based on them [Jesus' appearances]? Either we must decide to rest our belief on a foundation unstable and always exposed to fresh doubts, or else we must abandon this foundation altogether, and with it the miraculous appeal to our senses. . . . Whatever may have happened at the grave and in the matter of the appearances, one thing is certain: *This grave was the birthplace of the indestructible belief that death is vanquished, that there is life eternal.* . . . Belief in the living Lord and in a life eternal is the *act* of freedom which is born of God (162f).

Although it declines to take up a position on basic historical questions ("Whatever may have happened . . ."), this noble "fideist" option is more attractive than any "rationalist" approach. It appreciates that belief in Jesus as living Lord is *the* truth which should freely guide our existence and shape our hopes.

Nevertheless, all "fideists" ignore or play down our need and indeed responsibility as intelligent beings to illustrate the reasonableness of the faith option. In fact, public evidence and historical data converge with personal, experiential convictions to support faith. The best features of the "rationalist" and "fideist" approaches can be properly combined in a series of tests which taken together lend credibility to belief in Jesus as risen from the dead. It is an intellectually honest and humanly responsible act to believe in his resurrection.

(3) *Three Presuppositions.* Before proposing some convergent tests for checking and legitimating Easter faith, I want to recall three key presuppositions—three among many, of course. Engaging in the procedure which follows also implies, for example, a certain respect for the powers

and place of human reason. It implies too that one accepts God as creator of the universe. Otherwise it makes no sense to speak of resurrection as new creation. Nevertheless, here I wish to pick out only three major presuppositions to my argument.

First, the Easter faith which I am investigating holds that Jesus of Nazareth who was crucified under Pontius Pilate was raised personally and bodily from the dead. His resurrection was his own passage from earthly life through death to a final, transformed existence. Versions of Easter faith which, for example, reduce the resurrection to the continuing inspiration of Jesus' example not only fail to match the claim made by the apostolic witnesses but also do not call for any detailed discussion of public checks and evidence. On any showing, Jesus of Nazareth was a remarkable religious figure. There is no need to discuss at length relevant evidence and appropriate tests before we can reasonably allow ourselves to be inspired by his example. However, faith in him as personally triumphant over death does call for scrutiny and justification.

Second, belief in Christ's resurrection presupposes faith in a God who can and does intervene in human history and who, in particular, had already been specially present, active and revealed in the history of Israel. From the very beginning of Christianity the people's exodus from slavery to freedom and its commemoration in the Jewish Passover rite (see, for example, 1 Cor 5:7; 10:1–2; Mark 14:12, 14, 16 par) supplied the background for understanding and interpreting the resurrection of the crucified Jesus. New Testament Christians and then the Fathers of the Church remembered the coming out of Egypt and all that went with it as the great act of God which prefigured the even greater divine act in the paschal mystery. As the climax of the special divine involvement with the people, the resurrection of the crucified Jesus formed part of a larger picture. In a later chapter I shall discuss the meaning and truth of such a special presence and activity of God in human history. Here I simply want to note that those who follow a Deist line by systematically excluding such divine interventions will rule out in advance any evidence not only for Jesus' personal and bodily resurrection from the dead but also its background, the special (revelatory and redemptive) presence of God in Israel's history.

Third, it makes little sense to discuss the question of Jesus' resurrection unless we already agree that we have some substantially reliable information about his ministry, message and person. In particular, the discussion presupposes we can establish that with an extraordinary authority and compassion Jesus proclaimed God's reign. In revising the Mosaic law, forgiving sinners and acting as a final agent of revelation and salvation, Jesus claimed an authority and exercised a compassion which seemed more than human. If we do not accept some such account of his ministry, it seems pointless to examine evidence for his resurrection. We could volunteer no answers to those that ask who it was that underwent resurrection and why he was raised from the dead.

The early Christian formulation about "God who raised Jesus from the dead" (for example, Rom 10:9; 1 Cor 6:14; Gal 1:1) supposed that those who asserted this could give some account of who Jesus was and what he had been doing (my third presupposition). It also implied that those who confessed this new truth already knew something about the God revealed and actively present in the history of Israel (my second presupposition). Then the ordinary conventions governing the use of language argue that by "raised from the dead" the first Christians meant Jesus' own passage through death to a new, transformed existence (my first presupposition).

Assuming the validity of the three presuppositions, I ask: What ways are available for testing the truth of belief in Jesus' resurrection? Without taking back anything which has been said above about the place of commitment and confidence in the life of faith, I want to concentrate on the assertive proposition "He rose again," and ask: What counts as reasonable and relevant evidence for the truth of this proposition? What historical data and other public checks converge with personal checks to justify the confession of Easter faith? Are there any tests which taken together could lend credibility to confessing Jesus as risen from the dead? Is "He rose again" a true proposition, because in actual fact Jesus did rise from the dead?

(4) *Five Tests.* To validate the confession of Easter faith, I propose using five tests: partial continuity, coherence, reliable witness, vindication in public practice, and personal experience. Let me take them up in turn.

(a) A first test for belief in the resurrection could come from what was already believed about God on the basis of history and creation. Did this new truth ("Jesus has been raised from the dead") stand in *some* continuity with what the Jewish people already knew of God? Deuteronomy proposed this kind of test in the case of putative prophets (13:1–3, 5). In a similar way it seems reasonable to check the claim for the resurrection of Jesus by seeing whether and to what extent it drew support from prior beliefs about God.

Before developing this test, let me clarify what it does *not* involve. It is not precisely a question of whether Jesus' resurrection fulfilled particular predictions and expectations, whether Messianic or otherwise.

Nor am I talking about a perfect continuity between this new belief and prior beliefs about God. Rather I am asking: Did the new claim about Jesus' resurrection fit to some degree a pattern of divine activity which was already known and believed? Let us test the claim in this way.

The Israelites pinned their faith to Yahweh as the God of life, justice, power and fidelity. In many forms God gave and restored life to both individuals and the people. Yahweh was also believed to have consistently revealed himself to be supremely just, powerful and faithful. These ancient convictions about God, possibly supported by beliefs coming from other sources, eventually led many Jews to expect a resurrected life after death. A hope for a bodily resurrection at the end of time turns up in two apocalypses which are generally dated to the second century B.C. (Is 26:19; Dan 12:2–3). A book from the Greek canon records a similar expectation of a new life through resurrection (2 Macc 7:9–14; 12:44). Several apocryphal works like *Ethiopic Enoch* and *The Testaments of the Twelve Patriarchs* also attest such a hope for resurrection.[2]

In these terms the claim about Jesus' resurrection showed *some* continuity not only with (a) primordial truths about Israel's God but also with (b) the specific belief in resurrection which emerged in late Judaism. I say "some continuity." As Wolfhart Pannenberg and others have pointed out, to assert the resurrection of one individual (Jesus) before the end of the world introduced a new element. There existed an expectation that the end of the world would bring a general resurrection and judgment. No group in Judaism expected the final resurrection of *one* person alone. To quote Pannenberg:

> The primitive Christian news about the eschatological resurrection of Jesus—with a temporal interval separating it from the universal resurrection of the dead—is, considered from the point of view of the history of religions, something new (JGM, 96).[3]

Add too another new element that has already been noted: no Israelite envisaged the resurrection of a crucified Messiah. Yet the apostolic witnesses proclaimed the resurrection of Jesus in just such a scandalous way.

The point of the first test comes to this. Granted the real novelty of the claim about Jesus' resurrection, this claim was, nevertheless, not totally and utterly new but stood in some continuity with prior beliefs about God. What God was believed to have already done and revealed could be seen—at least in retrospect and at least partially—to have led toward the event of Jesus' resurrection. This is the logic behind the New Testament assertion that knowledge of the (Old Testament) Scriptures should have helped believers to expect the resurrection (for example, Luke 24:25–27, 32, 44–46; John 20:9). Normally this assertion is made in general. Only rarely are particular passages of Scripture cited in support of Jesus' resurrection (see, for example, Acts 2:25–28). But the central point is clear. Those who knew and understood God's revealing and saving activity recorded and interpreted by the sacred writers were or should have been prepared for Jesus' triumph over death.

To clarify its force, the test of partial continuity can be related to the earlier discussion on analogy (see Moltmann, Pannenberg and Sobrino in Chapters Two and Three). The claim about Jesus' resurrection should offer at least some analogy to the way God had acted before. Otherwise, if those who make this claim propose this resurrection as an utterly and absolutely new event and activity of God, it is hard to see how they could even talk about it. If Jesus' victory were alleged to be entirely new, totally anomalous and without any analogy whatsoever to the past, it would risk being quite unintelligible.

A similar point can be made if we express negatively this test of partial continuity in beliefs about God. If prior beliefs about God shed no light whatsoever on the claim about Jesus' resurrection, lend it no credibility whatsoever and stand in complete discontinuity with this new claim, we would have either to abandon those prior beliefs or to reject the asserted resurrection. It seems very difficult to maintain the notion of a God who acts in completely discontinuous ways and reveals truths which have no relationship whatsoever to each other. Provided, however, that we are satisfied that in this case there exists no such utter discontinuity between prior beliefs about God (which are presumed to be true) and the claim about Jesus' resurrection, we can move on to examine other ways of checking and possibly verifying this claim.

So far in discussing the test of partial continuity I have taken "prior beliefs about God" to be true beliefs about God entertained by the Jewish people. One might also ask about the continuity between (i) beliefs about God proclaimed during his ministry by Jesus himself and (ii) the claim later made by others about his resurrection. We could suppose that an examination of the relevant material (from the Synoptic Gospels) brought us to accept (i) that Jesus was *the* divinely endorsed agent of the final rule of God which offered human beings a new life here and hereafter. Do we then detect some continuity between (i) and (ii)? Does our acceptance of (i) even make it reasonable for us to expect and hold (ii)? Jesus showed exceptional obedience to his mission. When he went to Jerusalem for his last Passover, loyalty to his vocation kept him from escaping, even though his actions and words had set him on a deadly collision course with the authorities in the capital. Was it then totally surprising to hear the claim that the divine justice, power and fidelity had intervened to raise him from death to new life? Thus prior beliefs about Jesus and his mission could see in his resurrection their credible aftermath.

(b) The first test (partial continuity) can be followed by another, rather similar test, which takes the form of *coherence*. Is the meaning of the alleged resurrection coherent in itself and not evidently false? It would be more accurate to put the question in the plural. Can the various levels and patterns of meaning in the event of Christ's resurrection be systematically related in ways that are mutually consistent? If and when the various meanings are explained and shown to interrelate coherently such clarification inevitably helps to justify the truth of the claim.

In verifying the coherence of Jesus' resurrection, ever wider circles of meaning should be related and clarified. (i) The narrowest circle requires that we show that it is not evidently false to propose the personal resurrection of someone condemned by the political and religious authorities of his time and "abandoned" (Mark 15:34) by God to die on a cross. (ii) The next task is to illustrate how the resurrection of the crucified Jesus carried with it the revelation of the tripersonal God and "meant" the emergence of the Church with its community worship and universal mission. (iii) Finally, the widest circle of meaning entails relating the resurrection (as God's act of new creation) back to the original creation, and (as the real beginning of the end) forward to the *eschaton* (1 Cor 15:20–28). Does Jesus' resurrection cohere with the nature (creation) and final destiny of all things? Does a whole pattern of meaning come through the complete story in a way that is credible to our imagination?

Obviously those who do not or do not yet accept Jesus' resurrection will also fail to endorse many of the "other" beliefs involved in this test, especially those beliefs entailed by (ii) and (iii). Nevertheless, by relating the resurrection to all those "other" beliefs and vice versa, one aims to make sense of the whole Christian confession of faith. L. Scheffczyk's *Auferstehung: Prinzip christlichen Glaubens* (Einsiedeln, 1976) presents itself as a one-volume *summa* of Christian doctrines from the standpoint of Jesus' resurrection. Belief in that event serves to organize into a coherent whole the content of faith. In that book Scheffczyk does not intend to elaborate as such a justification for belief in the resurrection. All the same, by clarifying all major Christian doctrines in the light of Christ's resurrection and vice versa, he moves toward some kind of coherent totality of meaning which inevitably recommends the truth of the particular claim about the resurrection. Negatively speaking, if the alleged resurrection did not serve coherently such a total pattern of meaning, its plausibility would be severely jeopardized.

The second test, in looking to such coherent meaning, is asking whether the resurrection fits in with "other" beliefs in a pattern which is satisfying, attractive and even beautiful. Early in this chapter I mentioned Newman's conviction about faith being credible to our imagination. In particular, we are enabled to assent to Christ's resurrection because we find that it fits beautifully into a whole pattern of meaning. Beyond doubt, views differ here on whether and to what extent something which is beautiful points to what is true (and good). Keats, Shakespeare and other classic poets have had no difficulty in finding truth in and through beauty. Such modern scientists as theoretical physicists have at times followed suit by postulating, for example, the existence of quarks which satisfying patterns in the world of particles seemed to require. Admittedly repeated experiments can verify the existence of an extra quark, while no such experiments could verify the existence of the risen Christ. Moreover, in the case of the resurrection we deal with the fate of the *crucified* Jesus. To a degree his crucifixion is something cruelly unintelligible, hideously scandalous and absurd (1 Cor 1:23). To put it mildly, the crucifixion cannot be easily fitted into some coherent pattern of meaning. Nevertheless, whether we look at claims about Jesus' resurrection or something else, a beautiful pattern of meaning might well point us to the truth. At all events a lack of such coherence readily jeopardizes claims to truth made in a whole series of areas. The incoherent regularly looks implausible.

A final word on the second test. All major religions and, for that matter, ideologies also use their various teachings to propose a coherent view of the whole. Such a coherence test may be required, but by itself is insufficient to establish the truth of the given claims.

(c) The third test is a matter of historical *witness*. The New Testament records no direct evidence for the very event of the resurrection. It does not maintain that anyone was present to witness this divine intervention. Rather it claims that Jesus was seen alive by individuals and groups (for example, 1 Cor 15:5–8; Luke 24:34) and that his tomb was found to be empty (Mark 16:1–8 par). The implication is clear: this kind of positive (the appearances) and negative (the empty tomb) evidence was available because the resurrection had happened.

Two steps are involved here. First, the assertive propositions ("Jesus appeared alive" and "His tomb was discovered to be empty") correspond to real events in the lives of Peter, Paul, Mary Magdalene and other disciples. Second, the appearances would not have happened without a prior event—the resurrection itself. In the light of the appearances, the discovery of the empty tomb confirmed the event of the resurrection.

In *Jesus* Edward Schillebeeckx challenges this second test for Easter faith by asking: "What would a straight appearance of Jesus in the flesh prove?" (710, n. 119). Presumably Schillebeeckx thinks that nothing would be "proved" by such an event. But surely a bodily appearance of Jesus would at least be presumptive evidence establishing the fact that he lives and hence is risen from the dead?

Much more vigorously than Schillebeeckx David Hume questioned the validity of this second test. In his famous example Hume imagines a story that in 1600 Queen Elizabeth I died and was buried, but after a month appeared alive, resumed the throne and governed her kingdom for three more years before dying again. He would refuse to believe that "so signal a violation of the laws of nature" had taken place and would attribute to "the knavery and folly of men" this story, even though it was attested by the Queen's contemporaries and accepted by "all the historians who treat of England."[4] The example fails, of course, inasmuch as the early Christians never proposed that Jesus had been merely reanimated to resume life under normal human conditions and die once again some time later. But Hume's central point is clear: no amount of evidence and, specifically, no number of alleged appearances of someone who was dead and buried could ever count as a reliable sign that a resurrection had taken place.

Ultimately Hume's difficulty touches my second presupposition— that God can and does intervene in human history. Having denied that such interventions take place, Hume must rule out in advance Christ's resurrection from the dead and the major sign attesting that event, the appearances to individuals and groups of disciples.

This third test is at least partly an issue of correspondence. Do two assertions ("Jesus appeared alive after his death" and "His tomb was discovered to be empty") correspond to actual events in the past? This test clearly touches the value of the Easter witnesses who testified to their experience: "I/We have seen the Lord; his tomb was open and empty." Hence this test must also examine the status of the "authorities" in question.

To begin with, it may be worth noting that most of what we believe we believe on authority anyway. In such fields as the natural sciences and biology we accept innumerable things often simply on the word of the relevant experts. Even research scientists cannot possibly check for themselves the truth of much which they accept; frequently they have to take for granted the results established by others.

At the same time, however, believing in the resurrection means much more than simply accepting from a recognized scientist the results of certain experiments which we cannot repeat for ourselves. It also means much more than merely believing the word of a seemingly reliable witness for an historical event at which we were not personally present. Believing the apostolic witnesses to Jesus' resurrection (i) means accepting the word of persons who encountered the risen Jesus in a special kind of experience which, at least partly, was peculiar to them and hence lies beyond the range of possible experiences which we could simply as such repeat and hence verify for ourselves.[5] It also (ii) involves answering the fundamental question about the nature, meaning and destiny of our own human existence (1 Cor 15).

The quality of conviction exhibited by the Easter witnesses will obviously affect our readiness to trust them when they testify to their special experience of Jesus' living in a new way after his death. It would be difficult, if not impossible, to accept their testimony if they seemed less than fully convinced when either directly (for example 1 Cor 15:8) or indirectly (for example, Luke 24:34) they report their experience: "He appeared to me/us." The Gospels refer to some confusion and hesitation on the occasion of the Easter encounters (for example, Matt 28:17 and Luke 24:36–43). But these are only initial doubts and they trust the evidence of their experience in testifying with complete conviction to Jesus as living and therefore risen from the dead.

From the time of Origen and other Fathers the morally heroic quality of the disciples' lives has been often invoked as evidence that they were utterly convinced, and so radically changed, by their personal experience of the risen Jesus. "By their fruits" they were known to be convinced and truthful witnesses. Thus Saul the persecutor became the missionary to the Gentiles; Peter the broken failure became *the* official witness to the resurrection. In both cases their conviction led them eventually to death by martyrdom.

In substantiating this argument, one would have to establish what counts as moral excellence and heroism. Then we would need to be satisfied that morally heroic lives could not—at least over a long period of time—be supported by some experience which, while deeply moving, was in fact merely a case of subjective hallucination. (It seems most unlikely that deliberate lying about experiences of the risen Christ could have led the disciples to live in new, heroic ways.) Third, one would need to show that the Acts of the Apostles, Paul's letters and other sources allow us to conclude that the Easter witnesses, or at least the ones we have some information about, did truly demonstrate the quality of their conviction and conversion by lives of moral grandeur.

Finally, the force of this third test could be best illustrated by put-

ting it negatively. If the first disciples claimed to have seen the risen
Jesus but continued to lead thoroughly ordinary, unheroic lives, this
would count severely against their testimony. They would be witnessing verbally to an event of unique importance but without exhibiting
anything of that practical commitment which encounters with the risen
Christ could be expected to evoke.

(d) Just as the testimony of the first disciples can be evaluated by
the way they put into practice their encounters with the risen Christ, so
those who hear that testimony later can check it by the way it works out
in *practice* for those who accept its truth. What have been the results for
those who have trusted the word of the Easter witnesses and confessed
Christ's resurrection? What has been the quality of the commitment
produced by this confession? In other words, has the truth of the resurrection genuinely worked and shown up in practice by leading believers into deeper union with God and with one another?

This fourth pragmatic test is *not* a mere appeal to a certain consen-
sus—to the fact that in the course of nearly two thousand years millions
of people have believed in Christ's resurrection. (Many persons have accepted for a long time some very strange things about witchcraft, the
structure of the universe and human conception.) The question is
rather: What testable and valuable differences has belief in the resurrection made to human lives? As we saw in Chapter One, Origen,
Athanasius and other Church Fathers found such social and historical
confirmation for this belief by observing the creatively good effects it
had produced and continued to produce in the life of the Christian
Church. In effect they held that belief in the resurrection vindicated itself in lived experience by transforming the lives of the faithful. The
question then is: Have the lives of those who accepted Christ's resurrection proved (i) deeply satisfying and worthwhile to them, and (ii) productive, even heroically productive, for others?

This fourth test could also take the form of scrutinizing the contemporary life of the Christian community and the wider world for signs
of the risen Christ's activity. Resurrection faith claims not only that "he
rose again" from the dead but also that he has remained actively present
through the power of the Holy Spirit. If this is true, one can properly
expect to find here and now some observable traces of this presence. We
should look then for the public signs of the permanent reality and presence of the risen Lord—for example, in recognizable examples of saint-
liness. Do the personal witness of Christians and their various movements concerned with education, medical care, and work for refugees,
drug addicts, prisoners and the powerless poor reveal any testable and

valuable effects on human lives? Do such effects suggest the living presence of the object of Easter faith, the risen Christ himself?

(e) The fifth test moves from social confirmation for belief in the resurrection to the area of direct, *personal experience*. Does this belief illuminate my present reality, human concerns and future hopes? Does it both successfully reorder my picture of the world and offer me deep and permanent satisfaction in living by its light? This test recognizes that the apostolic testimony to Christ's resurrection will prove credible when that resurrection somehow rings true and is confirmed by my own experience. The question is pragmatic and personal: How does or could the truth of the resurrection show God's purpose for me and prove itself in the practice of my life? What kind of transforming experience might I expect to have from believing the resurrection to be true and relating in new ways to the God who has raised Jesus from the dead?

In looking at the photographs of people in childhood, adulthood and old age, in some cases one notes a deep shift of mood: from expectation to fulfillment, but then on to disappointment. In their own way such a series of photographs raises the question: When and how might we find the ultimate and peaceful fulfillment of our human life? Where might we find not just limited and temporary satisfaction, but deep and lasting happiness? Can such a goal finally come through our own achievement or through Christ's resurrection and the gift it offers, our sharing in his risen life here and hereafter?

The fifth and final test invites us to ask and reflect on such questions. It is only through facing them and pondering our personal experiences and expectations that this test will work.

Such then are five tests which can be used to verify the confession of Christ's resurrection. None of the checks should be isolated as if any of them could serve by itself. Taken together they work cumulatively to validate the proposition "He rose again." The first four tests raise questions which are more historical, public and "from the outside." The fifth test looks for favorable evidence "from the inside" in the ways that resurrection belief correlates "existentially" with my personal experience and expectations.

We need that fifth test, as it seems doubtful that anyone could be satisfied about the reality of Jesus' resurrection simply on the basis of the first four tests alone. That would be tantamount to saying: "Historically speaking, it is highly probable or even certain that Jesus rose from the dead, but I do not wish to be involved or even reflect on how that resurrection might illuminate and change my present life and future hopes." When people refuse to reflect personally and "from the inside" on the claim about Jesus' resurrection, it appears practically impossible to validate this claim for them merely "from the outside."

An anecdote about a well-known agnostic philosopher illustrates negatively this point about the essential role of personal testing and conviction. At the end of a lecture in which he rejected Christ's resurrection he remarked: "After all, it was a long time ago and we may hope it never happened." In a letter a friend of mine commented on the philosopher's closing remark:

> It was possibly meant to be flippant. But it seemed to me that [his] rationalism was suddenly revealed to be just a façade, the argumentation in appearance so impersonal to be just an attempt to justify an emotionally-determined stance.

This chapter has developed five convergent tests to justify believing in Christ's resurrection as a reasonable and responsible act. In Part 3 of his *Summa theologiae* Thomas Aquinas agreed that by themselves no particular reasons will establish the resurrection: "The individual arguments taken alone are not sufficient proof of Christ's resurrection, but taken altogether, in a cumulative way, they manifest it perfectly" (55, 6 ad 1). Aquinas' notion of the cumulative force of the signs and evidence suggests the right approach to legitimating Easter faith. It should also be noted that his talk of "manifesting" the resurrection "perfectly" does not correspond to "demonstrating" it strictly. As Chapter One of this book reported, he denied that arguments could prove the resurrection— in the sense of clearly and rigidly demonstrating it.

I hope these five ways of validating Easter faith may help two classes of people: those who already believe in the risen Jesus but want reassurance, and those who are drawn to examine the belief in resurrection yet feel that it could be an irrational, irresponsible leap in the dark. When I hear such talk about a leap in the dark, I wonder: Why leap? In what direction am I supposed to leap? Faith in the risen Jesus is an intellectually valid choice, as this chapter set out to establish.

At the same time, as I noted at the beginning of the chapter, divine grace and human freedom are essential to the making and living of faith. In believing we are led beyond the convergent signs and evidence to commit ourselves freely to a personal relationship with the risen Jesus. The reasonable tests that justify this faith and its central proposition ("He rose again") give us only a provisional verification. Full verification will come first with our own resurrection.

In proposing ways for examining and establishing reasonable evidence for Christ's resurrection, this chapter has left many relevant issues unexamined. Let me name only two. (i) The resurrection (prepared for by the incarnation) seems to be by far the strongest claim for divine intervention within human history made by any of the great religions. If so, is there a moral obligation to investigate the case for the proposition "He rose again"? Is it morally inexcusable not to do so? How much time should one give to gathering and examining the relevant evidence? What counts as an honest and adequate investigation of the claim about Christ's resurrection? (ii) To what extent is it advisable and even obligatory to consider the claims of other religions about what happened to Jesus (and what will happen to all of us) after death? What signs and evidence can other religions (and ideologies) invoke to back their rival claims?

To conclude. As I agreed at the outset, resurrection faith goes beyond the mere confession "He rose again." Yet it is reasonable to ask how we know that proposition to be true. The five tests I have proposed offer a cumulative set of checks for justifying and validating this confession of Easter faith.

6

The Focus of Revelation

In the bad old days before the Second Vatican Council (1962–1965) the resurrection often got treated as an introduction to Christian apologetics. It proved splendidly Jesus' claim to be a divinely-authorized messenger or else his claim to be the Son of God. But then his resurrection frequently dropped out of sight as theologians systematically articulated Christian beliefs in the Trinity, the Church or whatever else they were treating. The resurrection had done its work as a preliminary proof for Jesus' claims.

This procedure forgot that Jesus' resurrection was and remains ever so much more than a decisive argument for certain claims. It is much more than just a major revealed truth. When properly understood, it is *the* truth about God from which everything else follows. Paul takes Jesus' resurrection (together with ours) to be the specifically Christian way of presenting God. To be wrong about the resurrection is to "misrepresent" God essentially, since Paul defines God as the God of resurrection (1 Cor 15:15). One could not imagine a worse error in religion. It would be bad enough for our faith to be futile and for us to be still in our old state of sin (1 Cor 15:17). But to misrepresent God would be the most extreme religious mistake we could make. What Paul says negatively in 1 Corinthians 15:15 can be aligned with what he often says positively of the God who has raised Jesus and will raise us with him (for example, Gal 1:1; 1 Cor 6:14; 1 Thess 1:9f; 4:14; Rom 8:11; 2 Cor 4:14). Whether positively or negatively, Paul defines the God worshiped by Christians as the God of the resurrection.

From this basic truth everything else follows. Further Christian truths unfold what is implied in the resurrection of the crucified Jesus. Those other doctrines express in different ways and articulate in various areas the one foundational confession, "Jesus has been raised from the dead." What comes earlier and later in the Apostles' Creed can be rightly seen as introducing and unfolding the full sense of the belief "he rose again."

The cross, of course, is the great sign and characteristic of Christianity. Paul sums up his gospel as Christ crucified (1 Cor 1:18–24). Nevertheless, he does not say, "If Christ be not crucified, your faith is futile." Still less does he say, "If Christ be not crucified, we are even found to be misrepresenting God." The crucifixion without its sequel in resurrection would not reveal God, express our salvation and bring into existence the Church. The Preface to the Second Eucharistic Prayer does not stop with the words "for our sake he opened his arms on the cross." It continues: "he put an end to death and revealed the resurrection." In revealing the resurrection—that is to say, in revealing himself as risen from the dead—Christ, so to speak, revealed it all. The revelation of God reached its climax with Easter Sunday and the coming of the Holy Spirit.

Since the divine revelation achieves its purpose in the human faith that it evokes, what has been just said holds true of the faith which responded to the paschal mystery. With the resurrection faith received a new content which was not available before.

Concentrating on the content of what is confessed and believed, this chapter aims to show how the resurrection of the crucified Jesus works as the organizing center for Christian faith. Major beliefs about Christ himself, the Trinity, creation, the Church, the sacraments and other matters are based on the resurrection. Admittedly from the second century on the incarnation has often served to focus beliefs about the person and saving work of Christ, creation (understood as reaching its highpoint in his created humanity), the Church (as the extension of the incarnation) and so forth. Nevertheless, Christianity began with the disciples proclaiming not the incarnation, but the resurrection of the crucified Jesus. They knew themselves to be baptized into his death and resurrection (Rom 6:3ff), and their Eucharist celebrated the death of the risen Lord in the expectation of his final coming (1 Cor 11:23–26). In general, it is obviously consistent with all this to understand the resurrection as the focus and organizing center of Christian beliefs. Yet I can bear better witness to this vision of the resurrection if I show in some detail how it works for central articles of faith about Christ himself, the Trinity, creation, the Church and its sacraments.

CHRISTOLOGY

This resurrection revealed and illuminated Christ's relationship with the God whom he had called "Abba, Father dear." It disclosed that the life of Jesus had been the human life of the Son of God. By his resurrection from the death, Christ was now known to be declared "Son of God" (Rom 1:3–4). Hence for Paul to meet the risen Jesus was to receive a special, personal revelation of the Son that made Paul the great missionary to the Gentiles (Gal 1:16).[1]

Another key title from early Christianity, "Lord," reflected the post-Easter awareness that Christ shared in the divine majesty and being. Romans took up a pre-Pauline formulation which linked salvation with the confession of Jesus' resurrection and lordship: "If you confess with your lips that Jesus is Lord and believe in your heart that God raised him from the dead, you will be saved" (Rom 10:9). In Philippians Paul cited and adapted an early Christian hymn (or hymnic fragments) which called upon everyone in the universe to worship as divine Lord the crucified and exalted Jesus:

. . . he humbled himself and became obedient unto death, even death on a cross. Therefore God has highly exalted him and bestowed on him the name which is above every name, that at the name of Jesus every knee should bow, in heaven and on earth and under the earth, and every tongue confess that Jesus Christ is Lord, to the glory of God the Father (Phil 2:8–11).

Easter stories from the Gospels restate in a narrative form the call to adore the risen Jesus who is now revealed in his divine power and identity. In Matthew's Easter chapter Mary Magdalene and the other Mary leave the tomb, meet Jesus and "worship" him (28:9). Likewise the eleven disciples keep the rendezvous on the mountain in Galilee and they "worship" Jesus when they see him (Matt 28:17). According to the last Gospel, it is only in the Easter situation that anyone acknowledges Jesus in the terms adopted by Thomas, "My Lord and my God" (John 20:28). It took the resurrection to reveal that Jesus should be identified and worshiped as divine Lord.[2]

THE TRINITY

The essence of Christian faith entails accepting as true the good news that in the power of the Spirit the incarnate and crucified Son of

God has risen from the dead. Thus the doctrine of the Trinity points to and gathers up the self-revelation of God communicated through Christ's resurrection (understood in the light of the "prior" mysteries of creation, call of the Jewish people, incarnation and crucifixion, and the "posterior" mysteries of Pentecost and the eschaton).[3]

Mark recalls a kind of appearance of the Trinity at Jesus' baptism. The Spirit descended "upon him like a dove; and a voice came from heaven, 'Thou art my beloved Son; with thee I am well pleased' " (Mark 1:10f; par). At the resurrection the tripersonal God did not "appear" in any such way, and yet was revealed. Let us see some details.

(1) *The "Economic" Trinity.* Pre-Pauline formulations understood "God" (for example, Rom 10:9) or "God the Father" (for example, Gal 1:1) to have raised Jesus from the dead. The post-exaltation worship of Jesus as divine Lord takes place "to the glory of God the Father" (Phil 2:11), while the Holy Spirit makes it possible for men and women to acclaim Jesus as divine Lord (1 Cor 12:3).

Since Paul does not fully and clearly distinguish between the risen Christ and the Holy Spirit (see, for example, 2 Cor 3:17; Rom 8:9–11), he nowhere as such says that Christ sent or sends the Spirit. Luke and even more John draw a clearer distinction between the risen Christ and the Spirit. Hence they can speak of the risen Christ sending the Spirit as the Father's promised gift (Luke 24:49) or "breathing" on the disciples and giving them the Holy Spirit (John 20:22).

First-century Christians proposed thus a Trinitarian interpretation of the events of Good Friday and Easter Sunday. In those events they experienced the climactic revelation of God. That revelation had something threefold about it, as Peter's address at Pentecost emphatically appreciates:

> This Jesus God raised up, and of that we all are witnesses. Being therefore exalted at the right hand of God, and having received from the Father the promise of the Holy Spirit, he has poured out this which you see and hear (Acts 2:32f).

Undoubtedly we should be careful not to be anachronistic here. Christians had to pursue matters for several centuries before they could come to a clearer position on the divinity of Christ and the personal identity of the Holy Spirit. All the same, we find at the origin of Christianity a certain sense that the Father, Son and Holy Spirit were revealed as acting in our human history, above all in the events of Good Friday, Easter Sunday and their aftermath. The fully deployed doctrine of the Trinity can be correctly understood to be the developed interpretation of the triune interpretation of the paschal mystery.

To use the technical expression, this encourages us to begin with the "economic" Trinity, the triune God actively disclosed in the history Jesus enacted through his life, death and new life as risen from the grave. So often models of the Trinity have been drawn directly from creation and general human experience in the attempt to say something of the "immanent" Trinity—that is, of the Father, Son and Spirit in their eternal life.

(2) *The "Immanent" Trinity.*   From the time of Augustine there have been various attractive models of the immanent Trinity. Augustine drew on Tertullian to compare the two "processes" of the eternal divine life (which later got called "Filiation" and "Spiration") with human self-knowledge and self-love. The Father generates the Son as an act of thinking, while the Holy Spirit is the mutual love of Father and Son.

Bernard of Clairvaux at times used only the analogy of mutual love when speaking of the Trinity. In the eternal life of God there is the One who kisses, the One kissed and the Kiss, or the One who embraces, the One embraced and the Embrace. This image drawn from mutual love falters. Despite Bernard's orthodox intentions, it might insinuate only two persons in God.

In his reflections on the nature of love Richard of St. Victor (d. 1173) did better in showing how perfect love "demands" the existence of three persons in God. Perfect mutual love is so strong and secure that it does not jealously exclude a third party. In fact, the love of two persons for each other could not reach perfection unless each was willing to share that love with a third person. The lover not only loves the beloved as a second self but also wants the beloved to have the happiness of loving and being loved by yet another person. On this analogy one can picture the movement of love within the Trinity as follows: it proceeds from the Father's love for himself (*self-love*) through *mutual love* between the Father and the Son to the *shared love* of the Father and the Son for the Spirit.

Modern times have brought further images for portraying the eternal life of the Trinity. C.G. Jung (1875–1961), for example, drew on the human experience of psychological growth. In the child's state of consciousness the Father is the authority-figure who provides a ready-made pattern of existence, the parent to whose laws one submits. The Son is represented by the process of self-individuation and self-assertion when a growing human being seeks autonomy. The third phase, when an individual surrenders independence to share in some larger reality, symbolizes the Spirit.

Further threefold patterns of common human experience have been pressed into service. Indian thought contributes the triad: being, awareness of being and enjoyment of being. The personalist philosophy of Martin Buber and others has offered theologians the language of "I, Thou and We" when speaking about the ultimate relational reality of God.

A scheme drawn from the work of K. Graf Dürckheim has made me see something of the triune God as Life (the Father), Meaning (the Son) and Love (the Holy Spirit). In dramatic and less dramatic situations human beings can feel threatened by death in its various forms. They can be overwhelmed by a sense of injustice and meaningless absurdity. They can be abandoned, cruelly treated and hated. Then they can be given life, they can experience a deeper meaning and order in things, and they can know themselves to be the object of loving goodness. These experiences can make people long even more for some experience of life, meaning and love which will change everything. These experiences and longings point, I believe, to a God who is total Life, Meaning and Love. This view of the Trinity may be more compelling in a world which in some ways seems to be becoming more deadly, more absurd and more cruel.

All these images of the tripersonal God—that come, respectively, from human knowing and/or loving, psychological development, a philosophy of being, the language of community and the human experience of life, meaning and love—offer help, sometimes considerable help, toward portraying analogically the immanent Trinity. But they are all taken from created reality and general human experience, and not immediately rooted in that history of God's revealing and saving communication which came to its climax with the dying and rising of Jesus Christ. Christian reflection on God begins with the economic Trinity, the story which revealed the Father, Son and Holy Spirit. Only then can it move to think of the eternal existence of the immanent Trinity. Here, as elsewhere, history and thinking about history enjoys precedence over creation and thought based on created realities.

The special history of God's self-communication reached its peak with the events of Good Friday and Easter Sunday. The paschal mystery revealed God as the Giver, the Given and the Self-giving. For us all and for our salvation the Father gave up the Son (Rom 8:32). The Son was given up (1 Cor 11:23) or gave himself up (Gal 2:20). The Spirit, who personifies the process of Self-giving, gave Christ the new life of resurrection in which we too can share (Rom 8:11). To put things thus is to recover a sense of how the original Christian belief in the tripersonal God was clearly based on the resurrection of the crucified Jesus.

Whenever Christians make the sign of the cross "in the name of the Father, and of the Son and of the Holy Spirit," their invocation and gesture are associating belief in the Trinity with the paschal mystery. Even without realizing it, they are linking their faith in the tripersonal God with the events of Good Friday and Easter Sunday.

CREATION

In dealing with belief in the Trinity I have joined those who protest against the long-standing habit of moving away from history and collapsing the discussion into points for and against models of the immanent Trinity derived from created reality and the common experiences of human beings. What of a material creation and the whole cosmos? Does the resurrection illuminate or even focus belief about the nature and destiny not only of human beings but also of the entire material environment in which they live?

(1) *The Future of Creation.* The New Testament enshrines the conviction that the material world *will* share in the glorious destiny which Christ's resurrection promises to all men and women. This seems a plausible connection to make, seeing that here and now human beings belong essentially in a material environment. In the next chapter I plan to say something about our future, risen life. At this point let me only suggest that if our resurrection were to take us completely and utterly out of any kind of material environment, it is hard to see how that would be a bodily resurrection for us human beings. It would seem much more like an immortal existence for souls. In short, if there is to be resurrection for human beings, one should expect that somehow material creation will participate in that resurrection, the culmination of the new creation.

Paul writes of the created universe eagerly expecting the end. This is a vision of hope for human beings *and* their universe:

> The creation itself will be set free from its bondage to decay and obtain the glorious liberty of the children of God. We know that the whole creation has been groaning in travail together until now; and not only the creation, but we ourselves, who have the first fruits of the Spirit, groan inwardly as we wait for adoption as sons, the redemption of our bodies (Rom 8:21–23).

Its apocalyptic genre makes the Book of Revelation more exuberant than the letters of Paul. But its visions of the end express the same promise: our final life with God does not involve the elimination of our material environment, but rather "a new heaven and a new earth" (Rev 21:1; see 2 Pet 3:13). The new creation will bring a transformation of our cosmos.

How such a transformation will occur and what form it will take remains elusively mysterious. Nevertheless, nowadays it seems more credible to hold that the material universe will somehow share in the glorious destiny of human beings. The exploitation of our environment, pollution of our atmosphere and the advanced preparations for the nuclear annihilation of the human race have heightened the common awareness that for good or ill the fate of human beings and their universe—or at least our little corner of the material universe—are and will remain inseparably linked. Quite visibly human greed damages material creation and in that sense alienates it from God. Since our environment shares in the human condition of alienation from God, one can plausibly hope that it will share too in the final transformation of resurrection.

(2) *Present Creation.*   What is much harder to grasp and accept is that the resurrection has *already* changed the material world. Yet certain Church Fathers like Gregory of Nyssa and Ambrose make such a claim. In *De excessu fratris sui* Ambrose professes this belief: "In Christ the world has risen, heaven has risen, the earth has risen" (I, 2; PL 16, 1344). A similar cosmic picture of the reconciling impact of Christ's crucifixion and resurrection is found in Colossians. "All things in heaven and on earth" were not only first created "through" and "for" the Son, but also "reconciled" to God through the crucifixion and resurrection of the Son (1:15–20). Can one point to any differences that Christ's resurrection has made in the material universe? Are there any traces of this change which could help to validate the claims made by Ambrose, Gregory of Nyssa and the New Testament itself? The last chapter appealed to signs of Christ's resurrection in human beings and their relationships. Already this resurrection and faith in the risen Christ have left traces in the transformed lives and communities of believers. But can we detect any such analogous changes in the material world? How might one justify Ambrose in asserting not merely that in Christ the world will rise but that "in Christ the world has risen"?

A full answer here would linger on three items: physical miracles, the sacramental life of the Church, and the responsibility some Christians take for our material environment.

First, miracles. In listing his credentials as an authentic apostle,

Paul adds the signs, marvels and miracles that attended his missionary activity (2 Cor 12:12). These deeds which include but go beyond physical miracles were made possible through the power of the crucified and risen Christ (2 Cor 12:9f; 13:4). Miraculous events involving the material world can be one way the risen Lord makes his power felt even now.[4]

The sacramental life of the Church came into being with the resurrection of Christ. It uses material elements like water and oil and takes them in a new direction, investing these visible signs with the power to communicate a share in the life of the risen Lord. The Eucharist provides the supreme instance of how the resurrection has already changed the created world. The Eucharist lifts matter to a new level, spiritualizing and "christifying" it when bread and wine are transformed into the glorified body and being of the risen Christ. What happens here points ahead to the final state of the material universe when it will be publicly and fully under the risen power of the Lord.

Lastly, some and perhaps even many Christians have realized and acted upon the new dignity Christ's resurrection has given the material universe. Through the conscious collaboration of scientists, artists, farmers and environmentalists the resurrection has also left some observable traces on the material universe. Harvest festivals express not only our gratitude for blessings received but also the desire to act as responsible stewards toward a world graced by the resurrection of Christ.

(3) *Past, Present and Future.* Let me sum up three major ways in which Easter faith has modified and illuminated belief in the "Creator of heaven and earth." First, his resurrection led early Christians to acknowledge the pre-existent Christ as the agent of the world's creation, a role attributed by Jewish theology to the divine word and wisdom: "All things were created through him . . . and in him all things hold together" (Col 1:16f; see John 1:1–4; Heb 1:3; 1 Cor 1:24; 8:6). Despite their different nuances, these texts point to the same pre-existent Son through whom the world was created. They identify the Christ who died and rose as the agent of all creation.

Here and now through the risen Lord the created world has already been changed in anticipation of the end. One can validate Ambrose's view of what the resurrection has done to our material environment: "In Christ the world has risen, heaven has risen, the earth has risen." At the end the universe will share in the transforming power of the Lord's resurrection. The image of the "new heaven and new earth" expresses the last state to which our whole material environment will be called home.

As its final consummation that new creation reveals the point and purpose of what God did in creating "heaven and earth" (Gen 1:1).[5]

THE CHURCH

The resurrection of Christ gathered into the final community of faith those who live their lives in expectation of the consummation of God's kingdom. Apart from the resurrection one cannot rightly understand the origin and life of the Church, the community created through the crucified and risen Jesus. Neither the life of Jesus nor even his death by itself was enough to bring the Church into existence. John's image of the blood and water issuing from the crucified Christ (19:34–37) inspired a patristic tradition (which has lasted down to Sebastian Tromp, Pius XII's 1943 encyclical *Mystici Corporis Christi* [nr. 29], Hans Urs von Balthasar and Jürgen Moltmann) about the Church being born from the wounded side of Christ.[6]

Without collapsing one event into the other, John's Gospel links closely the crucifixion and resurrection. After his death but before his resurrection Jesus is pierced with a spear; blood and water flow from his side. The attentive reader should remember Jesus' words during the Feast of Tabernacles:

> On the last day of the feast, the great day, Jesus stood up and proclaimed, "If anyone thirst, let him come to me, and let him who believes in me drink. As the scripture has said, 'Out of his heart shall flow rivers of living water.' " Now this he said about the Spirit, which those who believed in him were to receive; for as yet the Spirit had not yet been given, because Jesus was not yet glorified (John 7:37–39).

The gift of the Spirit in and through the paschal mystery finally brought to life the Easter community of those who commit themselves to the crucified and risen Jesus.

The Church became and remains the place of the special presence of the risen Lord. There the promise is realized: "I am with you always, to the close of the age" (Matt 28:20; see 18:20). It is not that he is absent from other places and persons (see, for example, Matt 25:35–40). But it is in the Church and its life of prayer that the presence of the risen Jesus is most vividly experienced and acknowledged—above all at the Lord's Supper (1 Cor 10:14–22; 11:20, 23–26). There through the power of the

Spirit believers acclaim the risen and exalted Jesus as divine Lord (1 Cor 12:3; see Phil 2:11).

The paschal mystery elucidates not only the origin and ongoing life of the Church but also its function as sign and witness to all the human race. During his earthly existence Jesus was the visible sign and living symbol of his Father—a theme classically expressed by Jesus' words to Philip, "He who has seen me has seen the Father" (John 14:9). With his death and resurrection Jesus himself is no longer directly seen. His community comes fully into being as the visible, living sign of his saving intentions for all men and women of all times and places. For all their sinful failures, Christians are strengthened by the Holy Spirit to be the special sign for the whole world of the risen Lord's presence and powerful love.

SACRAMENTS

Here again one should cry out against any approach to the Church's sacraments which drifts away from the paschal mystery. Neither the life of Jesus nor his death was enough to set going the sacramental life of the Church.

Given the way the resurrection grounded and focused baptism, Matthew naturally associates the baptismal formula "in the name of the Father, and of the Son, and of the Holy Spirit" (Matt 28:19) with the solemn appearance of the risen Jesus with which the Gospel closes. Neophytes enter this community by being baptized into the crucified and risen Christ (Rom 6:3–12; Gal 3:27). They are "born anew" through their baptismal sharing in "the resurrection of Jesus Christ from the dead" (1 Pet 1:3). On the occasion of being baptized they confess their faith in Jesus as risen from the dead (Rom 10:9; see 1 Cor 15:1–11). Their new life means existing "in" the risen Christ, the inclusive figure into whom believers know themselves to be incorporated (for example, Rom 8:1; 16:7; 1 Cor 15:22; Phil 3:8f).

By being spiritually washed from sin and made alive to God at baptism, individual Christians form a single body with the risen Christ (1 Cor 12:12–13), and are engrafted into the very life of the glorified Son of God (John 15:5). Both these images—the head with its members, and the vine with its branches—imply that by means of baptism the unifying force of divine life and love, the Holy Spirit, flows not only through the risen Lord of the *ecclesia* but also through those who enter into the ecclesial community. Furthermore, since Christ and his Father are one

(John 14:9–10), those who are rejuvenated with water and anointed with the Spirit also share in the being of the Father.

Baptism, however, means more than passively participating in the existence of the risen Christ who was exalted by the Spirit of the Father (1 Pet 3:18). Whereas the "indicative" of Christian faith claims that the baptized share in a new way of being, the "imperative" of Christian faith challenges the baptized to share in God's salvific mission in history. How can we best describe what this mission entails? When we say that Jesus was raised up, we mean that his entire life and ministry were vindicated or justified by the Spirit of the Father (1 Tim 3:17). Jesus has allowed himself to be purified by John the Baptist, "for thus it is fitting for us to fulfill all righteousness" (Matt 3:15), preached the righteousness of the kingdom, and led a totally just life from his first baptism at the Jordan to his final baptism on Calvary (Mark 10:38–39). For this reason, Christians who are baptized by the Spirit of the risen Christ are to walk in the Spirit of the just Jesus (Gal 5:25). Baptismal grace enables Christians to be for others sacraments of the invincible justice won by the glorified Jesus. Being baptized into the resurrection of the crucified Christ therefore necessitates translating the interior renewal granted by the sacrament into social action on behalf of all humanity (which is in principle already liberated from injustice by the paschal mystery).

As for the Eucharist the disciples would never have begun "doing this in remembrance of the Lord Jesus" if he had not risen from the dead. Paul and the Synoptic Gospels report the origin of the Eucharist "on the night" when "the Lord Jesus was betrayed" (1 Cor 11:23)—that is to say, just before the events of the crucifixion and resurrection took place. John expressly links the Eucharist and our participation in Christ's resurrection: "He who eats my flesh and drinks my blood has eternal life and I will raise him up at the last day" (John 6:54). In the Eucharist Christians receive the risen Lord and through him they too will move to resurrection. In this direct way the Eucharist and the resurrection illuminate each other. The resurrection of the crucified Jesus has already taken place. Through visible signs the Eucharist makes powerfully present that resurrection which will fully come to human beings and their world.

Yet the Eucharist renders the resurrection present in an even fuller sense when Christians recognize the risen Jesus not only in his sacramental body on the altar but also in his ecclesial body gathered in prayer. For the Eucharist, as transubstantiated bread and wine, cannot be properly understood apart from the transfigured body of Jesus in heaven mystically united to the community of Christian worshipers. Hence Paul castigated those Corinthians who limited their encounter with the glorified Jesus to the reception of his sacramental body without also receiving him in the poor and hungry members of his ecclesial body. The words "without discerning the body" (1 Cor 11:29) have therefore two meanings: we can fail to perceive the risen Jesus either in the transformed elements or in those who have nothing to eat. At the back of this Pauline insight was the scandalous table-fellowship which Jesus offered to sinners during his lifetime (Luke 5:27–32). The risen Lord is the same one who once sat at table with harlots, publicans and other notorious outcasts so as to give himself to them by pardoning their sins, nourishing their broken bodies and spirits, and transforming their alienation into companionship; Jesus made them "bread-sharers" with each other and with the Father. Likewise, belief that the risen Lord is present in the Eucharist challenges Christians living in an egocentric society to prophetic acts of solidarity. These are based on the fact that the words "Take and eat" (Matt 26:26) spoken in the Upper Room can be properly joined to those of the final judgment scene, "I was hungry and you gave me food" (Matt 25:35). Just as at baptism the Spirit engrafts Christians into Christ the vine so that they can bear the fruit of justice, so at the Eucharist the Spirit unites Christians to Christ the bread of life so that they can produce the fruit of love (John 15:18). Christians who communicate with and act in the name of the risen Jesus, who in the flesh poured himself out for others, already participate in his resurrection, and look to the day when he will raise them and the cosmos to share unendingly in his life and glory.

Further, we might usefully note how the risen Christ exercises a primary ministry in and through all the sacraments. Whenever the sacraments are administered, the risen Christ is personally and effectively present. In his commentary on John's Gospel (tr. 6, 7) Augustine summed up this sacramental ministry of the risen Lord: "When Peter baptizes it is Christ who baptizes. When Paul baptizes, it is Christ who baptizes" (PL 35, 1428). With its talk about sacraments as personal encounters with Christ, modern theology has restated the Augustinian principle in a new form. In his 1979 encyclical *Redemptor hominis* John Paul II applies this language to the Eucharist and even more successfully to the encounter with the crucified and risen Savior realized through the sacrament of reconciliation (nr. 20).

In fact, all the other sacraments which have not been explicitly mentioned thus far are also means of participating in the person and mission of the risen Christ. At confirmation, those who were once baptized into the priestly people of God share more fully in Christ the high priest and are to assume a more active role in his mission of realizing God's kingdom. Through the anointing of the sick, Christians who are weak or at the point of death are more deeply united with the crucified and exalted Jesus, and along with the whole Church witness to his unending compassion and healing power. The vocational sacraments of orders and marriage link ordained and married persons to the glorified bridegroom who cherishes his bride the Church (Eph 5:29), and commission them to build up the domestic and local Christian communities in anticipation of the eternal wedding feast.

This chapter has only sketched the case for founding and focusing through the resurrection of the crucified Jesus those major doctrines which make up the content of Christian faith. To develop this case satisfactorily and establish that particular beliefs about Christ, the Trinity, creation, the Church, its sacraments and so forth interpret and articulate the basic Easter confession, one would need to write at least one large volume. Let me conclude the case for such a resurrection perspective by selecting an area within ecclesiology, the Petrine and Papal ministry, and arguing that this ministry is best understood and interpreted from that perspective.

PETER AS EASTER WITNESS

In interpreting the Petrine ministry and the papal office many theologians and others have commonly and consistently passed over a highly significant historical datum: the priority of Peter among the first official witnesses to the risen Lord. Yet this theme of Petrine witness to the resurrection can throw much light on the problems and procedures—both for those who maximalize the Petrine and papal ministries and for those who have minimalized them.

(1) *"The" Easter Witness.* Among those disciples who officially and authoritatively proclaimed Jesus' resurrection, Peter was the primary witness. Of course, John reports Mary Magdalene to be the first one to whom the risen Lord appeared. She brought the good news to the disciples: "I have seen the Lord" (John 20:14–18). According to another Gospel, Mary Magdalene and "the other Mary" met Jesus as they returned from discovering the empty tomb (Matt 28:9f). This brief encounter is the first appearance of the risen Christ recorded by Matthew. In these two Gospels the risen Lord himself (John 20:17; Matt 28:10) and an angel (Matt 28:7) told the two women (Matthew) or simply Mary Magdalene (John) to bring the news of the resurrection to the male disciples.

All four Gospels report how women discovered Jesus' tomb to be empty. In three Gospels an angel (Mark and Matthew) or two angels (Luke) explain why the corpse is missing: "He has risen" (Mark 16:6; Matt 28:6); "Why do you seek the living among the dead?" (Luke 24:5).

As messengers of the resurrection Mary Magdalene and other female disciples belonged to the core group which set the Church going. One could well speak of them as the "founding mothers" alongside the "founding fathers" of the Christian community. Nevertheless, it was Peter who took the primary role as official proclaimer of the Lord's resurrection. In that sense I wish to refer to his priority as Easter witness. But what is the evidence for this claim?

The list of resurrection witnesses in 1 Corinthians places first Christ's appearance to Peter: "He appeared to Cephas, then to the Twelve" (1 Cor 15:5). We should note that at this point in his letter Paul is quoting an early credal formulation which—according to reliable scholarship—dates from the first decade of Christianity.

Luke confirms this priority of Peter as Easter witness in a similar formulation which he derives from early Christian sources and introduces at the end of the Emmaus story: "The Lord has risen indeed, and has appeared to Simon" (Luke 24:34). Seemingly Luke inserts this item to head off any impression that the Emmaus appearance is the primary one. Even before Cleopas and his companion return, Peter's testimony has brought to Easter-faith "the Eleven" and "those who were with them" (Luke 24:33). The report from Emmaus and the later appearances of the Lord strengthen this faith, but do not create it for the first time.

Luke has prepared his readers for this role of Peter as the agent of faith in the resurrection. At the Last Supper Jesus warns that Peter will break down and deny him, but promises: "For you I have prayed that your faith may not fail; and when you have come to yourself, you must lend strength to your brothers" (Luke 22:32). The primary appearance of the risen Lord to Peter enables the apostle to play just that role. He comes to himself and strengthens his brethren in the power of his Easter-faith.

In Acts 1–12 Luke follows this up by reporting how Peter functions as the primary witness to the Lord's resurrection. Right from the day of Pentecost Peter acts as head of a college of Easter witnesses in announcing the good news: "This Jesus . . . you crucified and killed by the hands of lawless men. But God raised him up" (Acts 2:23f).

To be sure, Peter has other important things to do. He plays a decisive role in admitting Gentiles into the Christian community (Acts 10–11:8). Later Paul, Barnabas and James join him at the Council of Jerusalem to decide authoritatively against imposing on Gentile converts the obligation to observe the Jewish law (Acts 15:1–29). Peter and John lay hands on believers to bring them the gift of the Holy Spirit (Acts 8:14–17). Peter works miracles by healing the sick (Acts 3:1–11; 5:15f) and even bringing back to life a dead woman (Acts 9:32–43).

The first half of Acts presents various dimensions of the leadership role which Peter exercised in the life of the early Church. But the heart of the matter was his pre-eminence among the official witnesses to the resurrection of Jesus Christ (Acts 3:13–15; 4:10; 5:30–32; etc.).[7]

Mark's Gospel hints at the priority of Peter as Easter witness when the angel instructs the three women: "Go, tell the disciples and Peter that he is going before you to Galilee; there you will see him" (Mark 16:7). Here the Gospel reaches its climax neither with the discovery of the empty tomb nor even with the angel's announcement of the resurrection, but with the command to pass on the good news to "the disciples and Peter." Only Peter gets singled out for mention by name. Many scholars believe that this naming of Peter refers to that primary appearance of the risen Lord reported by 1 Corinthians 15:5 and Luke 24:34.

John's Gospel, albeit with modifications, also reflects Peter's status as primary witness to the Lord's resurrection. When Mary Magdalene discovers the empty tomb, she runs to inform "Simon Peter and the other disciple, the one whom Jesus loved." They both visit and inspect the grave (John 20:1–10). The appendix to the Fourth Gospel (Chapter 21) acknowledges Peter's function as resurrection witness and the pastoral role he receives from the risen Lord. Peter has taken six others out for a night's fishing. Dawn brings an encounter with the Lord on the shore. After breakfast Christ commissions Peter to feed his "lambs" and "sheep." Here Peter is established as shepherd of his Lord's flock on the far side of the resurrection.

Both Chapters 20 and 21 of John modify somewhat the place of Peter as primary Easter witness. In the race to the empty tomb the beloved disciple both outruns Peter and comes to believe, when he enters the tomb and sees the grave cloths tidily arranged. It looks here as if John's Gospel wants to represent the beloved disciple as first to believe. Chapter 21 likewise qualifies Peter's prominence as resurrection witness. The beloved disciple recognizes the stranger on the beach, even if it is Peter who flings himself into the water and gets ashore first to meet the risen Christ. The same beloved disciple will outlive Peter to continue the Easter testimony till the end of the apostolic age (John 21:18ff).

Nevertheless, Peter's priority as Easter witness remains substantially unchallenged in Chapter 21 of John. Moreover, in Chapter 20 a hint of deference toward this role of his can be spotted when the beloved disciple waits for Peter before entering the empty grave (John 20:3ff).

All in all, those last two chapters of John's Gospel do not intend to cut down Peter's role as Easter witness. Rather, his authority works to enhance respect for the beloved disciple who is present alongside him.

To sum up. On the basis of the New Testament evidence a broad range of scholars, Anglican, Catholic, Orthodox and Protestant, agree about Peter's leadership role in the early Church being associated with his pre-eminence as witness to the resurrection. And they do so, even though no detailed account of the appearance of the risen Christ to Peter alone has survived, unless one finds it in a masked form in various stories: the transfiguration (Mark 9:2–8 and par), the walking on the water (Matt 14:28–31), the miraculous catch of fish (Luke 5:3–11; [?] John 21:1–14), or the commissioning of Peter as head of the Church (Matt 16:17–19; John 21:15–19). Nuances differ and some scholars assign more weight to this conclusion. Yet I do not know any contemporary New Testament exegete who denies the special position of Peter among the official witnesses to the risen Lord.[8] *Peter in the New Testament* (New York, 1973; London, 1974), a study sponsored by the United States Lutheran-Roman Catholic Dialogue, speaks of "the important tradition about Peter having been the first of the major companions of Jesus' ministry to have seen the Lord after the resurrection." It concludes that "it is very likely that such a tradition provided the original context or catalyst for much of the New Testament material about Peter" (165). Unfortunately his priority as Easter witness then gets tucked away with the theme (developed in Christian apocryphal literature) of Peter as "the receiver of special revelation" (162ff). Nevertheless, *Peter in the New Testament* testifies to the basic datum: Peter had a primary role in witnessing to the Lord's resurrection.

(2) *Peter during Jesus' Ministry.* Of course, the position and ministry of Simon Peter in the emerging Church did not simply rest on the risen Christ's appearance to him. As normally happens in God's dealings with human beings, other factors were involved. We should not isolate the encounter with the risen Lord from earlier aspects of Peter's vocation and history. Let me fill this out.

Peter's priority as first Easter witness among the Twelve should not be taken by itself, as if this impressive and awesome fact *alone* accounted for his prominence in the emerging Church. The weight which Peter's witness to the risen Christ carried depended partly on his prior standing among the Twelve. What then was his position during the ministry of Jesus?

In answering this question, incidentally, we must not forget that even the Synoptic Gospels do not simply recall data from the personal history of Peter. They also use the figure of Peter to foster, interpret and symbolize Christian faith. At his own (secondary) level the Peter of the Synoptics, a little like Jesus himself, also blends historical reminiscence with the reflections of faith. Having allowed for all this, what do we find the Gospels reporting about Peter from the period of Jesus' ministry?

Peter always gets mentioned first among the Twelve (Mark 3:16) and among the smaller circle of three (Peter, James and John). Jesus takes those three with him on such special occasions as the raising of Jairus' daughter (Mark 5:37), the transfiguration (Mark 9:2–8) and the agony in the garden (Mark 14:33). Peter, James and John are the chosen witnesses of those events.

Luke reports how Jesus used Peter's boat as a platform from which to teach the people on the shore of the lake. When he had finished teaching, Jesus directed Peter to make a miraculous catch of fish. Peter was astonished at the result and "fell down at Jesus' knees, saying, 'Depart from me, for I am a sinful man, O Lord.' " But Jesus assured him and his partners, James and John: "Do not be afraid; henceforth you will be catching men" (Luke 5:1–11).

The Gospels also tell that Jesus gave Simon the name "Peter" or "Cephas"—that is to say, "rock." Matthew associates this naming with an extraordinarily important episode at Caesarea Philippi. There Peter acted as spokesman for the others and confessed Jesus to be the long-awaited Messiah or deliverer of his people (Matt 16:13–16). Jesus reacted by promising to make Simon Peter the foundation on which the new community of God would be built.

> You are Peter, the Rock; and on this rock I will build my church, and the powers of death shall never conquer it. I will give you the keys of the kingdom of heaven; what you forbid on earth shall be forbidden in heaven, and what you allow on earth shall be allowed in heaven (Matt 16:18f).

This promise expressed in Caesarea Philippi is matched by the risen Christ's commission to "feed the sheep" (John 21:15–17). That charge to shepherd the Lord's flock fulfills the promise of an authoritative leadership role made during the ministry.

(3) *Peter and the Other Apostles.* Although Peter was *the* witness to the resurrection, he was *not* the only witness. The traditional kerygma of the early Church appealed to further witnesses besides Peter. Others—

both individuals and groups—confirmed the truth of Christ's resurrection from the dead. The listing of various witnesses in 1 Corinthians 15:5–8 could have been partly prompted by the fact that, given the Jewish requirement of at least two independent witnesses, the other witnesses to the risen Christ were needed and in fact were available. At all events the risen Lord appeared also to others who were to propagate and guide the emerging Church. These other key leaders included not only the rest of the Twelve—whom Luke more accurately calls the Eleven after Judas' defection (Luke 24:33)—but also Paul.

All these apostles shared the responsibility of spreading the good news and caring for Christ's community. We have seen how the commission to Peter in Matthew 16:19 covered the task of "forbidding and allowing" or "binding and loosing." But the same expression is used two chapters later in the promise made to the disciples in general: "Whatever you forbid on earth shall be forbidden in heaven, and whatever you allow on earth shall be allowed in heaven" (Matt 18:18).

Likewise, although Matthew 16:18 singles out Peter as the rock upon which Christ's Church is to stand, elsewhere the New Testament calls *all* the apostles the foundation upon which the same Church is built (Eph 2:20). Peter is not to be isolated from these other leaders in their "foundational" function.

We have seen how at Pentecost and later Peter acted as spokesman in preaching the good news of the resurrection (Acts 2:14ff). When he did this, however, Peter "stood *with the eleven*" (Acts 2:14) and announced a resurrection of which "*we* are witnesses" (Acts 3:15). He spoke for and with a college or official group of Easter witnesses.

Moreover, the Book of Acts begins by telling us that the risen Lord had commissioned *all* the apostles to proclaim the good news to the entire world:

> You shall receive power when the Holy Spirit has come upon you; and you shall be my witnesses in Jerusalem, in all Judaea and Samaria, and to the ends of the earth (Acts 1:8).

Furthermore, the second half of Acts focuses on the leadership and apostolic authority of St. Paul. The meeting with the risen Christ on the Damascus road turned the persecutor Saul into the apostle Paul. Even if he was not one of the Twelve, Paul exercised a leadership role with an authority received directly from the risen Christ: "Am I not an apostle? Did I not see Jesus our Lord?" (1 Cor 9:1; see 15:8ff).

To be sure, Paul recognized the special position of Peter among the apostles. He recalled visiting Jerusalem with the express intention of getting to know Peter (Gal 1:18). According to Acts 15, Paul accepted the lead given by Peter at the Council of Jerusalem.

Nevertheless, Paul claimed to share with Peter parallel responsibility and apostolic authority. The leaders of the mother church in Jerusalem had recognized Paul's special mission to the Gentiles alongside Peter's special mission to the Jews:

> They acknowledged that I had been entrusted with the Gospel for Gentiles as surely as Peter had been entrusted with the Gospel for Jews. For God whose action made Peter an apostle to the Jews, also made me an apostle to the Gentiles (Gal 2:7f).

Undoubtedly, when dealing with the place and function of Peter in the early Church, we can succumb to the common temptation to decide what we like or dislike and then rustle up the evidence. I can put this point more solemnly. In evaluating the Petrine ministry we can easily slip into imposing on the New Testament material our own convictions as Anglicans, Roman Catholics, Orthodox, Protestants or whatever.

At the same time, however, at least two conclusions come through and are supported by reliable New Testament scholars. First, Peter held a special leadership role in the early Church, and this was associated not only with his function as *the* Easter witness but also with the position he had already enjoyed during Jesus' ministry. Second, the prominent role to which Peter had been called did not isolate him from Paul and the other apostles. Like them Peter was to exercise his leadership in the spirit of service, not domination:

> In the world, kings lord it over their subjects; and those in authority are called their country's "benefactors." Not so with you: on the contrary, the highest among you must bear himself like the youngest, the chief of you like a servant (Luke 22:25f).

(4) *The Shadow Side.* We have seen how the New Testament provides a general picture of Peter's prominence. He played a clear role of leadership through spreading faith in the risen Christ, opening the Christian community to Gentiles and overcoming threats to the unity of the Church (see, for example, Acts 11:4ff).

Nevertheless, we should not pass over the shadow side of things. From the outset human weakness affected the way Peter followed his special calling. Matthew reports how he started walking across the water, but became afraid, began to sink and had to be rescued. Jesus rebuked Peter: "O man of little faith, why did you doubt?" (Matt 14:31).

At Caesarea Philippi Peter confessed Jesus to be the Messiah, but could not accept that this entailed rejection, suffering and death. In the presence of the other disciples Jesus had to rebuke Peter severely: "Away with you, Satan; you think as men think, not as God thinks" (Mark 8:33).

After Jesus was arrested, Simon Peter followed him at a distance and went into the high priest's courtyard. There Peter three times denied his Master, even swearing under oath, "I do not know this man you speak of" (Mark 14:71). John's Gospel reports a matching scene after the resurrection. Three times Peter declares that he truly loves his risen Master. "Lord, you know everything; you know that I love you" (John 21:17).

Finally, there was an incident for which, admittedly, we have to rely solely on Paul's interpretation. At Antioch on one occasion Peter stopped eating with Gentile Christians. This put them under a false pressure to keep the Jewish law. The result was a confrontation with Paul, who held Peter to be at fault (Gal 2:11). Paul supplied the kind of fraternal correction which he believed Peter's weakness to require.

(5) *Beyond the New Testament.*   So far I have sketched some of the major themes which the New Testament indicates about the position and ministry of Peter. We should be careful to take the biblical evidence only as far as it can go. The New Testament provides us with some hints but not with a detailed blueprint about the precise ways in which the ministry of Peter should be continued in the Church till the end of history. As with other ministries the New Testament offers only fragmentary and unsystematic pointers.

What things do we not find in the New Testament itself? First, since Christians during the first decades expected an immediate *parousia*, they apparently gave little thought to the long-term way of institutionalizing and handing on various important ministries. Such questions turn up in relatively late strata of the New Testament (Acts 20:17–38; the Pastoral Epistles), only when the hope of an immediate *parousia* had waned and the early Church realized the need to preserve the Gospel tradition and clarify the question of succession for office-holders. As regards the way Peter's leadership should be or was in fact handed on, the New Testament contains no explicit directions.

Second, the Acts of the Apostles contain nothing about Peter's later life. They record Paul's coming to Rome (Acts 28:11–31) but not his martyrdom there. John's Gospel points to Peter's martyrdom (John 21:18f), but does not specify how and where it took place.

Nevertheless, Rome was the city where Peter and Paul taught and suffered death for their Master. The Church of Rome came to be recognized as possessing a unique responsibility among all the Christian Churches. The Bishop of Rome was acknowledged to be called in a special way to do two things. He was *both* to proclaim the saving truth revealed by Christ *and* to keep all Christians united in their faith.

Here "called in a special way" does *not* mean "called as the only one responsible" or "called exclusively." Peter's role of leadership did not isolate him from the other apostles: Paul and the rest also witnessed authoritatively to the good news and maintained unity among the churches. Likewise the special responsibility of the Bishop of Rome to uphold the truth about Christ and preserve Christian unity has always been a function exercised with other bishops.

(6) *Peter and the Pope.* What conclusions follow from this brief examination of Peter's role for interpreting the position of the Bishop of Rome? What light might all this throw on the nature of the papacy?

(a) The Church was founded on *all the apostles* (Eph 2:20). Together they were the primary witnesses to Jesus Christ. They proclaimed the resurrection of the crucified Savior, admitted all nations into the community and authoritatively guided the early Church.

Among this college of basic witnesses *Simon Peter* stood out as *the* witness and *the* foundation. His new name suggested his special function. To him alone were addressed the words: "On this rock I will build my Church."

(b) The mission given to Peter and the other apostles was partly but not totally handed on to their successors, the Bishop of Rome and the other bishops. I say "not totally," because certain functions died with the apostles. Under the risen Christ and through the power of his Holy Spirit they were called to bring the Church into being. Once achieved *this founding of the Church* could never be repeated. Pope, bishops and other Christians bear—in different ways—the responsibility of keeping the Church in existence. They are all called to maintain the good state of the community but not to found (or refound) the Church.

Hence the words "On this rock I will build my Church" do not apply to the Bishop of Rome in precisely the way they apply to Peter. In the case of the Pope the meaning would rather be: "On this rock I will preserve my Church in existence."

(c) Nevertheless, as I said above, the mission given to Peter and the other apostles was *partly handed on to their successors.* Let me indicate some details of this succession.

The Bishop of Rome has a relationship to his fellow bishops which is *like* the relationship of Peter to the other apostles. Together they share a special responsibility for spreading the good news, leading the Church with authority and maintaining the sacramental life of the community. The bishops with the Pope are the primary preachers, pastors and celebrants of the liturgy.

Among all the bishops, the Bishop of Rome like Peter has a special role of leadership to serve the whole Church with love (John 21:15–17) and through suffering (John 21:18f). His special service centers on maintaining the true faith and unity of all Christians.

(d) I noted earlier *the shadow side* of Peter's exercise of his ministry. Rather than being surprised at human weaknesses and limitations in Peter's successor, we should expect them. Even after the resurrection and the coming of the Holy Spirit, Peter could at least once appear to be limiting Christian freedom (Gal 2:11ff).

Among all the apostles only Peter is reported to have confessed his sinfulness so strikingly: "Simon Peter . . . fell down at Jesus' knees, saying, 'Depart from me, for I am a sinful man, O Lord' " (Luke 5:8).

The conclusion from this seems clear. The shadow side of the Papacy does not rule out Petrine succession. Rather, we should not be surprised if, like Peter, the Bishop of Rome will at times show human failure in the way he exercises his special function of leadership for the Church.

(e) Above I pointed out how Peter fulfilled his ministry primarily—although not exclusively—through being *the* official witness to Christ's resurrection. This suggests that among the various roles exercised by the Bishop of Rome the primary one could best be seen as that of being *the* proclaimer of the Lord's resurrection. I need to work this out in a little detail.

The pastoral jurisdiction and teaching function of the Pope could be helpfully contextualized by recalling the Petrine ministry as primarily witness to the risen Christ. The First Vatican Council (1869–1870) described the papal office as a "perpetual principle and visible foundation of the unity" which belongs to the episcopate and the whole Church (DS, 3051). The Pope serves as sign and instrument of this unity through being the primary, official proclaimer of the basic truth "He is risen."[9]

The Second Vatican Council's Dogmatic Constitution on the Church (*Lumen gentium*) put "preaching the Gospel" ahead of their pastoral and liturgical roles as the most important duty of bishops (nr. 25). No less than other bishops the Bishop of Rome must fulfill this duty which Paul VI called "the pre-eminent ministry of teaching the revealed truth" (*Evangelii nuntiandi*, nr. 67). Once again one can reasonably comment that the "Gospel" to be preached and "the revealed truth" to be taught come essentially from the resurrection of the crucified Jesus.

In recent years contacts between Catholics and other Christians have highlighted more and more the need to find real *unity* in confessing the *truth* of faith. How best can we describe that unity and truth? The key truth of Christian faith, as we have often seen, can be formulated by saying: "The crucified Son of God is risen from the dead to give us his Holy Spirit." The paschal mystery says it all. It is the basic truth to be maintained and passed on by Christians. They are baptized into Christ's death and resurrection (Rom 6:3f) to live together as God's new Easter people.

What more then could we expect from the Bishop of Rome than that like Peter he strengthen the whole Church's faith in Christ's resurrection? How could he better serve the unity of an Easter people than by proclaiming insistently the event which brought the Church into being: the resurrection of the crucified Jesus? Certainly the Pope must *also* lead the Church with loving authority and celebrate the sacraments. But his great task for all the world is to announce through word and deed the news which lies at the heart of Christianity: Christ is risen. Nothing can ever count against the power and joyfulness of that news.

The Lutheran-Catholic report, *Peter in the New Testament*, observes that "no matter what one may think about the justification offered by the New Testament for the emergence of the papacy, this papacy in its developed form cannot be read back into the New Testament" (8). In general we can only agree with this statement. Nevertheless, there is at least one yearly ceremony in which through his proclamation of the resurrection the Pope strikingly symbolizes and even parallels Peter's basic function as Easter witness. Each year millions of people see on television or hear on the radio the Pope's Easter broadcast. In thirty or forty languages he announces to the city of Rome and to the world the glorious news that lies at the heart of Christianity: "Christ is risen, Alleluia."

Of course, we should respect the great differences between our cultural and historical setting and that in which nearly two thousand years ago Peter carried on his ministry. Nevertheless, one need not strain to see some parallel between what the Pope does each Easter and what happened at the first Pentecost. In Jerusalem Peter announced Jesus' resurrection to

Parthians, Medes, Elamites; inhabitants of Mesopotamia, of Judaea and Cappadocia, of Pontus and Asia, of Phrygia and Pamphylia, of Egypt and the districts of Libya around Cyrene; visitors from Rome, both Jews and proselytes, Cretans and Arabs (Acts 2:9f).

Today the television cameras catch the faces of those who have come to Rome from all over our world, so that they can stand in St Peter's Square on Easter Sunday and hear from Peter's successor the good news which changed the world: "This Jesus God raised up, and of that we all are witnesses" (Acts 2:32). Peter's witness to the resurrection lives on strikingly in the Pope's Easter proclamation. In that special way each year the Bishop of Rome visibly serves and strengthens the Church's faith by re-enacting before all the world the role of Peter, the fundamental witness to Easter.

This chapter argued that major beliefs can be properly derived from the basic confession about the resurrection of the crucified Jesus. I took up the case of the Petrine and papal ministries to develop in some detail one example of this Easter perspective on Christian and Catholic faith. But this chapter has said little about something which engaged many Fathers of the Church, Aquinas, Barth and others: the place of the resurrection in Christ's work of redemption. To that we can now turn.

7

Redemption and Hope

Is there any way out of the pain and terror of the human predicament? Where can we find real life after birth and before death? Is there a personal life hereafter? What can any of us hope for?

Before his own death, Ernest Becker restated with fresh power the cruel conclusion to be faced by those who deny an after-life. Our human existence is essentially hopeless:

> We saw that there really was no way to overcome the real dilemma of existence, the one of the mortal animal who at the same time is conscious of his mortality. A person spends years coming into his own, developing his talent, his unique gifts, perfecting his discriminations about the world, broadening and sharpening his appetite, learning to bear the disappointments of life, becoming mature, seasoned—finally a unique creature in nature, standing with some dignity and nobility and transcending the animal condition; no longer driven, no longer a complete reflex, not stamped out of any mold. And then the real tragedy, as André Malraux wrote in *The Human Condition*: it takes sixty years of incredible suffering and effort to make such an individual, and then he is good only for dying. . . . He has to go the way of the grasshopper, even though it takes longer (*The Denial of Death* [New York and London, 1973] 266).

Where Becker cried out against an ultimate loss for which he could see no remedy, others encourage us to lower our sights and look to what we might achieve in this life. Shortly before he died, René Dubos, a bacteriologist who was professor emeritus at Rockefeller University, wrote an article "Reason for Optimism" in which he confessed: "As I lie here in a hospital bed in my 81st year, I am more convinced than ever that life can be celebrated and enjoyed under the most trying and humble of circumstances." He invited his readers not "to wallow in despair," but to overcome "the passivity born of pessimism" and rediscover "their innate celebration of life," so as to think "globally" and act "locally." Dubos concluded confidently:

> By using the five E's—ecology, economics, energetics, esthetics and ethics—*Homo sapiens* can create "humanized" environments that are stable, profitable, pleasurable and favorable to the health of the earth and the growth of civilization (*New York Times*, 4 March 1982).

Dubos optimistically settled for what we can create and celebrate here and now, whereas Becker found no final remedy for the human predicament.

The Easter faith of Christians, however, knows that through the resurrection of the crucified Jesus, God has revealed and inaugurated the definitive divine plan for saving human beings and their world. The resurrection was the beginning of that ultimate end when God will be "everything to everyone" (1 Cor 15:28). As Chapter One illustrated, from the beginning Christians have found in Christ's resurrection the basis for final hope and a new life already made available to them. Both within and beyond their liturgical celebrations they experience and express something of that new life. We do not face the ultimate, irremediable loss of going "the way of the grasshopper." Yet neither can we rest content to think of ourselves as autonomous self-redeemers, capable at least of creating more "humanized" environments. Easter faith calls us rather to cooperate with the glorious destiny which Christ's resurrection holds out to human beings and their world. The gift enables us to bear our responsibility for humanizing our world.

This chapter will reflect on what the risen Christ does for us here and hereafter. In other words, how might one experience the redeeming power of the resurrection in this life? What can one say about the resurrection we hope for?

REDEMPTION

(1) *John and Paul.* John's Gospel reaches its climax with the risen Jesus revealing himself to Mary Magdalene who brings the news of resurrection to the other disciples (John 20:11–18). Jesus then appears to them, gives them his peace and communicates his life-giving Spirit (John 20:19–23). A similar sequence encloses the Letter to the Galatians, where Paul moves from the revelation of Christ's resurrection (Gal 1:1, 12, 16) to all that followed redemptively for him (for example, Gal 2:20) and his Galatian converts (for example, Gal 3:1–5).

The apostle repeatedly bears eloquent witness to what it means to experience the power of the risen Christ (for example, Phil 3:8–11). The Second Letter to the Corinthians spells out what "the God who raises the dead" (2 Cor 1:9) has done for Paul's life and mission in terms of "consolation" (2 Cor 1:3–7), the Spirit who "gives life" (2 Cor 3:6), a new existence "in Christ" (2 Cor 5:17) and "strength" in the midst of many trials and "weaknesses" (2 Cor 12:9–10). After dedicating years to his ministry, the apostle acknowledges that the divine power of resurrection already manifested in the mission to the Gentiles will be shown in the conversion of Israel (Rom 11:15).

Over and over again the New Testament testifies that death, sin and the demonic forces which appear to govern the world are not really, or at least no longer really, its rulers. Believers know the life-giving power of God revealed and set at work through the resurrection and Lordship of Jesus (Col 2:6–15). By experiencing the powerful Spirit they know that the risen Christ is the true Lord of the cosmos (1 Cor 12:3; Phil 2:11), and that their own future resurrection has already begun inasmuch as they are "dead to sin and alive to God, in union with Christ Jesus" (Rom 6:11).

It is hard to know where to stop in citing evidence for the basic conviction of early Christians that the risen Christ mediates God's blessings to them. First Peter praises "the God and Father of our Lord Jesus Christ, who in his great mercy gave us new birth into a living hope by the resurrection of Jesus Christ from the dead" (1 Pet 1:3). Hoping in the risen Christ and believing in the good news of the salvation that he has effected makes it possible to "become incorporated" in him and receive "the seal of the promised Holy Spirit," which "is the pledge that we shall enter upon our heritage" at the end (Eph 1:12–14).

(2) *Experience Now.* That the New Testament richly reflects the way the first Christians experienced the risen Jesus' redeeming power is abundantly clear. The problem arises rather today. How far is that power accessible to us on a daily basis? What verifies now Paul's certainty that the risen Christ "makes his power felt" among us (2 Cor 13:3)? What effective signs of redemption can we experience and identify here and now?

Answers can center on three areas: (a) the Church's ongoing life of worship, (b) personal experiences, and (c) features of the world situation.

(a) As the Fathers of the Church vividly appreciated (Chapter One above), the sacramental life of the community symbolizes and enacts the

varied needs of human beings and the corresponding ways in which
Christ's redeeming power works. The Eucharist leads the way as the
sacrament where "hearts burn" and the risen Lord is known in "the
breaking of the bread" (Luke 24:13–35). The Emmaus story remains
paradigmatic for what believers expect and experience. The Scriptures,
the sacraments and, above all, the Eucharist bring them his powerful
and satisfying presence.

(b) "Sometimes Christ puts life where we least expect it." This remark by a friend points to the new life that comes into many deadly
situations where meaning has been shattered and relationships broken.
We can see the risen Lord's re-creating grace at work as it transforms
suffering and brings victory over evil.

Here believers frequently and rightly testify to experiences in
which the power of the resurrection changed them or others through the
mediation of support groups and basic communities. For me the most
striking way I have seen this power express itself has been in the transformation of some addicts. They have found a truly new life, not merely
a life without alcohol and other drugs.

(c) It is when we switch to the world situation that it can become
much more difficult to identify signs of the risen Christ's redeeming
power being effectively at work. At Christmas 1983 some friends in
Rome listed our common needs as follows:

Reconciliation between east and west; justice between north and south.
Prison systems reformed; reverence for human life.
An end to the nuclear threat; racial harmony achieved.
International enmities resolved; justice in all legal systems.
A halt to torture; work for the unemployed.
Amnesty for political prisoners; freedom of conscience for all.
Hatred turned to love; renunciation of violence.
Wealth shared; food enough for all peoples.
Arms production and sale stopped everywhere; technology at the service
   of human development.
A sharing style of living; homes for refugees.
Dismantling of all missiles; terrorism made obsolete; war outlawed.
Women freed to take full part in society; freedom of religion.
Careful use of the earth's resources; the environment kept safe for all
   generations.
The elderly cherished and cared for; the young preserved from
   exploitation.

The list ended with the invitation, "Here add your own." I would want
to add:

An end to the deliberate spread of misinformation; open and truthful communication everywhere.

Religious institutions at the service of personal faith; no more false syncretism, fanatical sects and self-seeking prophets.

Justice for minorities within dominant cultures; a more livable and human future for everyone.

But how much or how little of all this do we see happening in our world? Granted that no short-term, complete solutions are possible, what progress do we find taking place? Where are the signs that show Christ's risen power to be at work? From year to year and from century to century does our world look more redeemed?

Yet this may well be the wrong way of putting matters. Not only in (a) liturgical celebration, (b) personal experiences but even more in (c) the broader world situation their Easter faith invites believers to be active participants. Through their positive collaboration they can bring about signs of the risen Lord's redeeming presence, instead of merely waiting to observe them. In other words, belief in Christ's victory over death and evil entails actively "veri-fying" his saving power—in the sense of a collaboration which "makes true" and brings about at least some partial solutions to the problems I listed above.

Easter faith implies an obligation to set free those who suffer from economic injustice, cultural backwardness or any other form of human misery. Jesus' account of judgment places a hope for the coming kingdom in just such a context of responsibility for the alleviation of physical and mental suffering: "I was hungry and you gave me food" (Matt 25:35). The sequence is not: "I was hungry and you preached patience to me." There is a hard particularity about the duty imposed by any Easter hope for the coming reign of God, a particularity inculcated too by the story of the Good Samaritan.

The pressure behind responsible Christian service stems from a hope for the full redemption of human beings. Social and political action "verifies" the truth of our belief in Christ's victory and our final resurrection. Such action anticipates the ultimate freeing of our bodies which now face the sentence of death. To believe in Christ's resurrection is to place oneself under the obligation of actions shaped by that faith. It is hardly a coincidence that in 1 Corinthians Paul inculcates a full service of love (13:4–7) before going on to recall Christian faith in Jesus' resurrection and hope in our coming share in that resurrection (Chapter 15).

Although it places believers under a responsibility to "verify" actively and publicly the redemption effected by Christ's resurrection from the dead, Easter faith—as opposed to the views of René Dubos, Karl Marx and many others—does not reckon on some utopia to be achieved by innerworldly forces through the mutual cooperation of self-redeemed or self-redeeming human beings. Christians view the earth in the light of the coming kingdom of God, so that they should refuse to separate their hopes for that kingdom and their hope for this world. But at the same time the progressive dynamic of modern society in any of its good forms may not be identified with the full advent of redemption. Our Easter hope commits us to active intervention. Yet the coming of the final kingdom remains God's gift, not the end-result of our human actions.

(3) *The Sign of the Tomb.* Thus far this chapter has sketched some lines of response to the question: How do we experience the redeeming power of the risen Christ in this life? In Chapter Five of *Interpreting Jesus* and the last chapter of *Jesus Today* I have treated at length what it means for Christ's power to save us from our enslaved, contaminated and unloving state—or, to express our predicament another way—from our greed, fear and fatalism.

Before moving to reflect on the risen body and resurrected existence, however, I think it could be useful to insert something on the value of Jesus' empty tomb as a redemptive sign.

Here and there the New Testament notes how the Easter appearances also functioned as a sign of continuity between the earthly Jesus and the risen Christ (for example, John 21:7).[1] His pre-resurrection followers recognized him as the same person. The New Testament, however, offers little on the sign-value of Jesus' empty tomb. All the same, it is perfectly reasonable to go beyond the fact of the empty tomb (see Chapter Four above) to what it might express and symbolize.

First of all, the emptiness of Jesus' grave reflects the holiness of what it once held, the corpse of the incarnate Son of God who lived for others and died to bring a new covenant of love for all people. This "Holy One" could not "see corruption" (Acts 2:27).

Second, tombs naturally express the finality and irreversible loss of death. Jesus' open and empty grave readily suggests and symbolizes the fullness of the new and everlasting life into which he has risen.

Third, the empty tomb expresses something vital about the nature of redemption, namely that redemption is much more than a mere escape from our scene of suffering and death. Rather it means the transformation of this material, bodily world with its whole history of sin and suffering. The first Easter began the work of finally bringing our universe home to its ultimate destiny. God did not discard Jesus' earthly corpse, but mysteriously raised and transfigured it so as to reveal what lies ahead for human beings and their world. In short, that empty tomb in Jerusalem is God's radical sign that redemption is not an escape to a better world but a wonderful transformation of our world. Seen that way, the open and empty grave of Jesus is highly significant for our appreciation of what redemption means.

THE RISEN BODY

Chapter One above reported and commented on the fact that from the beginning of the Patristic era Jesus' own victory over death was generally not treated as a distinct theme but very often taken as grounding Christian hope for coming resurrection. Instead of collapsing into one his destiny and ours, this book has concentrated on the crucified Christ's resurrection. Now, however, I want to fashion some approaches to our risen, bodily existence. What could it mean to say "I/We look for the resurrection of the body"?

First of all, an introductory "confession" and a word of caution. I am well aware that (a) many people hold that death simply brings the extinction of our personal, human existence or at best a form of recycling—namely, the reabsorption of our material/spiritual being into some suprapersonal material/spiritual reality. (b) Others maintain the survival of our souls either as transferred to some enhanced state or else as reincarnated in a fresh body. Those who do not accept resurrection and especially group (a) may well find the reflections which follow a sheer waste of time, as absurd as looking for something north of the North Pole. Yet reflect we must. To put it mildly, I confess that it seems thoroughly odd to believe in Jesus' resurrection and hope for our own while steadfastly refusing to hazard any thoughts on what the resurrection of the whole person could be like. Can we then say something about the nature of the new, transformed life which will be "me" risen from the dead and not that of my spiritual successor or some duplicate?

Then a word of caution. Whatever way we try to depict a resurrected and glorified human existence, we should always remember the difference between Christ's case and ours.[2] By first confessing his resurrection and then expressing hope for ours, the Creed does not take the two cases to be absolutely the same. His corpse laid in the tomb near Golgotha entered directly into Christ's risen existence in a way which seemingly will not be true of ourselves. Of course, we are dealing here with mystery, the deliverance of Jesus from death and his final, glorious transformation. Nevertheless, once we accept that his tomb was found to be empty and did not become so through some human intervention (removal or theft of the corpse), we must conclude to some special divine activity. Someone could argue, I suppose, that God simply annihilated the corpse and, so to speak, fitted Jesus out with a totally new body or with a copy of the body laid in the tomb. Taken simply as such, the (divinely caused) disappearance of the corpse does not necessarily say anything about the nature of the material continuity between that corpse and the resurrected Jesus. Nevertheless, as we have seen, the New Testament seems to indicate some kind of direct continuity between the corpse laid to rest by Joseph of Arimathea and Jesus' risen existence. This continuity sets his resurrection apart from ours.

Reasons are available to render such a special continuity plausible. The corpse buried by Joseph of Arimathea differed in two ways from all other corpses anyone had ever or will ever place in a tomb. This corpse had been the body of the incarnate Son of God who had suffered on the cross to bring all men and women deliverance from evil. The *divine identity* and *universal redemptive role* of Christ puts his resurrection in another class. In rising from the dead, only he assumed his rightful divine dignity (for example, Acts 2:32–36; Rom 1:4) and became the effective Savior of the world (for example, Acts 4:12; 1 Cor 15:45). On both counts some peculiarly close continuity between the corpse laid in the tomb and Christ's risen, bodily existence can seem believable.

A partial reading of Paul could obscure the real differences between Christ's resurrection and ours. The talk about Christ being raised as "the first fruits of those who have fallen asleep" (1 Cor 15:20) and the apostle's gallant attempt to say something about "the resurrection of the dead" in general (1 Cor 15:42–51) does not necessarily bring out how different Christ's case is. Paul states that elsewhere. It is true only of Christ that his resurrection brought "justification" to all human beings (Rom 4:25). He alone has effected the resurrection of the dead (1 Cor 15:21): "As in Adam all die, so also in Christ shall all be made alive" (1 Cor 15:22). Paul does not say of any other risen person that "he must reign until God has put all his enemies under his feet" (1 Cor 15:25). In short, Paul does not present Christ's resurrection as being a precise prototype for ours.

His personal identity and saving function make it reasonable that Christ's dead body should be "incorporated" immediately into his risen existence and that hence he would enjoy "more" bodily continuity than we will. Furthermore, in his case a clear sign of continuity between his earthly and risen existence (the empty tomb) is infinitely more important than it is in the case of any mere human being.[3]

In what follows, however, I do not wish to stress the differences between Jesus' case and ours but rather reflect on the relationship between the earthly body and the risen body. Some insights into the possible meaning and nature of a personal, risen existence automatically bolster the position of those who look to share in Christ's resurrection and deny that we "go the way of the grasshopper."

I have just spoken of "some insights" into risen existence. No one can describe exactly and fully the life and activity of risen persons. To be able to do that we would need to have already experienced resurrection for ourselves. The limits in our experience condition the way we may conceptualize and describe the resurrection. Perhaps it would be wiser to say very little beyond speaking in general of a new life for the total person who will be transformed beyond the limitations and evil of our present existence. To the extent that the final reality of resurrection is more than a spatio-temporal reality, language fails. Even if I refuse to remain silent, at any rate I make no pretense here to say *how* resurrection takes place. I confine myself to reflecting on what its result, the risen bodily existence of a human being, could be like.

(1) *Matter and Spirit.* Nowadays it is common and reasonable to stress the spiritual and bodily unity of the human person. All the same, a certain dualism remains between matter and spirit. But it should be added at once that dualistic thinking about our present existence does not necessarily steer us to a Platonic conclusion in which "we" (as soul or spirit) are "in" a body or "have" a body. To speak of our present matter and spirit need not suppose that they are utterly, totally disparate realities which—like oil and water—will not mix. All matter has something spiritual about it.[4] A pure materiality that would be utterly "unspiritual" seems impossible.

The spiritualizing and personalizing of matter take place incessantly through eating and drinking. By being taken into a human body, matter becomes vitally associated with the function of a spiritual being. The world of art exemplifies a similar phenomenon. Paintings and sculptures are material objects. But by being organized and spiritualized in the hands of their maker, these works of art can embody a rich cargo of personal meaning. Believers acknowledge the same process in the life of the Church's sacraments, above all in the case of the Eucharist. There a piece of bread and a cup of wine are spiritualized and personalized in becoming the risen Christ's most intensely real presence.

Obviously matter can be understood and interpreted in many ways. Nuclear physicists know it as mainly empty space, the field of several basic forces. Electrons and other particles appear as either mass or energy. Nevertheless, eating, drinking, painting, celebrating religious ceremonies and further human activities disclose another face of matter: its possibility of being partly spiritualized and personalized.

The resurrection of the dead will mean the full personalizing and spiritualizing of matter, not its abolition. Through the Holy Spirit the human spirit will completely dominate matter. The body will clearly express and serve the glorified spirit of human beings. Accepting this demands a leap of the imagination. Four contrasts between the earthly and the risen body can carry us forward in making that leap.

(2) *Four Functions and Contrasts.* As human beings we are bodily, or—if you like—we are bodies. What can we appreciate about the nature of the human body now that could also point ahead to our bodily destiny in resurrection?

(a) First of all, our bodies obviously insert us into the material world. We become part of the cosmos and the cosmos part of us. Once upon a time people naively assumed a far-reaching autonomy and stability for the human body. They had not yet discovered that our life is a dynamic process of constant circulation between our bodies and our material environment. In *Resurrection and the Message of Easter* (London, 1974) Xavier Léon-Dufour puts it this way:

> In the universe there circulates a total body of "materials" which are the object of unceasing exchanges. For example, of the sixty million million cells which compose the human organism, five hundred million are renewed every day. . . . My body is the universe received and made particular in this instant by myself (239).

To adapt John Donne's words, no body is an island. An isolated bodily person would be a strange anomaly. Our bodies make us share in and incessantly relate to the universe.

An essential part of this insertion in the universe is our relationship to God. To be sure, for various reasons and in various degrees many people fail to live out this relationship. Nevertheless, as human bodily persons we participate in the universe, and that entails being related to God as the ultimate origin, ever-present partner and final goal of our existence.

Then our bodiliness creates the possibility of being *communicators*. Through our bodies we act, express ourselves, relate and communicate. Without our bodiliness there would be no language, no art, no literature, no religion, no industry, no politics, no social and economic relations, and none of that married love in which verbal and non-verbal communication reaches a supremely intense level. In short, without bodies we could have no human history. Through our bodies we build up that whole web of relationships with other human beings, the material universe and God which constitutes our story. Our bodies enable us to communicate, participate and play the human game.

Although our bodies permit us to communicate, at the same time they set limits to our communication. Being subject to the constraints of space and time, our bodies set us apart and restrict our chances of relating and communicating. People talk, hug, kiss, phone, write letters and in other ways try to make up by quantitative repetition what they lack qualitatively. Through sickness, old age, imprisonment and other causes, our bodies can bring us radical solitude and terrifying loneliness. That bodily loneliness finds its ultimate expression when the tomb encloses a newly-buried corpse.

Our material bodies do not merely separate and alienate us from one another, the world and God. Through weariness, physical weakness, sickness and sleep they alienate us from ourselves. Our bodiliness can make us feel not fully free to be ourselves and to be with others.

Here and now our bodies ensure our *continuity* (in the order of being) and our recognition (at the level of knowledge). To be and to be recognized as the same person we must remain the "same" body. Despite our constant and massive bodily changes, personal identity and continuity are somehow bound up with bodily identity and continuity. We are/have the same body, and therefore remain the same person. Bodily continuity points to personal identity.[5]

One might imagine the case of a murderer who not only repented and changed spiritually but also suffered a total loss of memory about his crime. Let us suppose that many years later he was arrested by the police. His physical appearance had changed with time, but fingerprints, blood tests and further bodily evidence could positively identify him as the same person who had committed the murder. We can bracket off the question as to what a law court might do in such a case. At all events one thing would be clear: bodily identity would establish the man's personal identity.

Fourth, at all stages in our human life we experience our bodiliness as the "place" and means of grace, happiness, sin and misery. The sacraments act as a massive reminder of this. Our personal communion in the life of God begins and grows through our heads being sprinkled with water, our hands smeared with oil and our mouths opening to receive the eucharistic elements. In ancient and modern hedonism the body takes on an exaggerated importance, as if the pursuit of happiness could and should be defined in terms of physical pleasure alone. Nevertheless, this exaggeration should not cover up the fact that all human happiness has something bodily about it. It is the same with sin and misery. It is hard to imagine either unhappiness or sinful human acts which could remain completely "unbodily." Through his silent miming of the deadly sins Marcel Marceau used to bring out brilliantly how all seven of them, including even pride and envy, have something bodily about them. In short, our body enters essentially into our life of grace, happiness, sin and misery.

(b) These four functions of our human bodies can help us refine what we say about the risen life. To begin with, resurrection brings matter its most intense participation in the life of God. By being raised from death, human beings as *embodied* spirits will not only belong again to the universe but also in a new way will share in divine life. As both *material* and spiritual beings they will receive their ultimate divinization so as "to live to God." In his bodiliness the risen Jesus himself is now a "piece" of this material world that has been inserted into the life of God—to be fully and finally with God (Rom 6:10).

Second, resurrection will maximize our capacity to relate and communicate. Let me select the supreme example. As risen from the dead, Jesus now relates to his Father, human beings and the cosmos in a way which has shed the constraints of his historical existence. Wherever, for example, two or three gather in his name, they find the risen Lord in their midst. Nothing expresses better the new communicative power of Jesus than the Eucharist, his worldwide presence and offer to communicate a life which will never end.

To hope for resurrection means hoping that we will be freed to go far beyond the limitations and triviality of so much communication in this world. We will be liberated to be truly ourselves and to be with others.

Perhaps the greatest difficulty in grasping something about the nature of risen existence gathers around the issue of continuity. As we saw, personal identity remains somehow bound up with bodily continuity. Irenaeus emphatically applied this principle to the personal identity that will be preserved in resurrection:

> With what body will the dead rise? Certainly with the same body in which they died, otherwise those who rise would not be the same persons who previously died (*Adversus omnes haereses* V, 13, 1).

But in what sense must we rise with the *same* body? What counts here as bodily sameness or identity? Even in this life the enormous and constant interchange of matter with our environment can make us wonder how far it is correct to speak of someone being the "same" body at six, sixteen and sixty. If it is difficult to say how we keep the "same" body within our human history, we will be even more hesitant about "explaining" and even maintaining bodily continuity between this existence and our risen life.

One answer here could be found by noting the connection between saying "I am my body" and "I am my history."[6] Through our bodiliness we create and develop a whole web of relationships with other people, the world and God. Our history comes from our body being in relationship. As bodies we have our history—from conception to death. As human beings we enjoy a bodily or embodied history. Through resurrection our particular embodied history will be raised from death. That human, bodily history which makes up the story of each person will be brought to new life. In a mysterious, transformed fashion the risen existence will express what embodied persons were and became in their earthly life. Put that way, the view of Irenaeus can make good sense:

> With what bodily history will the dead rise? Certainly with the same bodily history at the end of which they died; otherwise those who rise would not be the same persons who previously died.

I realize that to some this suggestion of mine can sound like pure poetry—in the pejorative sense of "pure poetry." Nevertheless, if one asks "What has made me what I am?" it has surely been my particular embodied history and not, for instance, merely the millions of molecules which in a passing parade have at different moments constituted my particular physical existence. Further, my whole bodily history is much more "me" than the body which breathes its last at seventy or eighty years of age. In short, I propose expressing resurrection as God bringing to a new personal life the total embodied history of the dead individual.

Here I would take issue with those who maintain that we will rise neither male nor female and add accordingly a sentence to Paul's list in 1 Corinthians 15:42–50: "It is sown male/female; it will be raised as human." If this were so, our personal history shaped by our sex, language, culture and other such factors would be radically flouted. We will rise with our integral history. Our sex forms an essential part of that history. If we were to rise as neither male nor female but as undifferentiated human beings, we would not be the same persons who had previously lived and died.

Lastly, here and now bodiliness enters essentially into our life of sin, grace and happiness. In our future existence our risen bodies will be the "place" where we will experience the full freedom and happiness of heaven. The truth of a beatific vision for our minds can obscure the essential bodiliness of risen life and even wrongly suggest that we will become pure spirits to contemplate the infinite beauty of God. Rather, both here and hereafter we receive God's loving presence through our bodily humanity. To apply and extend Tertullian's classic dictum (*"caro salutis est cardo"*), our bodiliness is the "pivot" of our grace now and of the glory to come.

This section has lingered over four points (participation, communication, continuity and salvation) which may help us leap imaginatively from our present to our future bodiliness. Seen in those terms, our present body points to and symbolizes, albeit inadequately, our risen body.

(3) *Physical Fantasies.* Over the centuries people have often taken final resurrection from the dead to involve a mere resuscitation of a corpse or at best an improved earthly body which enables the risen person to resume eating, sexual relations and other previous activities. This false interpretation turned up in a debate with Jesus initiated by some Sadducees (Mark 12:18–27). In our own century a crudely materialistic view of resurrection lay behind an appalling episode witnessed by a friend of mine. To stop them from rising from the dead, the dead bodies of government troops were dismembered by those who had ambushed and killed them.

It is a mistake to think of present human bodiliness in merely material terms and ignore or play down its spiritual and personal aspects. It is even more mistaken to take the risen body primarily in material terms. This happens with all those persistent speculations about our physical appearance in the life to come: "Will I look the same as I did at thirty?" Even in this life a person's external characteristics can suffer massive changes over the years, and he or she remains the same person. My maintaining my identical selfhood in a risen state does not depend on my enjoying an appearance similar to that of some optimum phase of my earthly life. Rather my remaining in resurrection the particular person I had been depends on *my* particular embodied history being raised from death to new life.

(4) *God's Special Activity.* Earlier in this book I noted how Bultmann's interpretation of the resurrection was partly shaped by his conviction about the world being a closed continuum of causes and effects. The astonishing advances of science have not only rendered obsolete the mechanistic determinism presupposed by Bultmann but curiously have

also produced a new humility. What do we really know about natural reality and forces? The natural causality of the weak force (which also creates radio-activity), the strong force (which holds together atomic nuclei), the electromagnetic force (which binds together atoms and molecules, as well as producing light and radio waves), and gravity remain mysterious. In the late twentieth century a growing sense of wonder at the material world and our immense universe (with its billions of star-systems) has produced a new willingness to admit the exercise of the special divine causality required by a final resurrection from the dead.

God respects the natural order of the world and its functioning. Yet the course of events is not utterly fixed and rigidly uniform. The resurrection of Jesus—not to mention other such matters as the role of God in Israel's history, the event of the incarnation, miracles, the writing of inspired Scriptures and special graces that touch human lives—involves some special divine action over and above the normal order of the world. To produce different effects like Jesus' resurrection God acts in ways that are qualitatively distinct and different from the ordinary divine work in creating and sustaining the world. Such different results are caused by special divine intervention.

A number of writers, including some Christian theologians, make a fuss over claims about God's special interventions. Let us remember too that in the case of Jesus' resurrection Christian faith asserts no such "small-scale" intervention as the instantaneous healing of a desperately ill person but a rising to a new life which has inaugurated the end of all history. Here I may clear away some difficulties by noting the need to distinguish between a mere (capricious?) interference and a loving intervention. Love intervenes but never interferes.

In Jesus' resurrection God's free love is effectively shown and present. It is a commonplace to remark on the presence and power of love in creating the conditions for a human life to grow and fully unfold. Easter faith postulates the freedom of God's re-creative love in an extraordinarily different kind of divine activity and intervention: the raising of the dead Jesus. Only the free, loving involvement of God makes adequate sense of that particular, yet universally significant, event.

8

The Resurrection and Love

By their fruitful love in the joys and sacrifices of their calling, married people will bear witness to that mystery of love which the Lord revealed to the world by his death and resurrection.

Vatican II, *Gaudium et Spes*, nr. 52.

In his resurrection the Son of God experienced in a radical way mercy shown to himself—that is to say, the love of the Father which is more powerful than death.

John Paul II, *Dives in misericordia*, nr. 8

Living in the land of Dante has made me realize that the Christian tradition lacks an essential element in its appreciation of Jesus' resurrection from the dead. Chapters One, Two and Three of this book studied the main ways of understanding and interpreting the resurrection which have turned up over the centuries. As I indicated at the end of Chapter Three, six or seven terms (event, faith, revelation, redemption, promise, hope and communication) gather up what has been said and written about the Easter mystery since the beginning of Christianity. What that whole history of interpretation fails to include is the theme of love. Recent theological reflection on the love involved and expressed in Jesus's resurrection has also been slight or simply absent.

This chapter will first review the little I have found written on the topic in our century and then propose some approaches to the resurrection as a mystery of divine and human love. The aim is to unpack what the liturgy of Eastertide cryptically suggests about the potent love of God that Jesus' resurrection revealed in action. In its own way this chapter comments at length on the Thursday prayer for the third and fifth week after Easter: "Almighty, ever-living God, make our hearts more open to your love in these days of Eastertide, when you have made known to us the depth of that love."

LOVE NEGLECTED

Some authors who use love as a major or even primary focus when discussing other Christological mysteries fail to do so when they come to the resurrection. Hans Urs von Balthasar is a case in point. His classic *Love Alone*[1] pointed the way for a theology largely developed around the divine glory and love in *Herrlichkeit* (1961–1969) and *Theodramatik* (1973–1979). *Love Alone* presents the incarnation (45) and the crucifixion (94–95) as mysteries of love, but does not really do the same for Christ's resurrection. At best this is only hinted at when von Balthasar describes both the crucifixion and the resurrection as "the dramatic appearance of God's trinitarian love"—that is to say, the revelation of "the Trinity's loving struggle for mankind" (120). Even this partial and passing link between love and the resurrection loses its impact, when the author at once switches to another idea, the power at work on the dead Jesus and then on his disciples:

> It was not a harmless "teaching" which tore the decomposing corpse of the sinner (!) from the grave that had been sealed for three days and which roused the disciples whose courage had gone, transforming them into witnesses to the Resurrection throughout the world (120; translation corrected).

The *Von Balthasar Reader*[2] provides a 50-page introduction and includes 112 representative texts to offer a comprehensive view of his key themes. In the context of the resurrection as trinitarian event, von Balthasar remarks that "God the Father . . . with the resurrection of Jesus . . . established the primitive Christian core of dogma: God is love" (113). Apart from this, the *Reader* neither reports nor quotes any exposition of the resurrection in the key of love. Von Balthasar's contribution to theology lies elsewhere.

If one examines the various writings on Christ's resurrection by von Balthasar's great contemporary, Karl Rahner, the yield on love is likewise slight. Apropos of the experience of the disciples at the first Easter, he observes in passing that this "experience includes the encounter" with Jesus' "love and fidelity."[3] But generally when he deals with the resurrection, Rahner's interests are different: the inner relationship of Jesus' death to his resurrection, the revelation of the resurrection, its redemptive force, the role of transcendental hope in the free act of accepting the resurrection, and so on.[4]

In a section (230–237) of his *Introduction to Christianity*[5] Joseph Ratzinger briefly expounds belief in the resurrection as "faith in the love that has conquered death" (237). He finds "*the* basic problem of human existence" in the fact that love demands indestructibility. But "this cry of love's cannot be satisfied . . . it claims eternity but in fact is included in the world of death". If we confront this common human problem, we can see how faith in Jesus' resurrection means believing in "the greater strength of love in the face of death" (230). Ratzinger interprets the link between love and death as follows:

> Only where someone values love more highly than life, that is, only where someone is ready to put life second to love, for the sake of love, can love be stronger and more than death (232).

Specifically, "Jesus' total love for men," which led him to the cross, was "perfected in total stepping-over to the Father" and thus became stronger than death, because in this passage he was taken up and totally "held" by the Father (233).

In what precise way does Ratzinger hold that love effected the resurrection? (a) Apparently the central point is the Father's love toward Jesus. What Ratzinger says later about our hope for resurrection and God as "the lover" who in the face of death "has the necessary power" (271) seems also to be the main thrust of the argument here. In the case of the Father's love for Jesus, "the power of love for another" was so strong "that it could keep alive not just his memory, the shadow of his 'I,' but that person himself" (232). In this way, Jesus was enabled to overcome death by "living on in another," whose love took the beloved Jesus "into its own being," and thus made possible "this existence in the other" (233).

(b) What role did Jesus' own (human) love play—and, in particular, his "total love for men"? Seemingly Ratzinger suggests that it also brought about the resurrection. As we have seen above, Jesus was someone who valued love more highly than life. Where (and only where) someone is ready to put life second to love, love can prove stronger than death. At the same time Ratzinger rules out the possibility of other human beings, apart from Jesus, exemplifying this power: "Our own love, left to itself, is not sufficient to overcome death; taken in itself it would have to remain an unanswered cry" (234). This argument clearly raises a question about the human powers of the historical Jesus. Did his generous, "total" love in some way literally effect his own personal, glorious resurrection? Did Jesus rise because his (human) love not only "demanded" that from the other (his Father) but also in and of itself proved stronger than death? It is not altogether clear that Ratzinger is saying this. I return to the point shortly.

(c) In any case Ratzinger's statement about Jesus' love (which sounds like a general principle), *"only* where *someone* is ready to put life second to love . . . *can* love be stronger . . . than death" (italics mine), obviously needs some qualifications. It is certainly not meant to rule out resurrection for those human beings and Christians who do love others but not in a way which shows that they are truly ready to put life second to love. (Apropos of this, the judgment scene in Matthew 25:31–46 presents the righteous as being rewarded with eternal life not because they have literally surrendered their lives through love, but because they helped the hungry, the sick and others in need.) Nor should the statement "only where someone . . ." be taken to exclude in principle the resurrection for judgment of those who, so far from putting life second to love, have sinned grievously against love. Despite "only," "someone" and "can," Ratzinger intends the statement not so much as a general axiom, but as a comment on the way Jesus' destiny once and for all put an end to death's power and opened up a new, definitive life. In that unique case the power of love proved stronger than death and brought for all human beings the new stage of risen life. Hence the resurrection means that "he [Jesus] who has love for all has founded immortality for all . . . *his* resurrection is *our* life." His love and only his love, "coinciding with God's own power of life and love, can found our immortality" (234).

In Ratzinger's brief treatment of the credal article, "rose again from the dead," the following links between love and Jesus' resurrection are made: God (the Father) was "the lover" who had the power to raise Jesus to new life—point (a); through the divine power Jesus' love proved life-giving for others—point (c). What is not totally clear is whether Ratzinger wants to maintain point (b)—that Jesus' self-giving (human) love also worked as a this-worldly cause to effect the resurrection.

Bela Weissmahr certainly does intend to hold (b). He argues that Jesus' utter surrender in love worked as an immanent cause in producing the resurrection or at least the great sign of the resurrection, the disappearance of his corpse from the grave. Ultimately the resurrection was a creative act of God, but Jesus' unique (human) love for God and neighbor also came into play to bring about that effect.[6] This interesting thesis is unfortunately not developed very much, even if the other matters which Weissmahr discusses have some relationship to love. The author remains faithful to the title of his article, which does not promise to restrict itself to the power of love.

Thus far I have sampled some contemporary Catholic writers. Apart from eight pages by Ratzinger and a briefly stated thesis by Weissmahr, there is scarcely anything to mention about attempts to elucidate Jesus' resurrection in terms of love. In his 1979 survey article on

"The Resurrection of Jesus in Catholic Systematics" (see fn. 4), John Galvin covers such authors as Rahner, Kasper, Küng, Schillebeeckx, Sobrino and von Balthasar, but (apart from a footnote reference to Weissmahr's article) has nothing to report on the theme of love. Recent discussions of the resurrection have dealt with other issues (see above, Chapters Two, Three and Four). A 1975 two-part study of the theological and exegetical writing on Jesus' resurrection (coming from a wide range of Christian authors) also had nothing to say about the topic of love.[7]

It occurred to me that Teilhard de Chardin might have analyzed the resurrection in the light of love. After 1930 he worked out a view of love as *the* most enormous and universal force in a world which is dynamically converging toward Christ, the one Omega point and unifying goal of everything. Then Teilhard often expressed a wish to die on the day of Christ's resurrection; in fact he did die on Easter Sunday 1955.

Drawing on the letters of Saint Paul, he wrote about the "cosmic attributes" of the risen Christ.[8] He saw the resurrection as a cosmic event in which Christ overcame matter's resistance to spiritual ascent, effectively assumed his functions as center and focus of the universe, and guaranteed the upward and forward development of the universe.[9] Nevertheless, Teilhard did not normally have a great deal to say about the event of the resurrection precisely as such. Rather, he spoke much more of the incarnation as it dynamically unfolded toward its future completion,[10] and was flanked by creation, on the one hand, and by Christ's redeeming death, on the other. Hence even though Teilhard acknowledged the risen Christ as the "Personal Heart of the Cosmos" who—rather in the role of the Holy Spirit—inspires and releases the basic energy of love which progressively carries both humanity and the universe toward its future goal,[11] nevertheless, he did not tend to associate love explicitly with the event of the resurrection. A note on the mystery of love from his unpublished personal retreat in 1945 typifies a mind-set which turned more easily toward Christological mysteries other than the resurrection: "Creation—*the generative aspect;* Incarnation—*the unitive aspect;* Redemption—*the laborious aspect.*"[12]

The present Pope draws some lines between the resurrection and God's merciful love in his encyclical letter, *Dives in misericordia* (30 November 1980). John Paul II speaks of "the Son of God, who in his Resurrection experienced in a radical way mercy shown to himself, that is to say, the love of the Father which is *more powerful than death*" (nr. 8). In this event which he personally experienced Jesus revealed a merciful love, which continues to show itself more powerful than death (and sin) for all who live "in a world that is subject to evil." Christ "has revealed in his Resurrection the fullness of the love that the Father has for him and, in him, for all people" (*ibid*). Here the papal teaching turns on two notions (experience and revelation) which surface throughout the whole encyclical. At the same time, even though John Paul II expounds the resurrection in the key of love, the treatment is slight and occurs in an article (nr. 8) which places considerably more emphasis on Jesus' cross as the sign of God's merciful love.

To conclude this first section I should also mention Rosemary Haughton's *The Passionate God*,[13] an imaginative attempt to interpret the essentials of Christian faith through the idea of romantic love. She calls Chapter Four, "Resurrection" (129–173), "the centre of the book" (129). Yet much of this chapter is spent exploring other, albeit related, themes like the role of Mary, the training of the disciples, and the passage to Calvary of a Jesus who was driven by "the inner logic of Romantic passion" (146). Apropos of the resurrection, the most significant thesis affirms Jesus being liberated to love his Father in a complete fashion: "the resurrection" was "the moment of breakthrough, the explosion of fully reciprocated love" which knew "itself free of all restriction." At last Jesus could "give back to the One he loved the unshackled fullness of love" (152f). In a later section of the book Haughton examines the life experienced by those baptized into the paschal mystery. There she speaks of the resurrection as "the leap by which the body of Jesus begins to live in those bodies of his lovers" (230). They are moving toward the final consummation which she calls "the unimpeded outpouring of divine love" (231). Haughton thus offers a few suggestive hints toward a presentation of Christ's resurrection in terms of love. But her book delivers its principal message elsewhere—in the reflections on the incarnation, "the supreme and constitutive instance of passionate breakthrough" (130).

THE NATURE OF LOVE

Having produced some contemporary evidence for my theory that little has so far been developed on Jesus' resurrection as a mystery of love, I want to consider what such an approach could entail. Not surprisingly it is a matter of exploring a number of reciprocal relationships: that of the Father toward the crucified Son, that of the Holy Spirit toward the Father and the Son, that of the risen Jesus toward his Father and himself, that of the risen Jesus toward all men and women, and that of human beings toward the risen Lord.

The reciprocal nature of love proved to be one of the major themes in *Dives in misericordia*. John Paul II emphasized that "merciful love is never a unilateral act or process" (nr. 14). In our century no one has insisted more on the mutual character of love than Maurice Nedoncelle (1905–1976). Of its very nature love requires a certain reciprocity. To love someone is to believe that my feelings are reciprocated or at least to hope that this will be so. Love necessarily has a bilateral quality to it. Life is really shared and enhanced where love is given, received and reciprocated.

To expound in any detail the love that was effectively revealed in the resurrection, one needs some account of what love means. Here I do not wish to indulge an enormous parenthesis and discuss at length what philosophers, theologians and others have written on the various forms of love—from the *Epic of Gilgamesh*, Plato, the Song of Songs, the *Bhagavadgita*, John and Augustine in the ancient world, through Abelard, Bernard, Aquinas and Dante, down to Martin D'Arcy, Denis de Rougemont, Gabriel Marcel, C.S. Lewis, Anders Nygren, Ceslas Spicq and many others in our own century.[14] My own experience, reading and reflection suggest the following working description of what true Christian love (and indeed genuine human love) should involve.

(a) First of all, love means approval. To love someone is, in a most radical way, to approve of, joyfully wonder at and assent to their existence. The lover rejoices over the object of his or her love and in effect says: "It is a beautiful thing that you exist, that you are there in the world. I want you to exist. I approve of you utterly."

(b) Love actively wills the good of others; it engages itself and works for their welfare and happiness. The New Testament clearly privileges this aspect of love. To a lawyer who questions him about inheriting eternal life, Jesus tells the parable of the Good Samaritan and twice insists on the activity of love in the service of God and neighbor: "*Do* this, and you will live. . . . Go and *do* likewise" (Luke 10:28, 37). In the original Greek Paul's version of love in 1 Corinthians uses fifteen verbs to present the active ways through which love expresses itself (1 Cor 13:4–7). These verbs point to action; 1 John likewise indicates that "love must not be a matter of words or talk; it must be genuine, and show itself in *action*" (1 John 3:18).

(c) Common experience constantly illustrates love's power to deliver others from all kinds of evil and danger. It can heal human wounds, both great and small. Authentic love brings to life those who have suffered spiritually, psychologically and physically. Love acts to transform persons who in different ways have become disfigured; love can make the ugly beautiful.

Two examples. The word "love" does not occur in the parable of the prodigal son (Luke 15:11–32). Nevertheless, it is the father's love which makes it possible for the prodigal to return home not in the role of a hired servant but with the renewed dignity of a true son who is received with loving joy. Love works to bring about the moral and spiritual transformation of the prodigal son: "This my son was dead, and is alive again; he was lost and is found" (Luke 15:24). In *Crime and Punishment* Dostoevsky illustrates the power of dedicated love to heal and bring new life to an ugly murderer.

(d) Love not only saves and changes what is already there, but it also generates and creates what does not yet exist. Human procreation is the usual and proper paradigm for this generative and creative power of love. At the same time such loving generativity extends beyond parenting to what all human beings should become as truly creative persons, lovingly involved for others.

(e) Besides "being for" others, love also welcomes others and desires to "be with" them. Where hatred breaks down interpersonal communication and rejects the presence of others, love seeks the presence of those whom it loves, and communicates with them (John 5:20; 15:15).

(f) Finally, love intends to be eternally faithful. It affirms immortality and wishes that its object would never die. In "A Metaphysic of Hope" Gabriel Marcel has classically established the thesis of his *Mort de Demain:* the communion of love maintains indestructibility. To love someone is, in effect, to say "You will not die."[15]

RELATIONSHIPS OF LOVE

Ever so much more could be said if one wanted to cover the whole ground very thoroughly. But even this brief, working description of love allows one to elucidate those relationships of love revealed and deployed when—to use the early Christian language Paul took over—God the Father raised the dead Jesus (for example, Gal 1:1; 1 Cor 6:14; 1 Thess 1:9–10).

(1) *The Ministry of Jesus.* The four Gospels—and in particular the Synoptic Gospels—depict a life totally energized by love. There was the vertical relationship of Jesus to his Father and his horizontal relationship of love to other human beings.

First, the ministry expressed itself as a dialogue of love and obedience toward the God whom Jesus called *"Abba"* or "Father dear." In a reckless way Jesus gave himself totally to the service of the present

(Matt 12:28 par) and future (Matt 8:11 par) rule of God, that final offer of salvation for sinful and suffering men and women. He identified himself with the divine concern to forgive and save human beings. This loving obedience reached its climax in the garden of Gethsemani where Jesus prayed: "Abba, Father, all things are possible to you; remove this cup from me; yet not what I will, but what you will" (Mark 14:36).

From the Father's side there came approval. In an account of Jesus' baptism Mark speaks of a voice from heaven: "You are my beloved Son; with you I am well pleased" (1:11). At the transfiguration of Jesus a voice "from the cloud" told the three disciples: "This is my beloved Son; listen to him" (Mark 9:7). But this reciprocal relationship of love seemed to reach its end on the cross. When Jesus cried out, "My God, my God, why have you abandoned me?" (Mark 15:34), there was no reply from heaven.

Second, on the horizontal level that same love which made Jesus utterly subject to his Father's will also drove him to be completely available for the service of those who needed mercy and healing (Mark 10:45a; Luke 22:27). When the Synoptic Gospels report Jesus' ministry they do not normally talk in explicit terms of love (Mark 10:21). Nevertheless, they summon up an activity inspired by love. He rejected no one but gave himself away in love for all.

This self-giving proved to be not only dangerous but also deadly. It meant pain when others refused to respond (Luke 13:34; 19:41), loss of freedom (Mark 14:43ff) and finally the radical diminishment of death.

Jesus freely faced those consequences. In *Interpreting Jesus* I drew together the evidence for maintaining that he anticipated and accepted the violent death to which his ministry of obedience (to God) and service (toward human beings) led (79–92). But the crucifixion looked like the final victory of hatred. It raised and left open the questions: could such love for God and neighbor ever bring personal fulfillment and happiness? Is it always and everywhere literally fatal? Did (and does) truly self-forgetful love ultimately produce only self-loss and self-destruction?

(2) *The Father and Jesus.* The resurrection embodied a love that effectively answered the questions left open by Jesus' death.

(a) In the first instance, one can characterize "the love of the Father" experienced in the resurrection (*Dives in misericordia*, nr. 8) as a stupendous act of approval. In a most radical way, the Father assented to and rejoiced over the (new) existence of Jesus.

(b) On Calvary the cry of abandonment brought no powerful word from heaven; the divine help was not forthcoming. But in the resurrection the Father's love showed itself supremely active. In raising the dead Jesus, it worked for his ultimate welfare and highest good.

(c) That love "healed" Jesus who had suffered the final wounding of death. It saved him from definitive decay and destruction (Acts 2:24–31). It brought him to new and everlasting life. Love transformed Jesus who had become disfigured and ugly, "a man of sorrows" who "had no beauty, no majesty to draw our eyes, no grace to make us delight in him" (Is 53:2f). In resurrection he was taken up into the radiance of divine glory (Luke 24:26; John 17:1; Phil 2:9–11; 1 Tim 3:16; 1 Pet 1:21).

(d) Within the life of the Trinity the Son is not created but eternally begotten—from all eternity born "from the womb of the Father" (the Eleventh Council of Toledo; DS 526). In the language of Nicaea, "there never was [a time] when he was not" (DS 125). With the earthly Jesus, however, a real death meant that there came "a time when he was not." In the resurrection the Father's love *re*generated and *re*created to new life the dead Jesus whose human existence had been terminated by crucifixion.

(e) To describe the resurrection as the Father's full and final welcome to the incarnate and crucified Son might sound poetical rather than properly theological. Nevertheless, it seems a reasonable gloss on that "going to the Father" (John 13:1) which runs as a leitmotiv through the last discourse in John's Gospel. Likewise the image of "being exalted at the right hand of the Father" (Acts 2:33f; Rom 8:34; Eph 1:20; Mark 16:19), besides indicating how the risen Christ is revealed in his divine glory and saving power, also points to his Father's lovingly receiving him into a full presence and perfect communion of life (Rom 6:10). Jesus' interpersonal communication with the One whom he called "Abba" was interrupted by death, only to be restored in a new and final way.

(f) Lastly, in raising Jesus from the dead, the Father showed the fidelity of his love (see 2 Cor 1:18). To name Jesus as "the Son whom I love" (Mark 1:11; 9:7) was tantamount to saying, "I will not abandon him to death" (see Acts 2:25–31). Human beings speak brave words of love, but know their weakness in the face of death. The Father's word of love, however, was powerful when spoken over the corpse laid to rest near Calvary: "You will not perish in death but will live forever."

(3) *Jesus Himself and the Father.* The resurrection effectively showed that the horizontal "going-out-to-others" and "being-for-others" which Jesus practiced, even at the cost of his life, finally meant a "coming-to-himself." His self-forgetfulness brought the ultimate self-fulfillment of

risen life. His earthly existence, which had been lived and lost in love, was raised to its definitive state as the supreme case of losing and finding one's life (Mark 8:35 par). His loving fidelity to his Father and to those he served made him give up all—only to receive all through the Father's fidelity to him. The utter self-giving of Calvary was more than matched by the greatest gift of all, the transformation of resurrection.

As raised to new life, Jesus could give back to his Father a "fully reciprocated love" (Haughton). Their dialogue, which at the level of Jesus' humanity had been interrupted by death, could now be resumed in a full and final way. In the resurrection Jesus "experienced the love of the Father" (John Paul II), and could thus respond in love—giving as well as receiving.

(4) *The Holy Spirit.* In the eternal life of the Trinity the Spirit is the personal and personified love between Father and Son. On the historical, earthly level the Holy Spirit empowered Jesus in his life of loving obedience toward the Father and caring service toward human beings (for example, Mark 1:10, 12; Luke 4:14, 18). Being full of the Spirit, Jesus worked in the power of the Spirit.

As the personal agent of the resurrection (Rom 8:11), the Holy Spirit could "spiritualize" Jesus' humanity to the ultimate degree possible (1 Cor 15:42ff) and restore in a transformed way that dialogue between Jesus and his Father which death had broken off. In these terms we can call the resurrection a trinitarian event of love—with the Spirit as the personal exchange of love between Father and Son.

(5) *Jesus and Humanity.* His new relationship to the human race forms another dimension of that mystery of love that is the resurrection of Jesus. The first Easter brought a liberation from the normal, earthly limitations of time and space. During his ministry Jesus' loving service of others had been limited by the ordinary conditions of human life. The radical transformation of resurrection liberated him to be actively present everywhere, so as to affect lovingly (and mysteriously) the lives of all men and women, to fashion a community of love which the New Testament presents through the figure of the groom/bride relationship (Eph 5:25ff; Rev 21:9), and to pour into the hearts of believers the Spirit of love (John 20:22; Acts 2:33; Rom 5:5). With his earthly body Jesus had reached out to touch lepers, embrace children, forgive sinners, break bread for the hungry and communicate the saving truth of God. Through his risen body that service continues and is enhanced: he ministers really, if under signs, in the whole sacramental system of the

Church. The gift of his risen presence in the Eucharist aims to bring his disciples to everlasting life (John 6:48ff), that final consummation which is "the unimpeded outpouring of divine love" (Haughton).

(6) *Human Beings and Jesus.* By its very nature, as I noted above, love looks for or at least invites reciprocity. Here we can apply to the situation of the resurrection some reflections which von Balthasar offers about the incarnation. He notes how a "glorious" or beautiful object attracts us. Beauty is deeply desirable and freshly satisfying. We want to stay in its presence. At the same time, the object we love always appears wonderful and glorious to us. In brief what is glorious draws forth our love, and what we love is or becomes glorious. Von Balthasar observes that this convergence of love and glory (or beauty) is exemplified in the incarnation, "where the divine logos *descends* [italics mine] to manifest and interpret himself as love, as *agape*, and therein as the Glory."[16] This relationship between love and beauty, which Saint Augustine classically formulated in his *Confessions* (X, 27), also bears strikingly on the situation of those who reciprocate the *risen* Christ's love.

After Jesus has risen and ascended (John 20:17) to enter into his final glory (John 17:1), John's Gospel reports Peter's protestations of love for his risen and glorified Lord (John 21:15–17). Radiantly exalted, Christ draws worship and wonder from the universe (Phil 2:9–11; Rev 1:12ff). This praise springs from love. Some Easter narratives, even though they do not explicitly state this, certainly hint at the risen Christ's glory and beauty which attract our human love and joyful worship (Luke 24:13–35; John 20:11–18).

John's Gospel calls to mind another aspect of the human response in love to the paschal mystery. Love makes it possible for the beloved disciple to "see" the empty tomb and on the basis of such an ambiguous sign to reach Easter faith (John 20:8). Love makes that disciple sensitively aware of the risen Lord's presence and capable of identifying the stranger on the beach at dawn: "It is the Lord" (John 21:7).

In the case of any Easter faith there is something of what Rahner calls the "circumincession of knowledge and love."[17] What he says about our relationship to mystery as such can be properly applied to the insight and love involved in a faith relationship to the Easter mystery. Because of the mutual conditioning between knowing and willing, love enables us to recognize the truth and know Christ's resurrection. The ultimate "incomprehensibility" of this mystery "forces knowledge to surpass itself and both preserve and transform itself in a more comprehensive act, that of love." This mystery is "the goal where reason arrives when it attains its perfection by becoming love" (43). In short, by remembering the role of love, we respect both the freedom of Easter faith and the mystery with which we freely relate through that faith.

The final words of Jesus' prayer to his "righteous Father" sum up what the crucifixion and resurrection are to bring for those who believe: "I have made known, so that the love with which you have loved me may be in them, and I in them" (John 17:25–26). The paschal mystery aims to establish a new community of love which through the Holy Spirit will exercise that love which defines the life of God. The last discourse in John's Gospel makes it abundantly clear that his love is to be directed not only toward the risen Lord himself but also toward his/our brothers and sisters (John 13:12–17; 34–35).

For one who believes in him something of Jesus' new beauty also shines through other men and women. In a special way they are all signs and sacraments of the risen Lord. They too invite our love, a love that transcends all "normal" human divisions (Gal 3:28) and a love made possible by the Spirit of the risen Christ.

At the beginning of *La Vita Nuova* Dante recalls the decisive moment in his boyhood "*quando a li miei occhi apparve prima la gloriosa donna de la mia mente* (when the woman whom my mind beholds in glory first appeared before my eyes)." The lifetime he spent exploring and interpreting his love for Beatrice hints at the challenge of Christ's resurrection. That mystery of divine love simply transcends any rational explanation to be readily comprehended by our minds. Easter first happened through the freedom of God's love and will never cease to invite the free, lifelong commitment of our love.

9

Communicating the Risen Christ

Back in Chapter Two I suggested that Bultmann's interpretation of the resurrection might be credited with at least raising a crucial issue: How is the risen Christ communicated? My closing chapter will first reflect on this challenge of communication and then add some afterthoughts on the whole of my book.

COMMUNICATION

Through being non-symbolic, non-experiential and non-liturgical, many recent Christologies have not appreciated and furthered the communication of the risen Christ.[1] Often they have been especially good at using scriptural and historical scholarship. But to the extent that they have persistently refused to explore relevant symbols, reflect imaginatively on profound human experience, and draw on the Church's liturgy, they have failed to play their part in communicating successfully the presence of the risen Lord.[2]

Here I do not want to spend time elucidating the link between (i) successful communication and (ii) symbols (including liturgical symbols) and human experience. Let me briefly state my conviction that any version of communication should pay attention to the interpretation of experience, the sharing (and constructing) of meaning, and the transmission of information. Communication takes place through symbols which genuinely unite people, interpret their religious and human experience, and make them partners in a mutual dialogue that shares and constructs meaning. In a multitude of ways experience conveys information and yields meaning through its immediate contact with reality. Liturgical symbolism—with its whole range of architectural, artistic, verbal, musical and bodily elements—offers illuminating and liberating communication.

Hence those who talk and write about the risen Lord in a non-symbolic, non-experiential and non-liturgical fashion fail to appreciate and use essential means for communicating him. Such theologians cannot expect to shed sufficient light on our common search for Christ and the images of him actually operative in people's lives.

I want first to substantiate briefly my broad claim that much recent Christology has not been adequately symbolic, experiential and liturgical. Then I can present some suggestions to help change this situation and so meet better the challenge of communicating the risen Christ and our belief in him.

(1) *Symbols, Experience and Liturgy.*   When North Atlantic theologians (and for that matter Latin American theologians) write about the risen Christ, how often does a sense of *symbolism* show up? Take, for example, the widespread absence of reflection on the rich range of meanings expressed symbolically by the shroud of Turin and the empty tomb.

In scholarly Christology today the shroud of Turin normally remains a forbidden topic. The enormous popular and scientific interest in the fourteen-foot-long piece of cloth kept in Turin Cathedral is unmistakable. Yet contemporary Christology cannot bring itself to acknowledge the existence of the shroud, let alone reflect on its symbolic meaning as a pictorial counterpart to Saint Paul's message about Christ being "crucified in weakness but living by the power of God" (2 Cor 13:4). The marks of the wounded body on the shroud encapsulize the fearful sufferings and "weakness" of Jesus' passion. At the same time, viewers have consistently sensed the majestic power and transforming peace which come through the battered face. The shroud repeatedly proves itself to be "powerful in weakness," a unique icon of the crucified and risen Lord.

Then a word about the significance of the empty tomb. I wonder how many people reject as an unhistorical legend the discovery of Jesus' open and empty tomb simply because theologians have failed to explore and point out what that tomb can express. For instance, the fact that Jesus' corpse was mysteriously but really "incorporated" into his glorious, risen existence vividly symbolizes, as we have seen, the nature of the final redemption which God initiated with the resurrection. Redemption does not mean an escape from this material creation, but its ultimate transformation. Generally one does not find in recent Christology any such interpretation of Jesus' empty tomb.

Then have recent Christologies been sufficiently *experiential?* Official Church teaching coming from the Second Vatican Council (*Gau-*

dium et Spes, nr. 4ff), the Latin American bishops (Puebla document, nrs. 87–92) and Pope John Paul II (*Redemptor Hominis*, nrs. 15–16) have recalled the various evil forces which human beings experience as enslaving and destroying them. It is our primordial anxiety about all forms of death, absurdity and hatred confronting us that makes us ready to hear the good news of the risen Jesus who offers life, meaning and love—both here and hereafter. Nevertheless, apart from a few like James Mackey and Jon Sobrino, contemporary Christological writing has generally remained non-experiential.[3] If basic human experiences of evil are ignored, will thoughtful readers comprehend and truly accept what theologians offer when they speak of the role of the resurrected Jesus as Savior of the world?

To conclude this sweeping set of complaints about the failure to communicate, I want to note the almost total absence of *liturgical* data in recent Christologies. How many Western European, North American or Latin American theologians draw on liturgical sources and devotional practices to explore and present the saving "work" and divine identity of Jesus Christ? And yet it is forms of worship, with the music and visual art which accompany them, that primarily transmit to believers what they experience and know about the risen Lord. Liturgy is the great vehicle of tradition which evokes and hands on belief in him as living and present.

If theologians, or at least Roman Catholic ones, had taken some notice of what their liturgy communicates, this should have decided for them the much-disputed question of the starting-point and center of Christology. The liturgy clearly supports starting with the paschal mystery and centering Christological thinking there. From the outset Christians knew themselves to be baptized into the death and resurrection of Jesus (Rom 6:3–5). Their celebration of the Eucharist meant proclaiming the death of the risen Lord until he comes (1 Cor 11:26). Today at Mass the acclamations after the consecration embody the same faith: "Lord, by your cross and resurrection you have set us free." We do not say, "Incarnating you destroyed our death, preaching you restored our life." Of course, the birth and ministry of Jesus are vitally important and should never be neglected. But a liturgically based Christology will take shape around the crucifixion and resurrection of Jesus. From that midpoint it can look backward (through his life, the incarnation, the history of the chosen people and finally right back to creation itself), and forward (through the coming of the Holy Spirit and the story of the Church on to the future consummation of all things).

Thus any Christology which follows the witness of Christian worship will center itself on the paschal mystery. That should enable it to communicate more effectively with believers who express and experience their faith primarily in terms of Christ's dying and rising. At the Eucharist Catholics say, "Dying you destroyed our death, rising you restored our life." In the Rite of Penance they hear the prayer of absolution which likewise points to the crucifixion and resurrection as the central mystery of redemption: "God, the Father of mercies, through the death and resurrection of his Son has reconciled the world to himself and sent the Holy Spirit among us for the forgiveness of sins." For Christians in general Holy Week and Easter Sunday form the climax of their yearly worship. A Christology which respects all that will be aligned with the familiar liturgical experience of believers and hence better able to communicate with them about their experience of belief in the risen Jesus as Son of God and Savior of the world.

Apropos of this last point, it is significant that even Walter Kasper, who has supplied one of the best Christologies from the 1970s, fails to be sufficiently liturgical. He rightly maintains that "the Jesus tradition" should not be removed

> from the context of proclamation, liturgy and parish practice of the Christian churches. Only where the message of Jesus Christ is alive and believed, where that same Spirit is alive who enlivens the writings of the New Testament, can the testimony of the New Testament be understood as a living witness. Even today, therefore, the community of the Church is the proper location of the Jesus tradition and encounter with Christ.[4]

Despite this stress on locating Christological reflection within the context of Christian preaching, worship and life, Kasper, nevertheless, does not appeal to this context when he argues for Good Friday and Easter Sunday as the proper center for such systematic reflection. His grounds are simply biblical and not liturgical:

> According to Scripture, Christology has its centre in the cross and the Resurrection. From that midpoint it extends forward to the *Parousia* and back to the Pre-existence and the Incarnation (*ibid.*, 37).

What has been presented so far in this chapter has been largely negative. It can all be put more positively as an appeal for future Christologies which would not only maintain the current advances in historical and biblical scholarship but also allow themselves to be symbolic, experiential, liturgical and hence better able to communicate the presence of the risen Jesus. To do that would be in effect to take a cue from one of the supreme Christologies of all time, that of John's Gospel.

The language and narrative of John are richly symbolic. In those formulae of self-presentation, such as "I am the vine, I am the good shepherd, I am the bread of life," Jesus (who is very much the risen Lord of the here and now) uses concrete images to reveal himself. He appeals to things we perceive in our world to express something about his mysterious divine identity and saving function. Further, the Fourth Gospel—from the meeting with Andrew in Chapter One to that with Simon Peter in Chapter Twenty-One—is full of individual encounters with Jesus which symbolize astonishingly well the deepest spiritual needs and problems of human beings. When we read those stories, they invite us to participate imaginatively with such persons as Nicodemus in Chapter Three, the Samaritan woman in Chapter Four and the crippled man in Chapter Five.

The liturgical dimension of John fits closely in with the Gospel's symbolic character. In the past some commentators may have gone overboard in finding a fully sacramental intention in its composition. All the same, the liturgical overtones of such sections as Chapter Six (the Eucharist) and Chapter Nine (baptism) are unmistakable.[5]

The symbolic and liturgical character of John's Gospel goes hand in hand with its experiential quality. It calls on its readers to experience the living Jesus in deeper and richer ways. Over and over again it shows us representative individuals who allow him to change and transform their lives. They come to "know" Jesus or, as we would say, "experience" him. Generally the mainline translations have been coy about rendering *oida* as "experience." At best they discreetly indicate this possibility in a footnote, as the Revised Standard Version does in *The New Oxford Annotated Bible* when it comes to the Samaritans' reaction to what they heard from the women about Jesus (4:39–42): "Faith based on the testimony of another (*the woman*) is vindicated in personal experience." It might have been simpler to have translated John 4:42 as follows: "They said to the woman, 'It is no longer because of your words that we believe, for we have heard for ourselves, and *experienced* that this is indeed the Savior of the world.' " So often in the Fourth Gospel "experience" catches the full sense of John's "know." Let me give one other example, Jesus' question to Philip: "Have I been with you so long, and yet you do not know me (= have not really experienced me)?" (14:9).

I want to suggest that a Christology built around the theme of the risen Christ's presence promises to be properly symbolic, liturgical and experiential. For the moment I wish only to note that John exemplifies these three qualities. The result is a portrait of Jesus and his interaction with others which nearly two thousand years after the composition of the Gospel continues to communicate splendidly and constantly elicit the "I-have-been-there" feeling. Whatever else John's portrait of Jesus may be, it certainly interprets experience, transmits information, shares meaning, invites participation and acts transformingly. In short, one can understand why this symbolic, liturgical and experiential Gospel is highly successful in communicating the risen Lord and his presence.

(2) *Communicative Presence.* In the light of John's Gospel, what shape could one propose for a Christology built around the communicative presence of the crucified and risen Jesus? Such an Easter Christology, as I have claimed, would be liturgical, symbolic and experiential.

It is no accident that the classic modern statement from the Church's magisterium about Christ's living presence comes from a document on liturgy, *Sacrosanctum Concilium* of the Second Vatican Council. That Constitution on the Sacred Liturgy acknowledges various forms of Christ's personal presence in liturgical worship:

> Christ is always present in his Church, especially in her liturgical cel-
> ebrations. He is present in the Sacrifice of the Mass not only in the
> person of his minister . . . but especially in the eucharistic species.
> By his power he is present in the sacraments so that when anyone
> baptizes, it is really Christ himself who baptizes. He is present in his
> word, since it is he himself who speaks when the holy scriptures are
> read in the Church. Lastly, he is present when the Church prays and
> sings (nr. 7).

A Christology of the risen Christ's communicative presence should base itself on the liturgy. It is in and through the liturgy that the Lord is specially present and revealed in a rich variety of ways. But we need also to look beyond the Church's worship and Christ's sacramental presence to many other signs and symbols of his dynamic presence.

In *Redemptor Hominis* John Paul II recalls that mystery of Jesus Christ, "in which each of the four thousand million human beings living on our planet has become a sharer from the moment he is conceived beneath the heart of his mother" (nr. 13). The living Christ comes to us behind those millions of faces; we can properly experience them as visible signs and sacraments of his invisible presence. A Christology of presence will ask: What does the mystery of his union with them say to us now as we seek to clarify and expound his person and saving work?

In particular, we should recognize those who suffer to be privileged carriers of his presence here and now. Left to ourselves, we would hardly turn to various sectors of human suffering for help in understanding and interpreting the continuing presence of the risen Christ. But this truth comes through clearly from the Gospels, Saint Paul's letters and other parts of the New Testament. Jesus named the hungry, imprisoned, sick and displaced persons as identified with him in a special way (Matt 25:31–46). Then he died in seeming failure and terrible pain, crucified between two criminals. That was precisely the moment when the Roman centurion broke through to the final secret of Jesus' identity: "Truly this man was the Son of God" (Mark 15:39). This event of powerless suffering remains paradigmatic. Paul discerned and interpreted the passion of his own missionary experiences as *the* place in which the crucified and risen Christ had proved peculiarly present and active in the apostle's life (2 Cor 4:8ff; 6:4ff; 11:23ff; 12:7ff).

Blaise Pascal pointed to Christ's continuing presence in all human suffering: "Jesus will be in agony till the end of the world. We must not sleep during that time" (*Pensées*, 552). One group whose history has consistently expressed that passion are the Jews, the chosen people who could also be called God's "symbolic people." No other race as such has symbolized as they do the divine intentions for human beings. Around 58 A.D. Saint Paul reflected on how this symbolic people, his own nation, spoke to him of God's mysterious plan for the whole world (Rom 9–11). The apostle wrote of the law, the covenants, the promises, the future salvation of Israel and the rest, but from his place in the first century he could not be aware of one overwhelming reality, the appalling history of suffering which his race would undergo. In the twentieth century, as in Paul's day, this symbolic people communicates many messages to those who care to look, pray and think. Among other things they are a living reminder of Jesus the Jew, God's suffering servant who rose from the dead. In a special way, their agony has embodied and symbolized his. The painful story of this symbolic people should enter into any adequate Christology, particularly one focused on the presence of the crucified and risen Christ.

Above and beyond the details of the Jewish story, there is the full range of other events which make up contemporary history. These events, which in a world of modern communications we all somehow experience, can also manifest the working out of salvation through Jesus' rising from the dead. Saint Paul sees all humanity and creation "groaning" together in a history of suffering as they move toward the fullness of liberating redemption (Rom 8:18ff). Through Christ the story of the world unfolds as a story of cosmic and human reconciliation (Rom 5:10–11; 2 Cor 5:18ff; Col 1:20ff). By means of its vivid scenarios and apocalyptic images, the Book of Revelation invites its readers to contemplate the victory of the suffering Christ in human history. Now it would be very odd to agree with the New Testament witnesses that his reconciling power is presently shaping world history toward the day of full and final salvation, while at the same time refusing to acknowledge any visible signs of his presence around us. In the "signs of the times" Christians note and seek to interpret current indications of Christ's personal presence and influence.

Further, the contemporary interest in dialogue with non-Christian religions (and ideologies) turns to other areas of modern experience which can enrich our sense of the ongoing presence of Christ. The Second Vatican Council initiated a theme which was taken up by Pope Paul VI, by the closing message of the bishops' synod of 1977 (nr. 15), and by John Paul II in *Redemptor Hominis* (nr. 11): the "*semina Verbi* (seeds of the Word)" which disclose here and now a kind of "inchoate" presence of Christ beyond Christianity. In *Evangelii Nuntiandi* Paul VI described non-Christian religions as "all impregnated with unnumerable 'seeds of the Word' " (nr. 53).

This attitude encourages us to acknowledge and reverence the risen Christ as, in some way or another, actively there in other religions even before any contact with the Gospel has taken place. These other faiths and their cultures have proved a matrix in which his saving revelation has also been effectively present. Some reflection on all this has its place in any theology of Christ's communicating and communicated presence.

T.S. Eliot's line "we had the experience but missed the meaning" bears applying here. We Christians have the experience of liturgical worship, human suffering, the Jewish people, contemporary history and the lives of those who espouse other religions or various ideologies. But we may miss much of the Christological meaning. The challenge is to interpret and articulate what all those symbolic realities communicate about the living Christ and his meaningful presence. The danger is that we can have all these experiences but simply miss Christ, who as *the* Meaning (upper case) transcends the various particular meanings (lower case) of life.

To conclude. A Christology of communicative presence is an Easter Christology ready to reflect not only on the historical Jesus but also the Christ of the liturgy, human suffering, the Jewish people, the signs of the times, and the various world religions. His living, communicative presence is the link between all those contexts. Very many symbols can appropriately evoke and express the experience of Christ and his meaningful presence. By raising questions about symbolism, liturgy, experience and presence, this chapter aims to encourage contemporary Christology to become more clearly what it should always be— properly effective in communicating the crucified and risen Jesus.

SOME AFTERTHOUGHTS

I cannot finish this work on Jesus' resurrection, I can only abandon it. But before doing so, I feel strongly the temptation to defend myself against critics. Some reviewers will doubtless attribute the reflections on the Petrine ministry in Chapter Six to the fact that I teach in Rome. Let me point out that Chapter Seven of my *The Resurrection of Jesus Christ* (= *The Easter Jesus*), which was written and published before I ever came to live on the banks of the Tiber, developed the first sketch of that approach. More critics may get after me for discussing some exponents of the swoon theory, non-scholarly writers (like Joel Carmichael and Ian Wilson) and the television program, "Jesus the Evidence." Here I simply beg to differ. Professional theologians should take note of such popular material which often commands a huge public. Some readers may wonder whether my opening quotation encourages a passive waiting around until life ends and the only real life of eternity begins. Those words from Léon Bloy were never meant to support any such disengagement from the earthly tasks that true Christian hope urges us to take up.

Let me admit in advance, however, that this book did not address some major issues connected with resurrection. Chapter Seven did not ask: What is the relationship of mind (and/or soul) to body? Why is it important for any view of the resurrection? Further, my proposal about our embodied history being resurrected must face the question: How can our history be resurrected in an existence which is not temporal? Any response would need to establish two points. (a) Time and eternity are not exclusively different. Just as some kind of eternal life can already be present in temporality, so there could be some kind of temporality in eternal life. (b) Time is more than a pure and mere succession of events (as Descartes and Hume would lead us to believe), but has also something cumulative about it. Every moment is a coming together of many things which are all somehow preserved. Likewise, or rather even more so, resurrected life could be a coming together of a whole, accumulated past which remains present in us.

This work began by proposing three "stations" of the resurrection. The point was this. We can learn about the first Easter not only by studying in the library but also by suffering in a slum and singing in a church. True theology entails praying and suffering as well as reading and thinking. As I end it, I hope that this book will encourage such an integral approach to the great mystery of the crucified Jesus' resurrection from the dead.

Appendix

Luminous Appearances of the Risen Christ

Views that the transfiguration story in Mark 9:2–8 derives from a retrojected Easter appearance associate luminous elements with resurrection traditions—a case which has been argued recently by James M. Robinson. He has served historians of Christianity by his work in organizing the publication of the Nag Hammadi papyrus codices (3rd to 5th century A.D.). But not all the conclusions which Robinson has reached on the basis of his study of gnosticism seem thoroughly convincing. In particular, he argues that even at the time Mark composed his Gospel, a gnosticizing trajectory had already begun and was in conflict with an orthodox trajectory. Mark initiated a process of correcting original traditions about Easter, in which "real bodiliness became increasingly prominent, no doubt at the expense of . . . glorious appearance." Once Mark started the process, later New Testament writings followed suit:

> The blinding light of the Damascus road gave way to a resurrected Christ who resembled a gardener, a tourist on the way to Emmaus, or a fisherman by the sea, and whose mode of existence was still bodily in that he could eat, be touched, and resume life on earth.[1]

According to Robinson, Mark had included no resurrection appearances, "perhaps because those available were so luminous as to seem disembodied."[2] The later evangelists provided resurrection appearances, but continued the process of blunting the gnosticizing quality of the Easter traditions by ending their Gospels with bodily as opposed to luminous appearances. Admittedly Luke included in Acts the Pauline tradition of an appearance in light from heaven, but he played it down "as hardly more than a conversion story."[3]

210

Robinson proposes then the following hypothesis. An early Christian tradition, which was not exclusively gnostic but which was to be suppressed by emerging orthodoxy, told of the risen Christ's appearance in light on a mountain. This original luminous visualization of Christ's appearance(s) survived at "mislocated" places: the transfiguration story in Mark 9:2–8; Paul's conversion as "an encounter with a blinding light, which according to Luke's chronology falls outside the period of resurrection appearances"; and the appearance to Peter which

> . . . because of its luminosity, ceded its position within the accepted
> period of resurrection appearances, and, rather than being simply
> lost, found a new location as the transfiguration story, which is
> clearly the same scene as that to which 2 Peter 1:16–18 refers.[4]

At the start of Christianity, however, were the appearances of the resurrected Christ understood to be (a) luminous (disembodied?) appearances of (b) a gnostic, albeit not exclusively gnostic, kind? Apropos of (b) others have rightly doubted whether the alleged gnostic trajectory began so early.[5] What Robinson calls a trajectory looks more like scholarly retrojection, or reading later documents too far back into earlier history. But in this appendix I want to discuss his case for (a).

To begin with, Robinson himself is tentative about several pieces of evidence he lines up. The assessment of Mark's transfiguration story as originally a luminous resurrection appearance to Peter he admits to be "contested."[6] The claim that the earliest evangelist, Mark, included no resurrection appearances because the only appearance stories available to him were luminous, disembodied ones is qualified with a "perhaps." Further, Robinson recognizes that a Pauline understanding of the resurrection body makes "it possible to affirm the bodiliness of a luminous appearance."[7] An appearance in light did not necessarily entail the resurrected Christ being in a disembodied state.

Yet despite this admission, Robinson seems in places to suppose that in the Easter tradition a "religious experience" could not have been an experience of something or rather someone bodily. He argues, for instance, that "the narrations of the empty tomb in the gospels tend to emphasize the continuity of the same body, lest the luminousness of the appearances suggest that it was *just a ghost, just religious experience*."[8] Certainly the Gospels tend to highlight such a continuity,[9] while Paul in 1 Cor 15:42–51 brings out the discontinuity between the physical, earthly body and the spiritual, risen body. But must "religious experience" be an experience of something or someone who is ghostly and disembodied? Just as on the side of the object (the resurrected Jesus) an appearance in light did not automatically mean that he could only be in a disembodied state, so on the side of the subjects (the disciples) such a luminous appearance did not automatically mean that their religious experience could only be one of someone ghostly and disembodied.

As part of his argument Robinson appeals to Rev 1:13–16, "the only resurrection appearance in the New Testament that is described in any detail, though it is usually overlooked due to not being placed at the end of a gospel." This appearance which "took place in the 90s" has

> . . . in common with Paul's much earlier but equally uninhibited luminous visualization of the resurrection in the 30s the fact that these are the only two resurrection appearances recorded by persons who themselves received the appearances, Paul and John of Patmos—and both these authenticated visualizations of a resurrection appearance were of a luminous kind!

The testimony of Paul and John of Patmos allows Robinson to conclude that "the original visualizations of resurrection appearances had been luminous, the experiencing of a blinding light, a heavenly body such as Luke reports Stephen saw (Acts 7:55–56)."[10]

All of this seems dubious. First, in Revelation the opening vision (presented with apocalyptic motifs which prepare the reader for the rich imagery to follow) is not a resurrection appearance in the sense of making the visionary into an apostle—that is to say, an official eyewitness to the risen Lord and a founder of Christianity. Elsewhere Robinson himself notes that "being a witness to the resurrection" was "the basic qualification for apostleship."[11] In Revelation there is no suggestion whatsoever that John of Patmos is now becoming "an eyewitness to the . . . appearance of the resurrected Christ,"[12] and so receiving this basic qualification for apostolic ministry. The vision functions in a quite different way—to introduce and communicate messages to seven churches of Asia Minor (Rev 1:17–3:22). The Book of Revelation does not attempt to describe the making of an apostle; in fact it looks back to the apostles who have already done their work as founders (Rev 22:14). Hence to maintain that Rev 1:13–16 describes one of the "resurrection appearances" both slips over the function within the book itself of that vision in apocalyptic glory, and ignores the link between such appearances of the risen Christ and apostolic qualifications (as recognized, in their somewhat differing ways, by Paul, Luke, Matthew and John).

Furthermore, what we find in Rev 1:13–16 is not a description in the ordinary sense, but rather a comparison, in which "the feel or value, the effect or impression of one thing is compared with that of another."

John of Patmos is "not giving a visual image which a skillful painter might reproduce." Rather,

> . . . he is telling his readers that if, for example, they will think of the feelings they have before a torrent in spate or beneath the brilliance of the midday sun, they will have some inkling of the sense of majesty and sublimity which he experienced in the presence of the heavenly Christ.

In short, Rev 1:13–16 does not purport to describe in detail the Lord's appearance, but uses traditional imagery to provide an "affective comparison" expressing the visionary's reaction to Christ's presence.[13]

What of Robinson's second authority? Paul hardly supports the attempt to set an experience which "took place in the 90s" on the same level as his own encounter with the risen Lord in the 30s. Paul differentiates between the fundamental post-resurrection encounters and all later experiences of the risen Jesus: "Last of all" Christ "appeared also to me" (1 Cor 15:8). With that appearance the series of meetings which qualified the recipient for apostleship was closed. Then Paul's "uninhibited luminous visualization of the resurrection [= of the resurrected Christ's appearance, presumably] in the 30s" does not come directly from the apostle himself. We simply do not have such direct reports from Paul as "an eyewitness" to a "luminous appearance of the resurrected Christ."[14] Where Paul himself writes of his encounter with the risen Jesus (1 Cor 9:1; 15:8; Gal 1:12, 16; and possibly Phil 3:8), he never visualizes it in an "uninhibited" way. Just possibly 2 Cor 4:6, which speaks of God shining "in our hearts to give the light of the knowledge of the glory of God in the face of Christ," may also refer to Paul's apostolic call-experience (as well as to general Christian experience). But Robinson does not invoke this passage. Rather, what he has in mind are some details in the three accounts of the appearance to Paul given by Acts (see 9:3; 22:6; 26:13). Certainly Luke does present that appearance as a luminous one "from heaven." But we are dealing there with three somewhat different versions which seemingly were in circulation in the early Church, not with a "visualization" of the appearance recorded and reported directly by Paul himself.

Then there is the third authority to whom Robinson appeals. What the dying Stephen is described as having seen of God's heavenly glory and of Jesus "standing at the right hand of God" was not a resurrection appearance which made him an apostle. Luke never claims that. Paul does not include Stephen when, on the basis of traditional material and his own experience, he lists witnesses to the resurrection (1 Cor 15:5–

8). Whatever we are to make of Stephen's experience, like the vision reported at the beginning of Revelation it is not on a par with the appearances to Peter, Paul, etc., and hence no guide to what "the original
visualizations of resurrection appearances" were like.

What I miss in Robinson's presentation is a clear sense of the difference between the foundational post-resurrection appearances and
other kinds of religious experiences. He assures us that "the luminous
visualization of resurrection appearances may be the kind of experience
that *in that day* would have been considered a vision."[15] Such a remark
passes over the fact that, although the New Testament calls certain phenomena "visions," apart from one passage (Acts 26:19) it never uses that
term of a resurrection appearance. Robinson himself observes that Luke
summarizes the meeting with "two men in dazzling apparel" (24:4) as "a
vision of angels" (24:23). That makes it all the more significant that Luke
(except for Acts 26:19) nowhere applies the word to a resurrection appearance. In the same context Robinson cites Paul who writes of "visions and revelations of the Lord" (2 Cor 12:1).[16] But these later ecstatic
episodes which took place "fourteen years ago" (2 Cor 12:2)—that is to
say, around 42 and so long after his initial call-experience (33/35)—are
not invoked by Paul to validate his fundamental role as apostolic witness
to the risen Christ. In the face of troublesome opponents who boast of
their high spiritual experiences, Paul refers (among other things) to some
extraordinary experiences of a "heavenly" nature which had happened
to him. But he does not put these "visions and revelations of the Lord"
on the same level as the once-and-for-all post-resurrection appearance
which made him one of those who through their public witness to the
risen Christ founded the Church. Of course, Paul offers practically no
details about the nature of such an appearance, but he is clear about its
special function in establishing him and others as apostles.

In developing his hypothesis about luminous appearances of the
resurrected Christ, Robinson claims that in the case of two eyewitnesses
(Paul and John of Patmos) the identification of such an appearance "as
the Spirit seems near at hand." He supports this claim by calling attention to 1 Cor 15:44–45 and 2 Cor 3:17–18.[17] But neither of these passages
refers as such to the historical appearance of the risen Christ to Paul. 1
Cor 15:44 speaks in general of the "spiritual" nature of risen bodily existence as opposed to the physical nature of earthly bodily existence.
When 1 Cor 15:45 calls Christ "the last Adam" and "a life-giving Spirit,"
it indicates that spiritual state in which his risen humanity confers life
by communicating to others the Holy Spirit (see Rom 1:3–4). Neither
verse intends to describe a particular appearance of the risen Lord, let
alone identify that appearance in terms of the Spirit. Nor does 2 Cor

3:17–18 have anything to say about such an appearance. When Paul states that "the Lord is the Spirit," he does so in a passage (2 Cor 3:1–18) where he makes an elaborate comparison and contrast between the old and the new covenants (the dead letter and the life-giving Spirit; the fading glory of Moses and his dispensation as over against the lasting glory of Christ and his dispensation, etc.), and emphasizes the liberating, transforming influence of the risen Christ here and now on believers: "the Lord *is* the Spirit." He neither says that "the Lord *was* the Spirit," nor in any other way testifies as an eyewitness that his encounter with the resurrected Christ was to be identified as an appearance of the Spirit.

As regards the Book of Revelation, we have already seen that its opening vision is not a resurrection appearance which qualified the recipient to be an apostle. Further, when John of Patmos recalls being "in the Spirit" and ends his seven letters with the exhortation "He who has an ear, let him hear what the Spirit says to the churches" (2:7, 11, 17, 29; 3:6, 13, 22), he is not describing and identifying some appearance of the risen Christ. Rather, the visionary knows that the Spirit who comes from the exalted Lord is working and speaking in and through him. In that sense what "the Spirit says to the churches" is what the exalted Lord wants to say to the churches.

To clinch his case for a primary identification of the appearance of the resurrected Christ with the Spirit, Robinson turns to Luke 24:37 ("they thought they were seeing a ghost"). He argues that here Luke rejects an identification of the risen Christ with the Spirit (to which Paul and John of Patmos are supposed to bear witness) and represents the Spirit as coming on the scene only fifty days later at Pentecost.[18] There seems to be some confusion here between the ongoing spiritual power of the risen Lord (to which Paul and John of Patmos refer) and his bodily reality experienced by those to whom he appeared at the outset of Christianity. In 24:37 and 39 Luke is rejecting, not some attempt to identify an appearance of the risen Christ with an appearance of the Spirit, but late first-century skepticism (from whatever quarter) about the factuality of the resurrection and the bodily reality of the risen Christ.

Finally, in line with his thesis Robinson detects various "vestiges" of the luminous visualization of the resurrected Jesus "in the otherwise very human appearances at the end of the canonical gospels." For instance, the failure to recognize at once the risen Lord (Luke 24:16, 31; John 20:14–15; 21:4) may also derive "from the luminous visualization," in which "it is quite understandable that one would not recognize a blinding light (Acts 9:5; 22:8; 26:15)."[19] Undoubtedly the appearances of the risen Christ were not and were not understood to be "a matter of normal vision, catching sight of a recognizable human companion."[20] However, this motif could well derive from another source (the initial failure of the disciples to recognize the risen Jesus whom they were not expecting to rise from the dead), and have been used by Luke and John to express two things: the transformation involved in Jesus' resurrection and the fact that seeing him risen to new life required more than ordinary human vision.

Robinson also takes "the sudden appearance and disappearance of Jesus" to be another motif (preserved at the end of Luke and John), which "originally developed in connection with luminous visualizations of the resurrected Christ."[21] Really? Could it be possible that it simply was like that—the risen Christ appeared and disappeared at will? Two evangelists maintained this motif which indicated so well that everything depended on the risen Jesus, who could not be sought out and observed like any ordinary person on the face of the earth but disclosed himself when and to whom he wished.

To conclude. If Robinson is correct and a tradition of luminous appearances of the risen Christ was primary, then Matthew, Luke and John did a remarkably good job in purging the tradition of that incipient gnosticism. What has struck most commentators about the Easter appearances in the Gospels is not the "vestiges" of luminous visualization of the resurrected Jesus which still remained, but rather the way these stories lack such traits (which most scholars would describe as apocalyptic glory rather than gnostic light). C.F. Evans' observation on the Emmaus encounter is typical: "The story is the furthest possible remove from the category of heavenly vision of the Lord in glory."[22]

Robinson's hard evidence for original luminous appearances of the resurrected Lord comes from gnostic sources.[23] This evidence is not only late, but may in fact derive (as a kind of decadent spin-off) from the earlier Gospel tradition rather than provide us with any independent information about the ambient in which Paul's letters, Mark, Luke, Acts, Revelation and even John were written.

Notes

INTRODUCTION

1. Wolfgang Goethe, *Faust*, Part One (Penguin Books, Harmonsworth, 1949) 152.
2. *Ibid.*, 55–56.

I. THE RESURRECTION IN THE STORY OF CHRISTIANITY

1. On Gnosticism see P. Perkins, *The Gnostic Dialogue* (New York, 1980).
2. See *ibid.*, 113–30, and R.E. Brown et al., *Peter in the New Testament* (Minneapolis & New York, 1973) 21 (fn. 27), 165.
3. *De praescriptione haereticorum*, 36; *Adversus Marcionem*, 4, 5.
4. I follow the translation of Henry Chadwick, *Origen: Contra Celsum* (Cambridge, 1953; reprinted 1979).
4a. J.N.D. Kelly strikingly confirms this in his *Early Christian Doctrines* (2nd ed., New York, 1960). It contains practically nothing on Christ's resurrection as such, but concludes with a treatment of Christian hope in our coming resurrection (459–89).
5. I follow the translation of M. Staniforth, *Early Christian Writings* (London, 1968).
6. On the symbol of the phoenix see also Tertullian, *De resurrectione*, 13.
7. See, for example, Tertullian, *Apology*, 48–50.
8. On such early Christian iconography see the literature indicated by R. Staats, "Auferstehung. Alte Kirche," *Theologische Realenzyklopädie*, vol. 4, 472–73.
9. For *De resurrectione* I follow the translation of E. Evans, *Treatise on the Resurrection* (London, 1960).
9a. On the problem raised by cannibalism see, for example, Athenagoras, *De resurrectione*, 4, 8.

10. *The Apostolic Tradition of St Hippolytus*, ed. G. Dix (rev. ed., London, 1968) 8–9 (= IV, 11).

11. *Prex Eucharistica*, ed. A. Hänggi & I. Pahl (Fribourg, 1968) 113.

12. See J. Leclercq, "Le mystère de l'ascension dans les sermons de saint Bernard," *Collectanea Ordinis Cisterciensium Reformatorum* 15 (1953) 81–88.

13. These notes, entitled *De Verbo Incarnato*, were produced in 1961 and used until at least 1964.

14. G.W.H. Lampe & D.M. MacKinnon, *The Resurrection* (Philadelphia & London, 1968) 97; see also 58f, 99.

15. *The Resurrection of Jesus Christ* (Valley Forge, 1973) 94, 95–96; in England this book appeared as *The Easter Jesus* (2nd ed., London, 1980).

16. I follow the translation of R. Wilken, *The Christians as the Romans Saw Them* (New Haven, 1984).

17. *The Scope of Demythologizing* (London, 1960) 86.

18. On the distinction between the apostolic witnesses to the risen Christ and all other believers see my *What Are They Saying About the Resurrection?* (New York, 1978) 58–60 and *Fundamental Theology* (New York & London, 1981) 89–91.

19. *What Is Man?* (Philadelphia & London, 1971) 41–53.

20. For the *Summa contra gentiles* I follow the translation by C.J. O'Neil (New York, 1957).

2. THE RESURRECTION IN MODERN THEOLOGY

1. I use the translation of E.C. Hoskyns (London, 1933); this work will be cited as *Romans*.

2. Up to the outbreak of the First World War we have the "early Barth" who followed the liberal Protestantism of Adolf von Harnack and others. Thus the three periods are: 1884–1914, 1914–31 and 1931–68.

3. Trans. H.J. Stenning (London, 1933) 11; this work will be cited as *Resurrection*. See Barth's *The Word of God and the Word of Man* (Boston, 1928) 86: "The theme of the bible . . . is the Easter message."

4. See *Kerygma and Myth*, vol. 1, ed. H.W. Bartsch (Harper Torchbooks, New York, 1961) 38ff, where Bultmann develops his thesis that the "resurrection" of Christ expresses the meaning of the cross.

5. *Credo*, trans. J.S. McNab (London, 1964) 95. Barth calls the resurrection "an event that occurred at a definite time in the past"—that is to say, at "a definite, datable time" (CD I/2, 115; see also CD III/2, 448, 451).

6. *Faith and Understanding* (New York & London, 1969) 83f.

7. *Kerygma and Myth*, vol. 1, 39. See Pannenberg, *Jesus—God and Man* (Philadelphia & London, 1968) 89.

8. On the Lukan and Johannine realism see my *What Are They Saying About the Resurrection?* 46–51.

9. *Word of God and Word of Man*, 90.

10. "Resurrection," *Sacramentum Mundi*, vol. 5, 323f, 329–33.

11. "Cross and resurrection form a single, indivisible cosmic event which brings judgment to the world and opens up for men the *possibility* of authentic life" (*Kerygma and Myth*, vol. 1, 39; italics mine).

12. "He stands before the Father at Golgotha burdened with all the actual sin and guilt of man and of each individual man, and is treated in accordance with the deserts of man as the transgressor of the divine command" (CD II/2, 758).

13. On the penal substitution theory and how it differs from the representative expiation theory see my *Interpreting Jesus* (London & New York, 1983) 145–57.

13a. In *Theology of the New Testament*, vol. 1 (London, 1965) Bultmann wrote: "The Church had to surmount the scandal of the cross and did it in the Easter faith. How this *act of decision* took place in detail, how the Easter faith arose in individual disciples, has been obscured in the tradition by legend and is not of basic importance" (45; italics mine).

14. *Faith and Understanding*, 83.

15. In *Theologische Literaturzeitung* 65 (1940) 245.

16. *Theology of the New Testament*, vol. 1, 295.

17. *An Existentialist Theology* (London, 1955) 186.

18. *Existence and Faith* (Cleveland, 1960) 291; see "Zur Frage des Wunders," *Glaube und Verstehen*, vol. 1 (Tübingen, 1966) 215.

19. For Bultmann the Easter stories in the Gospels also express an understanding of human existence in the light of the cross (*Essays* [New York, 1955] 258–59).

20. In *The Historical Jesus and the Kerygmatic Christ*, ed. C.E. Braaten & R.A. Harrisville (New York & Nashville, 1964) 42.

21. The review, which originally appeared in 1926, is found in *Faith and Understanding*, 66–94.

22. London, 1962.

23. *The Resurrection of Jesus of Nazareth* (Philadelphia & London, 1970) 119; hereafter *Resurrection*. Marxsen's essay "The Resurrection of Jesus as a Historical and Theological Problem," in *The Significance of the Resurrection for Faith in Jesus Christ*, ed. C.F.D. Moule (Naperville & London, 1968) 15–50, will be cited as *Significance*.

3. RAHNER KÜNG AND SOBRINO

1. "Dogmatic Questions on Easter," *Theological Investigations*, vol. 4, 127; hereafter ThI.
2. "Death," *Sacramentum Mundi*, vol. 2, 61 (= *Encyclopedia of Theology: A Concise Sacramentum Mundi*, 332; hereafter ETh); hereafter SM = *Sacramentum Mundi*.
3. *On the Theology of Death* (New York, 1961) 70.
4. What Rahner says in *Foundations of Christian Faith* about the genesis of resurrection faith corresponds largely to what he had already written on "The Resurrection and Human Experience" in SM, vol. 5, 329–31 (= ETh, 1438–40).
5. "Resurrection," *Theological Dictionary* (New York, 1965) 407.
6. A little later, when expounding the limits of demythologization, Küng does argue for the positive value of images and symbols (OBC, 412–15, especially pp. 414–15).
7. See my "Peter as Easter Witness," *Heythrop Journal* 22 (1981) 1–18, especially p. 6.

4. THE RESURRECTION AS EVENT

1. In *Resurrection* (New York & London, 1984) Pheme Perkins provides the material for another version of the effect-cause argument. Neither the Jewish background nor the teaching of Jesus himself sufficiently accounts for the given effect, the central significance which New Testament Christianity attaches to resurrection (75, 62f, 102, 317). Unless Jesus rose from the dead, we have no cause adequate to explain the disciples' Easter faith, preaching and theology.
2. *A New Life of Jesus* (London, 1879) vol. 1, 412. For a fuller discussion of the "swoon theory" see Chapter Five of my *Jesus Today* (Melbourne, 1986). To the bibliography given there add Muhammed Zafrulla Khan's *Deliverance from the Cross* (London, 1978) 102–3.
3. Frazer's propensity to slip over facts and indulge his fancy can be gauged from the preface to the 1900 or second edition of *The Golden Bough* (reprinted New York, 1935): "To a passage in my book it has been

objected by a distinguished scholar that the church-bells of Rome cannot be heard, even in the stillest weather, on the shores of the Lake of Nemi. . . . I make bold to say that by the Lake of Nemi I love to hear, if it be only in imagination, the distant chiming of the bells of Rome, and I would fain believe that their airy music may ring in the ears of my readers after it has ceased to vibrate in my own" (xxvi–xxvii). Frazer, incidentally, should not have needed correction from "a distinguished scholar." Any child in Nemi could have told him that even the loudest bells in Rome could not be heard thirty kilometers away. Apart from the distance factor, "the shores" of Lake Nemi are sheltered from outside sounds, as they lie deep below the rim of the volcanic crater.

4. See J. Jeremias, *New Testament Theology*, vol. 1 (London, 1971) 304.

5. On the whole attempt to explain Jesus' resurrection through the cults of Adonis, Attis, Osiris and other such figures in the mystery religions see V. Kesich, *The First Day of the New Creation* (Crestwood, New York, 1982) 38–47.

6. From M. Furlong, *Merton. A Biography* (London, 1980) 302.

6a. His thesis about "the cause of Jesus going on" associates Marxsen with those who reduce matters to the rise of a new consciousness. However, as we saw in Chapter Two, his position on the resurrection is more complicated than that.

6b. R. Pesch, "La Genèse de la foi en la résurrection de Jésus. Une nouvelle tentative," *La Paque du Christ. Mystère de salut*, ed. M. Benzerath et al., Lectio Divina 112 (Paris, 1982) 51–74, especially pp. 64–70. This essay also appeared as "Zur Entstehung des Glaubens an die Auferstehung. Ein neuer Versuch," *Freiburger Zeitschrift für Philosophie und Theologie* 30 (1983) 73–98.

7. On Schillebeeckx's reconstruction of the disciples' Easter experiences see further my *Interpreting Jesus*, 120–24 and *What Are They Saying About Jesus?* (2nd ed., Ramsey, 1983) 60–62.

8. On the visual vocabulary used to express the risen Christ's appearances see my *Interpreting Jesus*, 116–19 and J. Hug, *La Finale de L'Évangile de Marc* (Paris, 1978) 53–61; Hug also has a useful section on the vocabulary of the resurrection itself (*ibid.*, 40–45). Apropos of the encounters between the risen Christ and the disciples, Perkins (*Resurrection*, 94–95) fails to note how the language of seeing predominates in the witness of Paul, the Gospels and Acts. When discussing the nature of those encounters, she does speak of "some kind of external vision," but at once qualifies such a vision as "an ecstatic experience such as early Christians commonly attributed to the Spirit, equivalent

to other experiences of the Spirit" (198). I doubt both elements in this version of the Easter encounters. In various places the New Testament talks of ecstatic experiences but, as we will see, never attributes ecstasy to the disciples when they meet the risen Christ. Second, like others Paul distinguishes between experiences of the Spirit (common to all Christians) and the appearances which made him and others apostolic witnesses (experiences that were not and are not available to all Christians). The two texts Perkins refers to (Gal 2:20; 4:6) do not prove her case.

9. K. Dahan, "See, Vision, Eye," *Dictionary of New Testament Theology*, ed. C. Brown (Exeter, 1975–78) vol. 3, 511–18.

10. R.H. Fuller, *The Formation of the Easter Narratives* (New York, 1971) 46–49; for a discussion of Grass' view see Perkins, *Resurrection*, 138f.

11. H.S. Reimarus, *Fragments*, nr. 32; see C.H. Talbot ed., *Reimarus: Fragments* (Philadelphia, 1970) 200.

12. See, for example, K. Lake, *The Historical Evidence for the Resurrection of Jesus Christ* (London, 1907) 248–52; M. Muggeridge, *Jesus Rediscovered* (London, 1969) 50–51.

13. Marxsen, *Significance*, 25. He maintains that "the earliest story of the empty tomb" (from Mark) was not "intended to be an historical account" (*ibid.*). How does Marxsen know that Mark did not understand this story in an historical as well as a theological way? Or is it impossible for an historical event to be also theologically significant? Did Matthew and Luke make a mistake in taking Mark's tomb narrative (16:1–8) to contain an historical kernel? Or does Marxsen think that Matthew and Luke did not attribute any historical value whatsoever to Mark's tomb story?

14. Küng, OBC, 364.

15. Very few writers indeed have argued that Mark 16:1–8 is a creation of the evangelist himself—that is to say, that prior to the writing of this Gospel, there was simply no empty tomb story at all. In *Immortality or Extinction?* (Totowa, New Jersey, 1982) Paul and Linda Badham do so because of the way they interpret Mark's closing verse ("they said nothing to anyone about it, for they were afraid"): "This comment . . . implies that the empty tomb story formed no part of the generally received oral traditions about Jesus which circulated before the Gospels were written. It would be manifestly absurd for Mark to write that the women said nothing about it to anyone, if the story of their finding the empty tomb were generally known. The comment in fact only [sic] makes sense if Mark was conscious that he was adding a new element to

the generally received traditions about Jesus; an element which was not known prior to the publication of his Gospel, and which he therefore had to account for by claiming that his sources had hitherto kept this knowledge secret out of fear" (23–24). In short, "the story of the empty tomb was unknown before the appearance of Mark's Gospel" (*ibid.*, 24); the evangelist simply invented the whole story himself.

Many scholars, however, explain Mark's closing comment in ways that make good sense of it without claiming that the evangelist was consciously "adding a new element to the generally received traditions." A fear which leaves the women (temporarily) silent could belong to Mark's scheme of the "Messianic secret," or else be a way of maintaining the foundational role of the male disciples in preaching the resurrection. Or perhaps he wishes to insist on a period of astonished silence as the only appropriate reaction to the stupendous news of the resurrection (16:6). These and other reasonable views make sense of Mark 16:8 without claiming that the evangelist wanted to explain why the empty tomb story was simply unknown before he wrote his Gospel. In the program "Jesus the Evidence" even Helmut Koester did not allege that the empty tomb story was simply Mark's creation (see Chapter Four of my *Jesus Today*).

15a. See J. Jeremias, *Jerusalem at the Time of Jesus* (Philadelphia, 1969) 374–76; P. Lapide, *The Resurrection of Jesus* (London, 1984) 95–96.

5. BELIEVING IN THE RISEN CHRIST

1. See, for example, Rom 1:5; 16:26 (the obedient commitment of faith) and 6:8 (the confidence of faith).

2. G.W.E. Nickelsburg, *Resurrection, Immortality and Eternal Life in Intertestamental Judaism* (Cambridge [Mass.] & London, 1972).

3. Perkins illustrates the variety of beliefs about the after-life entertained in first-century Judaism (*Resurrection*, 37–56). Yet, despite that variety, no one expected the glorious, final resurrection of just one individual.

4. *An Inquiry Concerning Human Understanding*, ed. C.W. Hendel (New York, 1955) 138. Apropos of Hume, it should be added that he refuses to accept any necessary move from effects to causes. Hence, even if he agreed to the existence of the effect (the appearances of a living Christ), he could not or would not move to the alleged cause (the resurrection itself).

6. THE FOCUS OF REVELATION

1. See, for example, M. Hengel, *The Son of God* (London & Philadelphia, 1976).
2. See H. Bietenhard, "Lord, *kurios*," *Dictionary of New Testament Theology*, ed. C. Brown, vol. 2, 510–20.
3. On the Trinity see W. Kasper, *The God of Jesus Christ* (London, 1984).
4. On miracles see R. Latourelle, *Miracles de Jésus et théologie du miracle* (Montreal & Paris, 1986).
5. On creation see P. Smulders et al., "Creation," SM, vol. 2, 23–37 (= ETh, 313–28); J. Moltmann, *God in Creation* (London, 1985).
6. For details see J. Moltmann, *The Church in the Power of the Spirit* (London, 1977) 86, 374.
7. Luke draws on sources but builds up this picture of Peter's function as Easter witness.
8. See H. Conzelmann, *History of Primitive Christianity* (London, 1973) 40–41; O. Cullmann, *Peter: Disciple, Apostle and Martyr* (London, 1962) 59, 64, 223; C.F. Evans, *Resurrection and the New Testament* (London, 1970) 107; J. Fitzmyer, *The Gospel According to Luke X-XXIV*, Anchor Bible (New York, 1986) 1569; R.H. Fuller, *The Formation of the Resurrection Narratives* (New York, 1971) 35, 57, 112, 135f, 166; W. Marxsen, *The Resurrection of Jesus of Nazareth*, 58, 126, 159; Perkins, *Resurrection*, 83, 84–89, 120; P. Selby, *Look for the Living* (Philadelphia, 1976) 113; U. Wilckens, *Resurrection* (Edinburgh, 1977) 112–13.
9. The First Vatican Council described the papal primacy as functioning so that "by preserving unity in both *communion* and *the professio of the same faith* with the Roman Pontiff, the Church of Christ may be one flock under the one supreme shepherd" (DS, 3060; italics mine). Now the Church as a community of believers brings together those who confess Jesus as risen Lord and through sharing this faith are bound in love to each other. Their faith and communion are served by the Pope (as primary teacher and pastor) proclaiming through word and deed *the event* which more than anything else founded that community of believers: the resurrection of the crucified Christ.

7. REDEMPTION AND HOPE

1. In a distinguished and generally well-argued book (*The Divine Trinity* [London, 1985]), David Brown suggests that "proof of an Empty

Tomb is not even a necessary condition for the truth of the Resurrection" (130). Unless the tomb had been found empty, however, would the first Christians have persisted in their claim that the Easter appearances revealed the (transformed) continuation of the same person who was crucified and laid in the tomb? If after the appearances they had discovered the rotting corpse of Jesus, could they have remained convinced that they had truly encountered him risen from the dead?

2. Brown ignores this difference when he writes: "Most contemporary Christians would conceive of those who enter Heaven having something analogous to their original body rather than in any sense continuous with the same original physical particles. If such a discontinuity is acceptable in the case of other human beings, why not in the case of Christ? It cannot therefore be claimed in either case [that] the discovery of a rotting corpse would undermine the credibility of the contention that the individual in question had survived death" (*ibid.*, 131). It is right to invoke analogy so as to place the relationship between earthly and risen bodies. Further, any version of our resurrection built around some strict continuity with "the same original physical particles" has to face grave difficulties: With what original particles? Those we had at the age of fifteen? Or the different set we had at the age of forty-five? But my point here is this. Brown obviously supposes that what is conceivable in the case of our resurrection applies also to the case of Christ. For the reasons indicated in my text I doubt this. Moreover, if one agrees that there is some historical kernel to the story of the risen Christ appearing to Mary Magdalene near his tomb (John 20:14–18), could one imagine her gazing at the risen Lord and then turning around to see his rotting corpse in the tomb? How could she (or anyone else for that matter) cope with two bodies and a double sign: the decaying corpse indicating that Jesus was dead and the risen body indicating that he was alive?

3. For the original witnesses of the risen Christ his appearances provided the primary sign of continuity between his earthly and risen existence. For them the discovery of the open and empty tomb offered a secondary, negative sign of that continuity. If after the appearances they had found the rotting corpse of Jesus, they would certainly have called into question the continuity they had already accepted between the earthly Jesus and the risen Christ. Those who accept the resurrection of Jesus because they believe the original witnesses, by definition do not have the sign of the appearances. But they do have the empty tomb in Jerusalem as a sign of continuity between the earthly Jesus and the risen Christ.

4. Of course, one is dealing here partly with a question of definition. Matter could be defined in opposition to spirit and, if so defined,

would not have something spiritual about it. Nevertheless, all *human* matter has something spiritual about it. Moreover, all the atomic material in our universe is at least potentially human matter.

5. Brown holds that at least in principle there could be continuity of identity without (any?) bodily continuity: "bodily continuity is not necessary in order to guarantee continuity of identity." He explains: "what matters is continuity of character and memories. The importance of bodily continuity, like similarity of appearance, merely lies in providing a useful aide-mémoire" (*ibid.*, 131). As we shall see, neither "continuity of character" nor his personal memories would be enough to guarantee continuity of identity in the case of the criminal I imagine. Both these tests would be useless as well as mere "similarity of appearance" (which Brown correctly rejects). Bodily continuity would be decisive in establishing the continuity of the murderer's identity.

6. It could be said of an individual animal like the beautiful German Shepherd I know at Castel Gandolfo: "Jack is his body. Jack is his history." To bring out the fact that as human beings we also transcend our bodies and our history, we need to add, "I have my body; I have my history." We *are* more than our bodies and our history.

8. THE RESURRECTION AND LOVE

1. New York, 1969; the original, *Glaubhaft ist nur die Liebe*, first appeared in 1963.

2. Ed. M. Kehl & W. Löser (New York, 1982).

3. "Resurrection," SM, vol. 5, 329 (= ETh, 1438).

4. For a summary and a bibliography of Rahner's writings on the resurrection, see J.P. Galvin, "The Resurrection in Catholic Systematics," *Heythrop Journal* 20 (1979) 123–45, at pp. 125–30.

5. New York, 1969.

6. B. Weissmahr, "Kann Gott die Auferstehung Jesu durch innerweltliche Kräfte bewirkt haben?" *Zeitschrift für katholische Theologie* 100 (1978) 441–69, especially pp. 456f.

7. R.C. Ware, "The Resurrection of Jesus," *Heythrop Journal* 16 (1975) 22–34, 174–94.

8. *How I Believe* (New York, 1969) 80.

9. See C.F. Mooney, *Teilhard de Chardin and the Mystery of Christ* (London, 1964) 120, 135.

10. *The Divine Milieu* (New York, 1965) 30; *The Future of Man* (New York, 1964) 33.

11. For details see R. Faricy, *All Things in Christ. Teilhard de Char-din's Spirituality* (London, 1981) 13–31, especially pp. 17ff.

12. Quoted by R. Faricy, *ibid.*, 45.

13. London, 1981.

14. For various philosophical and theological approaches to love, see: J. Cowburn, *Love and the Person* (London, 1967); R. Carpentier & W. Molinski, "Charity," SM, vol. 1, 284–94 (= ETh, 186–88); M.C. D'Arcy, *The Mind and Heart of Love* (London, 1945); R.O. Johann, *The Meaning of Love* (Westminster, Md., 1955); C.S. Lewis, *The Four Loves* (London, 1960); E.V. Vacek, "Scheler's Phenomenology of Love," *Journal of Religion* 62 (1982) 156–77; D.D. Williams, *The Spirit and the Forms of Love* (New York, 1968).

15. *Homo Viator* (London, 1951) 29–67, especially pp. 57–63.

16. *Love Alone*, 45.

17. "The Concept of Mystery in Catholic Theology," ThI, vol. 4, 36–73, especially p. 42.

9. COMMUNICATING THE RISEN CHRIST

1. A noble exception to the general neglect of liturgical sources, G. Wainwright presents Christology from the angle of worship in *Doxology* (New York, 1980) 45–86.

2. I cannot explore here the reasons for much Western theology, and not merely Western Christology, having been non-symbolic, non-experiential and non-liturgical. The historical roots of the problem reach back at least as far as the Middle Ages.

3. Mackey, *Jesus the Man and the Myth* (New York & London, 1979); Sobrino, *Christology at the Crossroads* (see Chapter Three above). Schillebeeckx takes an experiential approach to the question of salvation in *Christ* (New York, 1980) 20–64.

4. *Jesus the Christ* (New York & London, 1976) 27.

5. For an introduction to the issues of sacramentalism and symbolism in John, see R.E. Brown, *The Gospel According to John*, Anchor Bible, vol. 1 (New York, 1966) CXI-CXIV.

APPENDIX: LUMINOUS APPEARANCES OF THE RISEN CHRIST

1. *The Problem of History in Mark and other Marcan Studies* (Philadelphia, 1982) 8; hereafter *Problem*.

2. "Jesus: From Easter to Valentinus (or to the Apostles' Creed)," *Journal of Biblical Literature* 101 (1982) 10; hereafter *Jesus.*
3. *Problem,* 9.
4. *Ibid.,* 30–31.
5. See, for example, J.A. Fitzmyer, *A Christological Catechism: New Testament Answers* (Ramsey, N.J., 1982) 12–14.
6. *Problem,* 29.
7. *Jesus,* 10.
8. *Ibid.,* 10; italics mine.
9. In their realistic and bodily presentation of the risen Christ's appearance, Luke and John clearly want to guard against errors. Robinson rightly observes their "apologetic" against "spiritualizing the resurrection away" (*Jesus,* 12). At the same time, these two evangelists also qualify their presentation by including details which indicate the transformed existence of the risen Lord. Closed doors do not prevent his coming (John 20:19, 26); he suddenly appears and disappears (Luke 24:31–36). See my *What Are They Saying About the Resurrection?* (New York, 1978) 48–51.
10. *Jesus,* 10.
11. *Problem,* 30.
12. *Jesus,* 13.
13. G.B. Caird, *The Language and Imagery of the Bible* (London, 1980) 147.
14. *Jesus,* 13.
15. *Ibid.,* 11; italics mine.
16. *Ibid.*
17. *Ibid.,* 13.
18. *Ibid.*
19. *Ibid.,* 15.
20. *Ibid.*
21. *Ibid.,* 15–16.
22. *Resurrection and the New Testament* (London, 1970) 105.
23. Robinson is not the first to propose that the appearances of the risen Christ were or at least were understood to be of a luminous nature. For example, in *The Formation of the Resurrection Narratives* R.H. Fuller concluded that the Easter appearances "involved visionary experiences of light, combined with a communication of meaning" (48). In reaching this conclusion, however, Fuller did not appeal to gnostic sources, and his reconstruction of the nature and function of the appearances in the earliest Christian traditions (*ibid.,* 47–49) differs markedly from Robinson's version.

Bibliography

Brown, R., *The Virginal Conception and Bodily Resurrection of Jesus* (London and New York, 1975), 69–129.

Carnley, P.F., *The Structure of Resurrection Belief* (Oxford, 1986).

Dunn, J.D.G., *Jesus and the Spirit* (London, 1975), 95–134.

Fuller, R.H., *The Formation of the Resurrection Narratives* (London and New York, 1971).

Galvin, J.P., "The Resurrection of Jesus in Catholic Systematics," *Heythrop Journal*, 20 (1979), 123–145.

Johnston, E.A., "Resurrection and Reality in Wolfhart Pannenberg," *Heythrop Journal*, 24 (1983), 1–18.

Léon-Dufour, X., *Resurrection and the Message of Easter* (London and New York, 1974).

Loewe, W.P., "The Appearances of the Risen Lord: Faith, Fact and Objectivity," *Horizons*, 6 (1979), 177–192.

Marxsen, W., *The Resurrection of Jesus of Nazareth* (London, 1970).

Moltmann, J., *Theology of Hope* (London and New York, 1967), 133–229.

Moule, C.F.D. (ed.), *The Significance of the Message of the Resurrection for Faith in Jesus Christ* (London, 1968).

O'Collins, G., *The Resurrection of Jesus Christ* (Valley Forge, 1973); published in England as *The Easter Jesus* (2nd ed., London, 1980).

————, *What Are They Saying About the Resurrection?* (New York, 1978).

Perkins, P., *Resurrection* (New York and London, 1984).

Perrin, N., *The Resurrection Narratives* (London, 1977).

Rahner, K., *Foundations of Christian Faith* (London and New York, 1978), 264–285.

Schillebeeckx, E., *Jesus* (New York, 1979), 320–397, 516–544.

Selby, P., *Look for the Living* (London, 1976).

Thrall, M.E., "Resurrection Traditions in Christian Apologetics," *Thomist*, 43 (1979), 197–216.

Ware, R.C., "The Resurrection of Jesus," *Heythrop Journal*, 16 (1975), 22–35, 174–194.

Wilckens, U., *Resurrection* (Edinburgh, 1977).

Williams, H., *The True Resurrection* (New York, 1974).

Index of Names

Abelard, 194
Adonis, 102–03, 221
Aesculapius, 113, 114–15
Ambrose, St., 155f
Anselm of Canterbury, St., 23, 34
Aquinas, St. Thomas, 21–32, 44f, 60, 63, 97f, 130, 146, 194
Aristotle, 29
Arnold, 29, 106
Athanasius, St., 14, 144
Athenagoras, 16, 30f, 60, 217
Augustine of Hippo, St., 14, 20, 89, 152, 160, 194, 199
Averroes, 30

Badham, L., 222–23
Badham, P., 222–23
Balthasar, H. U. von, 157, 189, 192, 199
Bambrough, R., 106
Barth, K., 22f, 27, 34–47, 51–57, 67, 70, 71–72, 75, 79f, 97, 128, 134f, 218
Basil of Caesarea, St., 20
Becker, E., 173f
Bernard of Clairvaux, St., 21, 152, 194, 218
Berten, I., 123
Bietenhard, H., 224
Blake W., 88
Blank, J., 123

Blinzler, J., 123
Bloch, E., 67
Bloy, L., 1, 209
Bousset, W., 111f
Brown, D., 224–26
Brown, R.E., 123, 217, 227, 229
Buber, M., 153
Buddha, 89
Bultmann, R., 22f, 25, 34f, 37f, 42, 44, 46, 47–59, 62, 65–67, 68, 71f, 75, 77, 80, 90, 97f, 100, 112, 128, 134f, 186, 201, 218f
Bunyan, J., 64

Caird, G.B., 228
Calvin, J., 23
Campenhausen, H. von, 123
Carmichael, J., 107f, 209
Carnley, Archbishop P.F., 229
Carpentier, R., 227
Celsus, 8, 9–13, 30f, 33, 102, 106f, 119, 122
Chadwick, H., 217
Chesterton, G.K., 131
Clement of Rome, St., 8, 9, 14–15, 16, 30, 60, 71, 88
Collingwood, R.G., 131
Confucius, 89
Conzelmann, H., 224
Cowburn, J., 227
Cullmann, O., 52, 224
Cyril of Jerusalem, St., 16, 20